The King Who Never Was

Michael De-la-Noy

THE KING WHO NEVER WAS

The Story of Frederick, Prince of Wales

PETER OWEN

London & Chester Springs PA

PETER OWEN PUBLISHERS
73 Kenway Road London SW5 0RE
Peter Owen books are distributed in the USA by
Dufour Editions Inc. Chester Springs PA 19425–0007

First published in Great Britain 1996
© Michael De-la-Noy 1996

ISBN 0–7206–0981–X

A catalogue record for this book is available from
the British Library

Printed and made in Great Britain
by Biddles of Guildford and King's Lynn

For Edna and Peter Thomas

Acknowledgements

I am grateful to the following for their invaluable help: Mr Hubert Chesshyre, Chester Herald; Sir Thomas Chitty, Bt.; Mr Peter Day, Keeper of Collections at Chatsworth; the Duchess of Devonshire; Mr Cyril Eland; Professor Edward Gregg; Mr Jeremy Harte, Curator of the Bourne Hall Museum, Ewell; Mr Eeyan Hartley, Keeper of the Archives at Castle Howard; Lady Hesketh; Mr Christopher Lloyd, Surveyor of the Queen's Pictures; Mr Michael Melia of the National Maritime Museum, Greenwich; Dr Richard Mortimer, Keeper of the Muniments at Westminster Abbey; and Miss Elizabeth Steele, Curator at Raby Castle. The portrait of Prince Frederick with his brother and five sisters by William Aikman, in the Devonshire Collection at Chatsworth, is reproduced by kind permission of the Chatsworth Settlement Trustees.

M. De-la-N.

'The longer I live the more difficult I find it to arrive at the truth' – Lady Irwin, lady-in-waiting to Augusta, Princess of Wales, to her father, the 3rd Earl of Carlisle, 1 February 1733

'The follies and vices of royalty are always noted: their virtues are taken for granted and rarely receive recognition' – John Brooke, *King George III*

Illustrations

(between pages 128 and 129)

1 Princess Sophia, Electress of Hanover
2 George I
3 George II
4 Caroline of Brandenburg-Ansbach
5 Frederick Louis, Prince of Wales
6 *The Music Party*
7 The children of George II
8 William Pitt the Elder
9 Sir Robert Walpole
10 The young George III with his brother and their tutor

Contents

	Abbreviated Family Tree	12
	Dramatis Personae	14
1	Hanover's Good Fortune	17
2	A Murder in the Family	32
3	Abandoned	44
4	'They Are All Mad'	64
5	'Von Big Lie'	81
6	Homes and Gardens	100
7	'No Excise!'	119
8	Marriage	138
9	Expelled from Court	157
10	The Patriot Prince	178
11	'An Unwearied Friend to Merit'	194
12	'Thy Will Be Done'	207
	Notes	221
	Select Bibliography	231
	Index	233

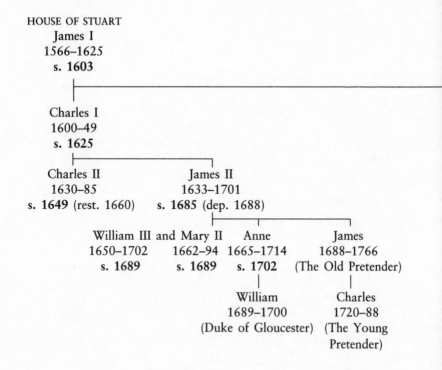

HOUSE OF STUART
James I
1566–1625
s. 1603

HOUSE OF STUART
James I
1566–1625
s. 1603

Charles I
1600–49
s. 1625

Charles II   James II
1630–85   1633–1701
s. 1649 (rest. 1660)   s. 1685 (dep. 1688)

William III and Mary II   Anne   James
1650–1702   1662–94   1665–1714   1688–1766
s. 1689   s. 1689   s. 1702   (The Old Pretender)

William   Charles
1689–1700   1720–88
(Duke of Gloucester)   (The Young
Pretender)

ABBREVIATED FAMILY TREE OF
FREDERICK, PRINCE OF WALES

s. = date of succession

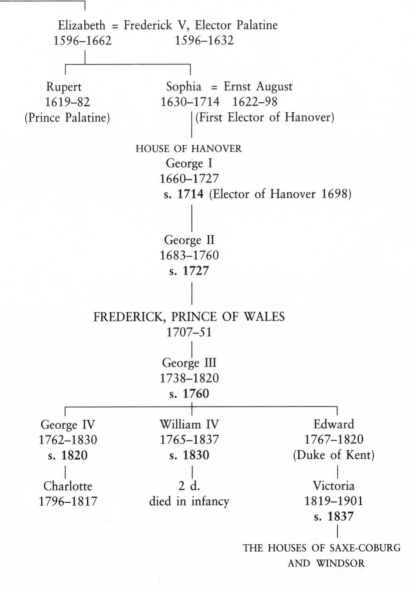

Elizabeth = Frederick V, Elector Palatine
1596–1662   1596–1632

Rupert   Sophia = Ernst August
1619–82   1630–1714 1622–98
(Prince Palatine)   (First Elector of Hanover)

HOUSE OF HANOVER
George I
1660–1727
s. 1714 (Elector of Hanover 1698)

George II
1683–1760
s. 1727

FREDERICK, PRINCE OF WALES
1707–51

George III
1738–1820
s. 1760

George IV   William IV   Edward
1762–1830   1765–1837   1767–1820
s. 1820   s. 1830   (Duke of Kent)

Charlotte   2 d.   Victoria
1796–1817   died in infancy   1819–1901
s. 1837

THE HOUSES OF SAXE-COBURG
AND WINDSOR

Dramatis Personae

While resident in Brunswick-Lüneburg the Hanoverian royal family were naturally known by the German spelling of the names with which they had been baptized; on the accession to the throne of Great Britain of the Elector Georg Ludwig they adopted English spelling. Their German spelling has been retained up to 1714, and because the Elector and his son, the Electoral Prince, were both called Georg, their second names, Ludwig and August respectively, have been retained to help avoid confusion.

AMELIA (1710–86), second daughter of George II and Queen Caroline. Sister of Frederick Louis. Known in the family, and referred to by Lord Hervey in his memoirs, as Emily.

ANNE, THE PRINCESS ROYAL (1709–59), oldest daughter of George II and Queen Caroline. Sister of Frederick Louis. Married William of Orange-Nassau.

ANNE (1665–1714), younger daughter of James II. Married George of Denmark (1653–1708). Succeeded her brother-in-law William III in 1702. Second cousin twice removed to Frederick Louis.

CAROLINE OF BRANDENBURG-ANSBACH (1683–1737), wife of George II and mother of Frederick Louis.

CAROLINE ELIZABETH (1715–59), third daughter of George II and Queen Caroline. Sister of Frederick Louis.

CHARLES EDWARD (1720–88), elder son of the Old Pretender and grandson of James II. On his father's death in 1766 he claimed to be Charles III but was later styled Count of Albany. Known as the Young Pretender.

FRIEDRICH LUDWIG (FREDERICK LOUIS, 1707–51), elder surviving son of Georg August (George II), created Duke of Gloucester in 1717, Duke of Edinburgh in 1727 and Prince of Wales in 1729. Married Augusta of Saxe-Gotha (1719–72). Father of George III.

14

GEORG AUGUST (GEORGE II, 1683–1760), only son of Georg Ludwig (George I), and on his father's accession in 1698 as Elector of Hanover known as the Electoral Prince. Father of Frederick Louis. Created Duke of Cambridge 1706 and Prince of Wales 1714. Succeeded his father as George II in 1727. Married Caroline of Brandenburg-Ansbach.

GEORG LUDWIG (GEORGE I, 1660–1727), oldest son of Ernst August, Elector of Hanover, and Sophia of the Palatinate. Succeeded his father as Elector of Hanover 1698 and Queen Anne as George I in 1714. Married Sophia Dorothea of Lüneburg-Celle (1666–1726), from whom he was divorced in 1694; hence she was never Electress or Queen of England, and was known after her divorce as Duchess of Ahlden. Father of George II and grandfather of Frederick Louis.

GEORGE III (1738–1820), oldest son of Frederick Louis. Succeeded as king in 1760 on the death of his grandfather, George II. Married Charlotte of Mecklenburg-Strelitz (1744–1818). Father of George IV and William IV.

GEORGE WILLIAM (1717–18), second son of George II and Queen Caroline. Brother of Frederick Louis.

JAMES II (1633–1701), second son of Charles I. Created Duke of York. Succeeded his brother Charles II in 1685. Deposed 1688. Father of Mary II and Queen Anne, and father-in-law of William III.

JAMES FRANCIS EDWARD (1688–1766), son of James II by his second wife, Mary of Modena. Styled Prince of Wales in exile, and on the death of his father in 1701 was recognized by Louis XIV of France as James III. Known as the Old Pretender.

LOUISA (1724–51), fifth daughter of George II and Queen Caroline. Married Frederick V of Denmark. Sister of Frederick Louis.

MARY (1722–72), fourth daughter of George II and Queen Caroline. Married Frederick II, Landgraf of Hessen-Kassel. Sister of Frederick Louis.

SOPHIA OF THE PALATINATE (ELECTRESS OF HANOVER, 1630–1714), a granddaughter of James I, mother of George I and great-grandmother of Frederick Louis. Married Ernst August, Elector of Hanover (1622–98). Nominated in Act of Settlement 1701 as heiress presumptive to Queen Anne.

WILLIAM AUGUSTUS (1721–65), Duke of Cumberland, known as 'Butcher' Cumberland. Youngest son of George II and Queen Caroline. Younger brother of Frederick Louis.

1

Hanover's Good Fortune

Frederick Louis (baptized Friedrich Ludwig), Prince of Wales from 1729 until his death in 1751, was born at Hanover in 1707, probably on 3 February.[1] His father was Prince Georg August, Duke of Cambridge,[2] the twenty-three-year-old son and heir of Georg Ludwig, who in 1698 had succeeded his father, Ernst August, as Duke of Kalenberg, and in 1705, on the death of his uncle Georg Wilhelm, had inherited the Electorate of Brunswick-Lüneburg. This was a new, small but wealthy and strategically important domain in north Germany, watered by the Aller and the Weser and with access to the North Sea. It was always referred to in England by the name of its capital city, Hanover. In 1708 Hanover was to become the ninth electorate of the Holy Roman Empire, a once formidable alliance founded in the ninth century by Charlemagne, but since the severence of its links with the Pope sometimes scornfully dismissed as neither Holy, Roman nor an empire. In its heyday the Holy Roman Empire, dominated by the Hapsburgs, had played a crucial role in the maelstrom of medieval European politics; now it was an informal grouping of Germanic states, still, however, with an emperor elected from among its sovereigns, hence the terms 'elector' and 'electorate'. Members of its ruling families were accorded the status of princes and princesses and were styled Highness.

At the time of Frederick's birth his accomplished great-grandmother Sophia, Princess Palatine, the widow of the first elector, was an old lady of seventy-seven; but she was physically and mentally alert, and she was looking forward with the keenest anticipation to the distinct possibility of becoming Queen of England. Under the Act of Settlement of 1701[3] she and her Protestant successors had been named by the English Parliament as heirs presumptive to Queen Anne. In 1707, the year of Frederick's birth, Anne was thirty-five years younger than the Electress, but after

losing eighteen children she was already worn out with dropsy
and futile child-bearing (at one time she suffered three miscarriages
in thirteen months). Indeed, by the turn of the century, in her
own thirty-fifth year, Anne had already become an invalid, and it
seemed increasingly likely that she would be the last of England's
Stuart monarchs. Sophia, on the other hand, although she too
had endured the loss of three sons and a much-loved daughter
(another son, Maximilian, had disgraced himself by embracing
the Roman Catholic faith), was in excellent spirits and the possessor,
she was pleased to boast, of a perfect digestion.[4] This was just as
well, for like many of her family she relished food and drink. She
also enjoyed long, brisk walks in her garden. Milton's biographer,
John Toland, noted that the Electress had 'ever enjoyed extraordinary
health', and had not 'one wrinkle on her face, nor one tooth out
of her head'. She read without spectacles, was fluent in five languages,
and was generally agreed to be 'a woman of incomparable knowledge in divinity, philosophy, history and the subjects of all sorts
of books'.

It was not only from Anne's pathetic failure to produce an heir
that Sophia stood to gain the thrones of Great Britain and Ireland;
Anne's Whig ministers were determined to bar from the succession
anyone who was a Roman Catholic, which of course included the
Catholic heirs of Anne's father, the deposed King James II. Had
this not been so, Prince Frederick would have had nothing more
to look forward to than the eventual inheritance of Brunswick-
Lüneburg, with a population of perhaps 750,000, a flourishing
wool and linen trade and wealth derived from the silver mines of
the Harz Mountains. Hanover itself possessed a fine opera company,
and an opera-house that seated two thousand, but as a centre of
commerce it lagged some way behind London, a city now dominated
by Wren's magisterial cathedral dome, so architecturally ravishing
it was waiting to be recorded by Canaletto just as soon as he
could tear himself away from Venice. Of Hanover's three royal
palaces, only one, the Schloss Herrenhausen, could begin to compare
– certainly as far as its park and gardens were concerned – with
the splendid homes at Queen Anne's disposal: St James's Palace,
Windsor Castle (the east wing not so long ago remodelled on
Renaissance lines by her uncle, Charles II), Hampton Court (built
by Cardinal Wolsey), Kensington Palace (formerly Nottingham House
and purchased by William III in 1689), and Greenwich Palace,

romantically situated on the bank of the River Thames, now in full flood as a commercial and domestic thoroughfare. Since the early years of the seventeenth century, Greenwich had been enhanced beyond measure by the Queen's House, built by Inigo Jones for the wife of Charles I; more recently, the gardens had been laid out for Charles II by Le Nôtre. And in England the nation's wealth was more evenly distributed than in the electorates of north Germany; you did not need to be royal to build and pay for such masterpieces as Blenheim, Castle Howard, Easton Neston or Chatsworth, nor to embellish them with paintings and sculpture acquired on the Grand Tour.

Queen Anne's England had its problems, of course. With a population of about seven million, a poor harvest could mean agricultural poverty; London was beginning to spawn its slums, which by Frederick's time were to become a disgrace. Parliament had a mind of its own and frequently expressed it. And although they often made brilliant contributions to foreign policy, the Queen's ministers schemed and bickered in a way that would have caused open-mouthed amazement at the court in Hanover, where the Elector reigned as a benevolent despot. For Sophia and her successors to add the problematical splendours of England to their own agreeable but relatively modest possessions it was necessary only that Anne should not confound medical opinion by giving birth to a healthy heir – and that they should fail to follow James II's path to Rome; the Bill of Rights, passed after the Glorious Revolution of 1688, had barred the Crown to Roman Catholics. As to the matter of a Stuart heir, Anne's husband, Prince George of Denmark, was to die in 1708, and in theory the Queen could have married again. Indeed, in November 1708 addresses were passed, at the instigation of the Whigs, in both Houses of Parliament asking the Queen to remarry, but as we know, she never did. Barring heirs to Anne, or an equally unlikely stampede of Hanoverians to Rome, after his great-grandmother, grandfather and father, Frederick had been born to ascend the throne of Alfred the Great. It was a not inconsiderable prospect for someone who, had politics and medicine taken different courses, might have expected to live and die in almost total obscurity.

By the beginning of the eighteenth century what was left of Frederick's Scots blood (his great-great-great-grandfather, James I, had been King James VI of Scotland) had been thoroughly diluted with German, although in many respects he seems to have avoided inheriting too many of the conspicuous genes of his paternal Guelph[5] ancestors, observable in certain members of the British royal family even today. There had been madness in the seventeenth century in a branch of his mother's family. More dangerous was the hereditary and often very debilitating Stuart porphyria passed on by his great-grandmother Sophia to George III and at least three of his sons, but which fortunately passed Frederick by, as it had done his grandfather George I. But Sophia was distinctly and very recently British, and inordinately proud of the fact. Her mother, Elizabeth, who married Frederick V, Elector Palatine and King of Bohemia, was a daughter of James I. One of her brothers, Prince Rupert, had fought for their uncle, Charles I, throughout the Civil War, and had ended his life as Governor of Windsor Castle. James II had been Sophia's first cousin. Elizabeth of Bohemia, Sophia's mother, gave birth to thirteen children, of whom Sophia was the twelfth. When the Act of Settlement was passed only two of Elizabeth's children remained alive, Sophia and an older sister, Louise, who had converted to Roman Catholicism in 1657 and became Abbesse of Maubuisson. Ten of Sophia's brothers and sisters had no descendants, and those descendants who did exist had, like the Abbesse, become Roman Catholics. There had been grandchildren of Charles I closer to the throne than the offspring of Charles II's sister, but they too had died without issue, so that a considerable element of luck had gone to producing Sophia as the nominee of the English Parliament.[6]

But it was politics that played the decisive role. James II's conversion to Roman Catholicism while heir presumptive to his brother Charles II was the initial cause of James's disaster and the House of Hanover's good fortune. With two Protestant daughters, Mary and Anne, waiting in the wings to succeed him, James might have survived as king despite his fervent religious beliefs had his second wife, Mary of Modena, who was also an ardent Catholic, not given birth, on 10 June 1688, to a son.[7] It now seemed likely that a permanent Roman Catholic dynasty was to be established in England, with all the attendant dangers of a too close alliance with Catholic France, even with the possibility of stirring up another civil war. Thoroughly alarmed by the birth of Prince James (Prince of Wales until 1701 and known to history as the Old Pretender), seven of the country's leading Protestants invited William of Orange, a grandson of Charles I and husband of James's elder daughter Mary, to invade. On 4 November William landed in England unopposed. Within a month his father-in-law had fled.

Between 11 December 1688 and 13 February 1689, a period now known as the Interregnum, the throne of England remained vacant. Although it could be argued that treason on the part of his subjects, including his daughters, had been the cause of James's undignified departure, by his manner of leaving the country the King was deemed to have abdicated, and a hastily elected Convention settled the matter by offering the crown jointly to William and Mary. Such a course of action was against all precedent, but since Parliament had executed its sovereign in 1649 the power to make and unmake monarchs had rather gone to its head. William was invested with the executive authority during his lifetime, so that in effect Mary reigned while William ruled. They had no children, and with the line of succession by no means secure, and with William anxious to ensure Protestant Hanoverian support in his opposition on the Continent to French expansionism, the new king immediately informed the Privy Council that Princess Anne had agreed to Sophia, Duchess of Kalenberg, being named heiress in the event of neither he and Mary, nor Anne herself, producing children. (Children by William of a second wife were to take precedence after Anne and her heirs.) No formal steps were taken at this time, however, for that very year, 1689, on her sixth wedding anniversary, Anne gave birth to her fourth child, Prince William, created by his namesake and godfather, the King, Duke of Gloucester at his christening; and as the young prince, after a precarious start, began to thrive, so the need to make firm contingency arrangements about the succession appeared to melt away.

Mary II died of smallpox in 1694. Far worse, 'to the inexpressible grief of their Royal Highnesses, and sensible sorrow of the whole kingdom', on 30 July 1700, also almost certainly as a direct result of catching smallpox, the eleven-year-old Duke of Gloucester, the last surviving child of Anne and Prince George, always so delicate (he had failed to talk until he was three or walk until he was five), died too. The poor child suffered from water on the brain, and his death can have come as no great surprise to those (and they included a hundred servants, now all thrown out of work) who had watched over him. The incompetent ministrations of the wealthy Dr John Radcliffe, a notorious quack like so many members of his profession, but ultimately the benefactor of Oxford's Radcliffe Infirmary, did little to help.

With the Duke of Gloucester's death it was now perfectly obvious that to all intents and purposes the struggles of the House of Stuart to survive were over. No one was more concerned by Gloucester's death than King William, who was in The Hague at the time and promptly wrote to his sister-in-law to say: 'It is so great a loss for me and for all England that my heart is pierced with affliction.' But it is doubtful that he cared much about the boy himself, or the bereaved parents; what concerned William was the lack of an officially recognized Protestant heir after Anne.

Anne too had affairs of state on her mind. There was no guarantee that on the eventual death of William III her half-brother, Prince James, would not be brought over from the château of Saint-Germain-en-Laye, twelve miles from Paris, or invade. Her fears on the matter could only have been increased when, on the death of her father in 1701, Louis XIV of France rashly recognized the prince as James III. Rumours spread to the effect that Anne was so fearful for her own rights that she had promised to take measures to ensure her brother's succession on her death if she were permitted to succeed William.[8] The situation was felt by everyone to be so unstable that William's ministers now decided to enact legislation, and Parliament passed the Act of Settlement in the summer of 1701. While riding in Richmond Park the following year William was thrown from his horse, an accident which exacerbated his tubercular condition and from which he died. Thus five years before the birth of Frederick Louis his great-grandmother found herself heiress presumptive to the throne of England.

It was the Act of Settlement which really settled once and for all the vexed question of the Divine Right of Kings, over which the Civil War had been fought, for the Act hedged about with a list of restrictions the scope of the sovereign's prerogatives. He or she might not, for example, leave the country without Parliament's consent, the sovereign must be a communicant member of the Church of England, and the nation was not to be taken to war in defence of a foreign power without the consent of Parliament. No foreigner was to be sworn a member of the Privy Council, and the sovereign was not to dismiss a judge or block a move for impeachment. Charles I had believed that 'Parliaments were altogether in his power', for 'their calling, sitting and dissolutions'.

Half a century and two revolutions later the germs of constitutional monarchy had been sown, and it was the flight of Charles's younger son James II that laid the foundations in England of political and legal freedom.

A copy of the Act of Settlement, together with the Garter for Frederick's grandfather, Georg Ludwig, was sent to Hanover, where 'one of the largest houses in the whole city' was assigned to the English suite. 'The Elector's own servants waited on them every morning with a silver coffee and teapots in their own chambers. Burgundy, champagne, Rhenish and all manner of wines were as common as beer.' The electoral court had good cause to offer generous hospitality, for the death of the young Duke of Gloucester had profoundly affected Queen Anne, who began her lonely twelve-year reign with no serious prospects of producing any more children, prone to depression (she is thought to have suffered at the end from senile dementia) and to severe physical illness. By 1703, when she was only thirty-eight, her arms and legs were horribly swollen, and she was writing to the Duchess of Marlborough to say she could 'walk a little with ye help of two Sticks'. Eighteen months later she was not even able to 'set her foot to the ground' and had to be lifted into her coach on a chair. Her eyes, too, began to give trouble, and in 1705 it was noted that 'The Queen's right hand is bound up so that she can't write.' During the summer of 1706 one of the Scottish Commissioners for the Union of Scotland and England, Sir John Clerk, paid a visit to Kensington Palace and recorded in his journal that the Queen was 'labouring under a fit of the Gout, and in extreme pain and agony'. Her face, he wrote, was 'red and spotted' and 'the foot affected was tied up with a pultis and some nasty bandages'.[9]

No wonder Sophia believed she might soon be able to exchange the petty politics and physical restrictions of Hanover and the Schloss Herrenhausen for Hampton Court. At Herrenhausen her son, who did not like her and never consulted her on matters of state, had confined her to one wing. The reason for this was that Sophia was in frequent correspondence with her niece, Elizabeth-Charlotte, Duchesse d'Orléans, reputed, in an age of rampant gossip, to be the greatest gossip in Europe. 'I do not care when I die so long as it is written on my tomb that I was Queen of England,' Sophia used to say. 'And a very good queen she would have made', in the opinion of one distinguished modern historian, Charles

Chenevix-Trench, the biographer of her grandson, George II.[10] In the end Sophia's tomb bore only the inscription *Magnae Britannae Haeres*, 'The Heiress of Great Britain'. Sophia could make herself slightly ridiculous, by pretending, for example, to a greater understanding of the British constitution than she really possessed, and by wishing to be styled Princess of Wales, a title reserved exclusively for the wife of the Prince of Wales,[11] but she was left in no doubt of her newly acquired political prestige by the numbers of bet-hedging place seekers who now found it convenient to call at Herrenhausen, request an audience and pay their flattering respects.

In 1676, entirely thanks to Sophia's influence, the philosopher and mathematican Gottfried von Leibniz was appointed librarian at Herrenhausen. It was he who coined the controversial dictum 'All is for the best in the best of all possible worlds', an optimism satirized by Voltaire in *Candide*. Leibniz became a close friend and confidant of Sophia, and it was in part his stimulating company that helped alleviate the tedium of life in Hanover for those not simply intent upon eating and strutting around in military uniforms. There was music, too. Although not a Hanoverian, a young and promising composer by the name of George Frederick Handel was appointed *Kappelmeister* to the Elector's court, and it was to Georg Ludwig's credit that he became an early patron of one of the great geniuses of the eighteenth century. But in 1711, while Anne was still alive, Handel, by now twenty-six, found life in Hanover so boring that he decided to visit London, which to all intents and purposes became his home from then on. Contests over performance of his mature works were to form one of the spirited dramas of Prince Frederick's life in London.

Sophia's desire to end her days in England exceeded her son's and grandson's partly because, like Handel, she found court and domestic life at Herrenhausen so tedious ('I never knew a greater Sobriety,' John Toland reported home), and also because she does not seem to have shared their antipathy for a race described as the 'most divided, quarrelsome nation under the sun'. Georg Ludwig could not help recalling how, well within living memory, the English had beheaded their king, established a republic, then changed their minds and restored the monarchy, only to depose another king and invite a taciturn prince from Holland to rule over them. English politicians plotted; their tradesmen rioted. As Hanover expanded and became ever more prosperous (on the death of his uncle, the

Duke of Celle, Georg Ludwig inherited additional land and wealth),
the Elector and his heir could see little to be gained from trying
to govern a nation increasingly averse to autocracy, and possibly
a good deal to be lost. But perhaps because the considerable difference
in age between Sophia and Anne gave the Electress reason to
believe that if she did not hurry matters along she might not,
after all, set foot in England, with the aid of Leibniz, who had
become her principal adviser, she began to intrigue with English
politicians for a household befitting the heiress presumptive, for a
pension and for an invitation, preferably from the Queen herself,
to take up residence in England.

On purely pragmatic grounds the Elector was against the idea
of his mother leaving Hanover, and Queen Anne was anxious
that he should say so publicly, thus strengthening her own hand
against the Tories, bent as they were on mischief. The Duke of
Marlborough, at the height of his fame following the Battle of
Blenheim (fought on 13 August 1704), was planning visits in 1705
to Berlin and Hanover. Anne wrote to him to say:

> The disagreeable proposall of Bringing some of the house of
> Hanover into England (which I have bin afraid of soe long) is
> now very neare being brought into both houses of Parliament
> which gives me a great deal of uneaseynes, for I am of a temper
> always to fear ye worst. There has bin assurances given that M.
> Schutes [Baron Ludwig von Schütz, the Hanoverian envoy in
> London, who, like the Elector, believed the Tory plan was to
> cause dissention between the courts of St James and Hanover]
> should have instructions to discourage the propositions, but as
> yet he has said nothinge of them, which makes me feare there
> may be some alterations in theire resolution at ye court of Hanover.
> I shall depend upon your friendship & kindness to sett them
> right in notions of things heare, & if they will be quiet I may be soe
> to, or els I must expect to meet with a great many mortifications.

So concerned was the Queen that she even sent for the Archbishop of Canterbury to solicit his opposition to the plan to invite
Sophia to England, and Marlborough told Sidney Godolphin, the
Lord Treasurer, 'I am very much of your mind that if *the elector*
be responsible, as they say he is, it will be very easy to convince
him that the jorny of *Electress Sophia* is very unseasonable, and

may be prejudicial to his interest.' Meanwhile the Tories pressed ahead, with Lord Haversham moving an address to the Queen in the House of Lords, humbly requesting her to invite the Electress to reside in England. Haversham's motion was easily defeated, and the Queen believed until her dying day that by wishing Sophia to live in England the Tories had been trying to undermine her own authority. She suffered, if truth be told, from a certain degree of paranoia. Keen, nevertheless, for the Hanoverian succession to take place in due time without the danger of a Jacobite intervention, the Queen now supported Whig proposals for a Council of Regency to be established to tide the country over from the moment of her eventual death until the arrival in the kingdom of her heir, be it Sophia or Georg Ludwig. (The term Jacobite was coined from Jacobus, the Latin for James.)

The Act of Regency became law in February 1706. At the same time, legislation was passed granting English nationality to all Protestant members of the House of Hanover. It was left to Sophia's unofficial representative in London, Pierre de Falaiseau, a former Prussian diplomat, to explain to the Electress and to Leibniz why it was the Whigs had been against Sophia coming to England but in favour of the Hanoverian succession. 'In their judgement,' he wrote, 'these were the most convenient means to succeed in this affair without shocking the Queen, and I can tell you frankly that those who believe that the goal could have been reached by any other means or highhandedly know neither the Queen, who is very opinionated and quite ferocious, nor England.'

Even before the Act of Regency had been passed Queen Anne was thinking up a way to gratify her Hanoverian relatives, and she asked the chancellor of the Order of the Garter, Gilbert Burnet, a famous Bishop of Salisbury and formerly tutor to the Duke of Gloucester, to examine the records and see whether (excluding an English sovereign and the Prince of Wales) the Garter had ever been worn simultaneously by a father and son, as she wished to create the Electoral Prince an Extra Knight Companion. Burnet's answer seems to have been satisfactory, for on 5 April 1706 Georg August was granted the Garter, and the Queen sent Lord Halifax as her special envoy to Hanover, to invest Prince Georg on her behalf and to take with him a copy of the Act of Regency. But while he was there fresh trouble brewed up, for Halifax discovered that Georg August 'had a mind to be an English duke'. When the

Queen heard about this request, she realized at once that if the Electoral Prince were made a peer he could exercise his right to take his seat in the House of Lords, and even if that did not result in Georg taking up permanent residence in England, it would entail a prolonged and unwelcome visit. Anne's vanity was on a par with her illustrious predecessor Queen Elizabeth's, and the actual sight of a healthy male heir who was not her son was more than she could have endured. Eventually, however, the Queen hit upon a compromise. In November 1706 she created Georg August Duke of Cambridge, but informed him that the present state of war in Europe prevented him from travelling to England.[12] Nothing could have been more ridiculous, hence no hint to stay away could have been dropped in stronger terms. The choice of dukedom had a sting in its tail, too. In 1677 Anne's stepmother, Mary, had given birth to a boy baptized Charles and created Duke of Cambridge. After his father, then still Duke of York, he had been heir to the throne. Anne, aged eleven at the time, paid her baby half-brother a visit while infected with smallpox, the child caught the disease, and died.

With the birth in 1707 of Georg August's son Frederick, England was now assured, under the Act of Settlement, of four monarchs in direct succession. On the Continent, the war being pursued in defiance of French aggrandizement was continuing to embellish Anne's reign with military glory. Blenheim had been followed by Marlborough's triumph against the French in 1706 at Ramillies. In 1708 there was fought the third of the Duke's great victories, at Oudenarde, a battle in which Frederick's father played an heroic part, much to the chagrin of his own father, the Elector, who had been persuaded to command the armies of the Upper Rhine. When Marlborough linked up with Prince Eugène of Savoy, Georg Ludwig missed the action. Like many a son in search of independence, Georg August had chosen to serve not under his father but about as far away as he could get, with the army on the Moselle. Although young and inexperienced, he had under his command twenty squadrons of Hanoverian cavalry. As the future George II's biographer has explained: 'In an age when the accepted military practice was to plan and fight battles in exact formations and with stately deliberation, Marlborough was to force a confused battle encounter, in which all would depend on quick decision, rapid movement and seizing the fleeting opportunity.'[13] Maréchal

Vendôme, the French commander, was enjoying a leisurely picnic when the Allied army suddenly bore down on him. Georg August was in the thick of battle. His horse was shot from under him, and as an officer was helping the Prince into the saddle of his own horse, he too was killed. The Prince's undoubted courage and fearlessness that day did his own reputation a great deal of good, both at the time and in the years to come, as King of England. Indeed, he was to bore his wife and children to death with his martial reminiscences. Certainly at Oudenarde George II's efforts put into the shade the conduct of his grandmother's rival claimant to the throne, Prince James, who, at Vendôme's insistence, watched the battle from a safe distance at the rear. (In 1709 James had an opportunity to redeem himself at the bloody battle of Malplaquet.) Unfortunately, the glory with which Georg August covered himself also became a major cause of disharmony between himself and his father, for Georg Ludwig, having missed the engagement, ever afterwards felt resentment against the Duke of Marlborough and intense jealousy of his son. The attitude taken up by Georg Ludwig became an object lesson for Georg August in poor relations between a father and son, one which was to prove a disastrous preparation for his own almost unbelievable rows with Frederick.

As Anne tottered towards an early grave, reasons other than those of vanity can be seen to have inclined her against any visits to England of the Hanoverian royal family. For all her protestations of goodwill towards them, the bestowal of the Garter on both the Elector and his son, and of a dukedom on the Electoral Prince as well, her feelings of guilt and family obligations could never quite obliterate her doubts about the Act of Settlement. She would have known that on his deathbed her father had named her as one of his three greatest enemies whom he had asked God to forgive. His son, Prince James, was her half-brother, and despite all the rather absurd rumours about his having been smuggled into Mary of Modena's bed in a warming-pan (rumours Anne pretended to believe for the rest of her life, for it was greatly in her own interest for the rumours to be true) there was no question he was legitimate, and in the eyes of many of Anne's subjects not just the rightful heir but *de facto* king. In May 1711 James wrote to the Queen to say he was sure she would prefer her 'own brother the last male of our name to the Electress of Hanover, the remotest relation we have, whose friendship you have no reason to rely on, or to be fond of, and who will leave the government to foreigners of another language, and of another interest'. James may not have read the Act of Settlement, which forbad the government of England being entrusted to foreigners, but the gist of the letter was designed to unsettle the Queen's determination on a Protestant succession. It also echoed sentiments born out by others. On 12 January 1714 Sophia's own devoted niece, Elizabeth-Charlotte, since 1701 Dowager Duchesse d'Orléans, was writing to Sophia to say: 'Queen Anne must be well aware in her heart of hearts that our young king is her brother; I feel certain that her conscience will wake up before her death, and she will do justice to her brother.' The Duchess, like her aunt, may not fully have comprehended the workings of the British constitution, for it was not in Queen Anne's power to dispose of her crown as she thought fit. But despite the Act of Regency it is evident that such a letter can have done little to shore up Sophia's expectations of a trouble-free accession. The Hanoverian settlement had found few enthusiastic supporters on the Continent, and it was well known that the English Church, the armed forces and even Parliament were liberally populated with Jacobite sympathizers. Toasts to King James III were openly proposed; even his birthday was celebrated in England. Up to the last moment there always seemed to Sophia every reason to establish some sort of foothold in the country prior to the death of Queen Anne, notwithstanding a motion introduced in the House of Lords on 5 April 1714 stating that 'The Protestant Succession in the House of Hanover is not in Danger.'

When Queen Anne declined to sanction a proclamation offering a reward for Prince James 'dead or alive' should he ever enter her kingdom, alarm bells rang anew. Sophia's Baron Schütz, who had long believed that the court at Hanover should have given him orders to demand a writ summoning the Electoral Prince to Parliament as Duke of Cambridge, called on the Lord Chancellor, Lord Harcourt, to make just such a demand. He did so on the strength of a letter he had received from Sophia, which she later asserted amounted only to instructions to *ask* Lord Harcourt why the writ had still not been issued – a fine piece of hair-splitting on Sophia's part. Schütz, of course, protested that he considered the letter constituted instructions to *demand* the issuing of the writ. Harcourt took the matter to the Queen, and that evening it was discussed at an emergency Cabinet meeting. Schütz was later informed by the Earl of Oxford, now Lord Treasurer, that because Schütz had not consulted the Queen personally he had never seen Her Majesty 'in a greater passion'. She went so far as to demand the envoy's recall to Hanover. To Georg Ludwig the Queen wrote:

> . . . as the rumour increases that my cousin the Electoral Prince has resolved to come over to settle in my lifetime, in my dominions, I do not choose to delay a moment to write to you about this. . . . I then freely own to you that I cannot imagine that a Prince who possesses the knowledge and penetration of Your Electoral Highness can ever contribute to such an attempt; and that I believe you are too just to allow that any infringement shall be made on my sovereignty which you would not choose should be made on your own. . . . I am determined to oppose a project so contrary to my royal authority however fatal the consequences may be.

Prince James declined to renounce his faith, and Anne hastened to assure bishops and temporal peers alike that she favoured the Hanoverian succession. Nevertheless Sophia and her son would not leave well alone, and in April 1714 they drew up what amounted to an impertinent list of demands: they wanted a member of the Electoral family to reside in Great Britain 'for the security of [Anne's] royal person, and for that of her kingdoms, and of the Protestant religion'; they wanted a civil list income for Sophia; they wanted James 'the Pretender' removed from Lorraine to Italy; and they wanted British titles for all the princes of the House of Hanover. Anne became convinced that the Elector intended sending his son to England, come what may. So she wrote in unequivocal terms to Sophia, to the Elector and to the Electoral Prince to inform them all that no member of the Electoral family would be allowed to enter Great Britain during her lifetime.[14]

Sophia was playing at cards at Herrenhausen when her letter was delivered. She left the table to read it, and then spent the rest of the evening walking up and down the garden in a state of great excitement. It took her two days to regain her composure, when she appeared in public at dinner with the Elector. After dinner she went for a late afternoon walk with her grandson's wife. Again she became agitated, began to walk at too brisk a pace, and according to an eye-witness,

> ... suddenly became pale, and ... fell forwards in a fainting fit. The Electoral Princess [Frederick's mother, Caroline] and the Countess von Pickenburg, who were with her, supported her on either side, and the chamberlain to her Electoral Highness helped them to keep her from falling. The Elector, who was in the garden hardby, heard their cries, and ran forward. He found her Electoral Highness unconscious and he put some *poudre d'or* in her mouth. Servants were promptly called, and between them they carried the Electress to her room, where she was bled. But she was already dead, and only a few drops of blood came out. ... The doctors say that she has died of apolexy.

Whatever the precise cause of Sophia's death, she was eighty-four years of age, and missed becoming Queen of England by two months. Frederick's grandfather was now heir presumptive. Anne replaced Sophia's name with his in the *Book of Common Prayer*, and Georg Ludwig continued to pester the ailing Queen for permission for a member of the Electoral family to live in England. But he need not have bothered. On 30 July 1714 Anne suffered what appears to have been a stroke, leaving her 'speechless, motionless and insensible'. She lingered for a couple of days, dying, at the age of forty-nine, early on the morning of 1 August. It was a Sunday. Even before he could possibly have known for certain that Anne was dead, the Principal of St John's College, Oxford, a diehard Whig, ordered prayers for 'King George' to be said at morning prayer. When someone pointed out that the Queen might not yet be dead he retorted, 'Dead, she's as dead as Julius Caesar.'

2

A Murder in the Family

Frederick Louis was seven when his grandfather became King of England, Anglicizing his names to George Lewis and creating Frederick's father Prince of Wales. Georg was not entirely a stranger to England. When he was twenty and ostensibly on the Grand Tour he had arrived at the court of his uncle Charles II, for it was Prince Rupert's idea that Georg should marry his cousin Princess Anne, the fifteen-year-old younger daughter of the King's brother, the Duke of York.[1] He arrived in London on 6 December 1680, to find his prospective father and mother-in-law decamped to Scotland, in hiding, in effect, from a House of Commons intent on excluding the Duke from the succession because of his conversion to Roman Catholicism. The House of Lords threw out the projected Exclusion Bill, but even so, Princess Anne could not have seemed much of a catch at the time. Her father's marriage to a commoner, Anne Hyde, had drawn from Georg's mother Sophia the comment, 'née d'une famille fort médiocre', and Anne, daughter of the future Earl of Clarendon, was generally regarded as perfectly fitted for the role of mistress but scandalously unsuitable, not being royal by birth, to become a princess, yet alone perhaps one day queen. She was fortunate not to have been accorded a morganatic marriage. As it was, the wedding was conducted without ceremony and kept secret for six months. However, by the time she sat for a portrait by Lely, which now hangs in the Queen's Gallery at Kensington Palace, she looked every inch a royal duchess.

York's younger daughter was a big girl and her face was pitted by the marks of smallpox. Georg was more interested in military matters than in matrimony, and he was written off by many who met him as a boorish young man. Neither Anne nor Georg spoke a word of each other's language, and their first meeting, which lasted half an hour, was more in the nature of a faintly embarrassing family encounter between a gauche pair of cousins than the preliminary to a courtship. Georg remained in England for four months but he never made a formal proposal of marriage, and Anne had a lucky escape, her eventual marriage to Prince George of Denmark proving exceptionally happy. But the young German prince did not entirely waste his time; he received an honorary doctorate at Cambridge and sat for a portrait by Godfrey Kneller, and when he came to the throne he rewarded the painter with a baronetcy. An initial report that Anne was infatuated by Prince Georg of Hanover seems inflated, and stories which were spread much later that she opposed the Hanoverian succession because as a young girl she had been spurned by him are ridiculous. It is a strange fact, however, that had they married, Georg would have become the consort of the Queen of England whose throne he was ultimately destined to mount.

Instead of Anne of York, Frederick's paternal grandmother turned out to be another of Georg's cousins, Sophia Dorothea of Lüneburg-Celle, and she became engaged to Georg, with catastrophic consequences, only after more glamorous potential brides had turned him down. Sophia Dorothea, pretty but scatter-brained, was half French by birth and entirely French by temperament. The last thing she wanted was to be cloistered in a petty German dukedom not more than spitting distance from her own childhood home at Celle (the Hanoverian Electorate had yet to come into existence) with a loutish young man whose idea of married bliss was to go campaigning, eat too much and play at cards. But most likely she was pressured into marriage by her mother, who considered her daughter had been settled 'with the most pleasant prince in Germany, and the richest'. The moated castle at Celle, with its 180 rooms, belied the size of the town itself, situated some twenty miles north-east of Hanover; there was a population of perhaps ten thousand. It was here that Sophia was brought up and here where she left her heart when she left home to marry, for the castle was a romantically domed and turreted fantasy that perfectly matched her own impressionable and sensual nature. To Celle, soon after marriage to Georg, she longed to return. But at least the marriage was consummated, for when Sophia Dorothea was only seventeen Frederick's father was born, on 10 November 1683. (Once resident in England, he celebrated his birthday on 30 October.) Five years later Sophia's boredom was considerably lightened when a wealthy young adventurer by the name of Philipp von Königsmarck arrived at court. At twenty-three, Count von Königsmarck, descended from the Brandenburgs, and Swedish by nationality, was 'admirably well made', in the opinion of his sister, 'handsome, with flowing hair and sprightly eyes; in one word, an equal mixture of Mars and Adonis'. She might have added that his handsome appearance and amorous exploits were exceeded only by his indiscretions.[2] Not that Sophia Dorothea allowed herself to be swept off her feet all at once. Nor was she the first partner in her marriage to commit adultery. By the time that Sophia and Philipp had become lovers, in 1692, Georg already had a daughter by his mistress Melusine von der Schulenburg, seven years younger than Georg, and eventually the mother by him of three girls, passed off, when he became king, as her nieces. (Her name is sometimes spelt Schulembourg or Schulemburg.)

While in the Netherlands, Philipp wrote to Sophia to say if, like his desire, he were able to take wings, he would 'this moment be in your lovely arms, tasting the sweet delights of your lips'. He told her he resented even having to discuss regimental matters with a brother officer, for that constituted time wasted when he could be thinking about her. 'I hope,' he wrote, 'after all these assurances that you will not ask me again whether I love you. If you still doubt, it will kill me.' He said he had a pet bear with him (he also had thirty servants, fifty horses and heavy debts), and if ever the Princess were to fail him, *he* would not fail to bare his chest and let the bear tear out his heart.

These were the declamations and empty threats of a conventional womanizer rather than the tender wooing of a sincere and sophisticated lover, but their effect was to break down any resistance Sophia may have thought it prudent to put up against the Count over a number of years, and to banish all regard for her reputation and safety. It was not long before she received a letter from von Königsmarck to say he had slept like a king, and he hoped she did likewise. 'What joy! What rapture! what enchantment have I not tasted in your sweet arms! Ye gods! what a night I spent!' In case Sophia should still doubt his love for her, he took to signing his letters in his own blood. It was all too melodramatic to be genuine, and as the Count was disreputable enough to sleep as well with Countess von Platen, the middle-aged, double-chinned mistress of Sophia's father-in-law, it is hard to feel much sympathy for his eventual fate, sealed when he broke off relations with the

Countess. On receipt of a note of assignation, the reckless von Königsmarck made his way to Sophia's bedroom in the Hanoverian royal family's town house, the Leine Palace, on the night of 1 July 1694. The note may have been forged by Countess von Platen; she certainly informed Georg's father, in Berlin at the time of the murder, what was afoot, the Count was arrested and was never seen again. Rumours multiplied. He had been stabbed; he had been strangled. That however he met his death he was buried in quicklime beneath the floor-boards was the story Horace Walpole believed, and published in his *Memoirs*. Others said he had been bundled into a sack weighted with stones and deposited in the River Leine, which conveniently ran beside the palace.

A wonderfully embroidered and bloodthirsty account of the murder was circulated by Thackeray, when he was lecturing about the first four Georges in America 161 years after the event, but he may well have been basing his version of events on a rash of poorly researched books published in the wake of the scandal.[3] He said that Sophia Dorothea had had 'a hundred warnings', but that on the night of the murder 'her carriages and horses were prepared and ready for the elopement'. Four guards, says Thackeray, were told to arrest the Count.

He strove to cut his way through the four men, and wounded more than one of them. They fell upon him; cut him down; and, as he lay wounded on the ground, the Countess, his enemy, whom he had betrayed and insulted came out and beheld him prostrate. He cursed her with his dying lips, and the furious woman stamped upon his mouth with her heel. He was despatched presently; his body burnt the next day; and all traces of the man disappeared.

Who the eye-witnesses to this Gothic horror were, Thackeray does not divulge; and Countess von Platen died in 1706, taking with her to the grave any dire secrets she may have possessed.

Ignorant for some time of her lover's fate, Sophia seems to have been quite keen on the idea of a divorce on the grounds of her refusal to cohabit with Georg, for, failing to take account of Hanoverian vindictiveness, she naïvely imagined that a divorce would set her free to marry von Königsmarck. A divorce she certainly got, on 28 December 1694, when Georg saw to it that a specially convened Consistorial Tribunal declared his marriage to 'the illustrious Princess' dissolved; and because Georg did not care to be laughed at as a cuckold, the grounds were indeed stated to be her 'continued denial of matrimonial duty and cohabitation'. But while the terms of the divorce permitted Georg to remarry, Sophia was forbidden to do so. She was barred from seeing her children or from receiving visitors, and was sent packing back to Celle, where her father refused to speak to her.

Although supplied with an income, ladies-in-waiting, servants and the semblance of a court for the rest of her life (and she was still only twenty-eight), Frederick's grandmother was submitted to house arrest at the castle of Ahlden – in reality not much more than a modest timbered house. She wrote letters and received visits from her mother, but at Ahlden she remained, virtually incommunicado and in unremitting disgrace, until the day of her death in 1726. Announcing her end in the *London Gazette*, her former husband named her 'Duchess of Ahlden'. He countermanded court mourning at Hanover, very probably initiated on the instructions of Prince Frederick, by that time nineteen years of age, and would not even permit his son to go into private mourning for his mother, from whom he had been forcibly separated for ever at the age of eleven. Although the drama of Sophia's exile had occurred twelve and a half years before Frederick was born, a tacit understanding throughout the Hanoverian royal family that in no circumstances was her name to be mentioned or her whereabouts referred to hung like a sinister and intriguing secret over the impressionable years of his childhood. As for the future George II, his father's treatment of his mother – and of himself, by denying him a mother – helped develop in him a dangerous disregard for family relationships which goes some way towards explaining his later appalling conduct towards Frederick.[4]

The great mystery of Frederick Louis's life is why both his parents hated him so much. In the case of his father, the antagonism may have been in part genetic. Georg Ludwig had no time for his mother, Sophia; and from his father, Ernst August, Frederick's grandfather had inherited the short temper so characteristic of the Hanoverians, together with their bulbous eyes, receding chins and uninquiring minds. Georg Ludwig was said to be 'not much addicted to any diversions besides hunting'. If one monitors the influence of Guelph traits, both physical and emotional, up to the present time, one can see how deep-rooted they were. The preposterous behaviour of George III's unpopular brood was in a class of its own, but Queen Victoria and Edward VII both inherited an exorbitant love of food amounting to gluttony, while Victoria, Edward, George V and George VI were all renowned for their uncertain tempers. Victoria, Edward VIII and George VI suffered from depression. Elizabeth II can exhibit quite irrational impatience; and her sister is prone to famous tantrums. No royal family in Europe other than the Spanish Hapsburgs had been so tainted as the Hanoverians with unfortunate and seemingly ineradicable genes. All the direct descendants of George I to inherit the throne of England have possessed an obsessive interest in etiquette and uniforms, and Frederick's father was no exception. Lord Chesterfield said of George II: 'No one is more exact on all points of good breeding, and it is the part of every man's character that he informs himself of first.' But compared with his own father, Georg August was well educated, speaking French, Italian and English. What seems so deplorable is that despite a sound grounding in the classics, he openly despised learning. Poetry and painting bored him, and although he went to the trouble of learning from his bluestocking grandmother the English language as well as the history of the land over which he expected one day to reign, he failed to imitate her interest in theology or philosophy. His memory for historical events could unfortunately sometimes let him down. At a levee one day, a baronet, Sir Wolstan Dixie (an 'abandoned brutal rascal' in the opinion of Samuel Johnson), was presented to George II as Sir Wolstan Dixie of Bosworth Park. The King, vaguely recalling something to do with Richard III, said, 'Bosworth, Bosworth! Big battle at Bosworth, wasn't it?' 'Yes, sir,' replied Sir Wolstan, 'but I thrashed him.' In a perfect world, Georg would have been a professional soldier – or at least an heroic and battle-scarred prince, never a king condemned to converse with tedious people like bishops and politicians.

There is another strange trait in Hanoverians. Many, especially the boys, start life with delightful good looks, their faces taking on a distinctly froglike appearance in early middle age. In his own youth, Georg August was quite an attractive young man; yet few of his contemporaries would have regarded him as possessing even the remnants of good looks by the time he became king. It was fortunate that through marriage to intelligent outsiders a number of Hanoverians from time to time introduced refreshing new blood into the line, so that not every descendant of the first Elector of Hanover is recognizably a 'Hanoverian'. One such benefactor was Frederick's mother, Wilhelmina Charlotte Caroline, daughter of John Frederick, Margrave of Brandenburg-Ansbach. Ansbach was a small town situated in modern Bavaria, and it was here, in the palace, that Caroline was born, on 1 March 1683, so that she was seven months older than her future husband. Whereas the domain of the margraves was small and impoverished (in 1791 the last margrave, Caroline's nephew, actually sold his margravate to the King of Prussia), the palace was an enormous edifice of four storeys with a cloistered courtyard and ornate west-facing façade. Caroline's father had previously been widowed, and her mother, much younger than her father, was Eleanor, daughter of the Duke of Saxe-Eisenach. It was from her auburn-haired mother, with her large blue eyes, that Caroline inherited her own robust good looks.

Caroline was only three when her father died, and ten years later he was followed to the grave by Caroline's mother. Perhaps it was the effect of being deprived of parents at the age of thirteen that hardened her heart when she came to leave her son Frederick to his own devices when he was only seven; perhaps, because she pulled through her own adolescence in remarkably fortunate circumstances, she imagined everyone else was equipped to cope with emotional deprivation. The Elector of Brandenburg, the most powerful Elector in north Germany, who was to become King Frederick I of Prussia in 1701, assumed the role of her guardian, so that she spent her adolescence in the cosmopolitan atmosphere of Berlin. The Electress of Brandenburg, Sophie Charlotte, was a daughter of Sophia of Hanover, so that long before Caroline and Georg August met, Caroline would have learnt almost all there was to know about the Hanoverian dynasty, and of its prospects of one day moving to England. She also acquired from Sophie Charlotte a proficiency in languages, for the wife of her guardian spoke French, English and Italian. Not for nothing was she Sophia's daughter. Sophie Charlotte was also an accomplished musician, and she studied the scientific discoveries of Isaac Newton and the philosophical theories of her mother's friend Leibniz. In short, Sophie Charlotte presided over the intellectual aspect of the court in Berlin while her husband fussed over protocol.

Frederick gave his wife her own palace in the city in which to create a miniature Versailles, a château called Lützenburg, renamed Charlottenburg and visited, some 150 years later, by Queen Victoria. For many years after the Second World War Charlottenburg, now open to the public, ended up in the eastern sector of Berlin. Le Nôtre, who had landscaped the gardens at Versailles for Louis XIV, was called in, to provide terraces, statues and fountains. Indoors, it was said that entry could be gained more effectively through wit and talent than by means of rank or wealth. Religious disputations took place; the proposition that marriage had been ordained for pleasure as well as procreation was debated. It was at Charlottenburg that exiled Huguenots met Jesuits, to Charlottenburg that Handel came, from Saxony, as a boy, where Leibniz gravitated south from Hanover for visits, and where French, because it was considered more eloquent, was spoken rather than German. It was in this heady climate of radical enlightenment that for nine years Caroline, the future queen consort of England, was brought up. The Electress – Queen of Prussia after 1701 – became to her more than a guardian, more a guardian angel, almost her adopted mother. One peculiarity, however, differentiated the civilized Queen and her devoted pupil: Sophie Charlotte took no interest in politics, whereas Caroline was to share with Sophia of Hanover, whom she met in Berlin, a very considerable love of power. Caroline's upbringing could not have been in greater contrast to that of Georg August. She was engulfed in affection and lived in a sophisticated environment, in a palace furnished with exquisite taste. Georg's home was haunted by the indignity of his mother's imprisonment, and what intellectual life there was at Hanover was orchestrated in only one wing of Herrenhausen, where Georg's grandmother stumped up and down impatiently awaiting her call to destiny.

Sophia heartily approved of Caroline. She wrote from Hanover to Berlin to tell Leibniz: 'If it depended on me, I would have her kidnapped, and keep her always here.' By the time Caroline was twenty-one she is said to have acquired a supple figure with a stately bearing, and by 1704 she was high on the list of eligible if impecunious German princesses. 'Everyone predicts the Spanish crown for her,' Leibniz, employed throughout Europe as a roving diplomat, reported to the Hanoverian Minister of State on 25 October 1704, but negotiations for Caroline to marry the Archduke

Charles, titular King of Spain and elected, in 1712, Holy Roman Emperor, faltered, most probably because Caroline believed the Archduke's future to be less than totally assured. She was also extremely reluctant to become a Catholic, Rome's religion being the only one she could not tolerate. Nevertheless she was placed under considerable pressure by the King of Prussia, and consented to allow a Jesuit priest to argue with her. Although Caroline acknowledged the cleric's kindness, he eventually reduced her to tears. 'The dear Princess of Ansbach is being sadly worried,' the Electress Sophia, who was staying with her daughter in Berlin, noted on 27 October 1704. 'She has resolved to do nothing against her conscience, and Urban [the Jesuit] is very able, and can easily overcome the stupid Lutheran priests here. If I had my way, she would not be worried like this, and our court would be happy. But it seems that it is not God's will that I shall be happy with her; we at Hanover shall hardly find anyone better.'

But from the point of view of the Electress things began to look up, for on her return home she wrote to Leibniz: 'Most people here applaud the Princess of Ansbach's decision, and I have told the Duke of Celle that he deserves her for his grandson. I think the Prince likes the idea also, for in talking with him about her, he said, "I am very glad that you desire her for me."' She added that she had mentioned the possibility of an engagement between Caroline and Georg to the Prime Minister, who was 'not opposed, but does not wish it so much'. With his mother locked away, Georg August was dependent on his grandmother for what passed for family affection in Hanover, and of course for reports on his prospective bride, for Georg himself had not yet set eyes on her.

Had the Queen of Prussia had her way, Caroline would have married a boy whom Georg August, with good reason, had learnt to detest: the Queen's only child, Frederick, later Frederick William I. He became the father of Frederick the Great. Frederick William's childhood temper was so uncertain and violent that he had no conception how to play in a normal way, and the beatings he administered to Georg, dress rehearsals for the manic thrashings he later administered to his children, left the future hero of Oudenarde emotionally scarred for life. The Queen's desire to see the Crown Prince married to Caroline was quite simply because she wanted Caroline for a daughter-in-law, but neither Caroline nor Frederick William cared for one another. Soon, however, Queen Sophie Charlotte's role in Caroline's life was to come to a tragic end. In the new year of 1705 she set out for Hanover, to stay with her mother. The weather was atrocious, and at Magdeburg she became so unwell she had to be put to bed. She struggled on, but by the time she arrived at Herrenhausen she was a dying woman. She declined the ministrations of the French chaplain, and told her weeping lady-in-waiting not to pity her. 'I am at last going to satisfy my curiosity about the origin of things, which even Leibniz could never explain to me,' she said. As to her husband, her death would afford him the opportunity of giving her a magnificent funeral 'and displaying all the pomp he loves so much'. Her mother, the Electress Sophia, was prostrate with grief next door, but her brothers Georg Ludwig and Ernst August were with her when she died. She was only thirty-seven, a brave and remarkable princess and the most formidable influence by far on the future Queen Caroline of England.

Caroline was on a visit to her brother at Ansbach when her beloved mentor died, and in reply to a homily from Leibniz on the wonders of divine providence she wrote, with a touch of rather unconvincing melodrama: 'Heaven, jealous of our happiness, has taken away from us our adored and adorable Queen. The calamity has overwhelmed me with grief and sickness, and it is only the hope that I may soon follow her that consoles me.' Fresh pressure was brought upon her by King Frederick to marry the Archduke Charles, but Caroline's brother, now Margrave of Brandenburg-Ansbach, stiffened her resolve against any change in her religion and assured her she might live with him as long as she pleased. With the death of the Queen she had no desire to return to Berlin anyway, and the coast was now clear for the Electoral Prince of Hanover to pay court. In June 1705 Georg August arrived at Ansbach, attended only by his former governor, Baron von Eltz, and a valet. He was supposed to be travelling incognito, and his visit took on the nature of a charade, for not only did he assume a false name but presented himself at the palace in disguise. Everyone knew who he was but they all kept up appearances by pretending not to recognize him, so that in the event of rejection he could beat a dignified retreat. Georg had already received a snub from Sweden. He also deemed it wise to cloak his visit in as much secrecy as possible in order to keep the King of Prussia in ignorance.

Queen Anne's envoy at Hanover had some inkling what was afoot, and it seems that Georg's interest had been thoroughly awakened by his grandmother's first-hand reports of Caroline's charm and accomplishments. 'In what concerns the Prince's own inclinations in this business,' the envoy reported to London, 'His Highness hath not hitherto appeared so much concerned for the character and beauty of any young lady he hath account of as the Princess of Ansbach.' He added: 'There is in this court a real desire of marrying the prince very soon.'

When Georg arrived at Ansbach he pretended to be a Hanoverian nobleman planning to meet up with friends from Nuremberg – but having failed to effect a rendezvous, and finding Nuremberg dull, had come on to Ansbach. He was duly received by the Margrave, invited to supper and cards, and was then presented to Caroline. On the strength of a few moments' conversation he persuaded himself he had fallen in love and dashed back to Hanover. Anne's envoy reported on 19 June: 'The Electoral Prince is returned and gone to Herrenhausen. He was about two hours with the Elector alone, and the Elector's appearing afterwards in good humour at table makes it to be imagined that there hath nothing happened but that he is well pleased with.' But the envoy was not really certain if Georg had been to Ansbach or had been wooing a princess of the House of Hesse, which says quite a lot for Georg's efforts at cloak-and-dagger diplomacy. When von Eltz again left for Ansbach, to negotiate in detail, all the English envoy was able to report was: 'He hath disappeared secretly.' On 23 June 1705 von Eltz, having arrived at the Ansbach court in the guise of 'Herr Steding', was writing to the Elector to say he had been presented to the Margrave and to Caroline, and that Caroline had granted him a private audience, expressing surprise and agitation when von Eltz broached the subject of marriage to Georg August, for 'she had never flattered herself that anyone in Hanover had so much as thought about her'. She confirmed that negotiations between herself and the King of Spain had been completely broken off, and apparently she told von Eltz she would infinitely prefer an alliance with the Electoral House of Hanover to any other – perhaps because for the past four years the House of Hanover had been nominated to succeed in England. Two days later von Eltz was writing to his master to say the Margrave had consented to Caroline's engagement, and that he had offered as a dowry everything left to her in the will of her stepbrother. His letter concluded: 'I have so much good to tell concerning the Princess's merits, beauty, understanding and manner that your Electoral Highness will take a real and sincere pleasure in hearing it.'

What Caroline lacked by way of chattels she made up for, according to the marriage contract, with a truly amazing string of titles: Princess of Brandenburg in Prussia, of Magdeburg, Stettin and Pomerania, of Casuben and Wenden, Duchess of Crossen in Silesia, Electress of Nuremberg, Princess of Halberstadt, Minden and Cannin, Countess of Hohenzollern. . . .

Poor Sophia, it was only now that her son informed her of Georg August's betrothal. Like everyone else, she had been kept in the dark over his visit to Ansbach, but she repressed her justifiable resentment. Someone else with more than a passing interest in the affair was Georg's mother, who heard the news during a visit to Ahlden from her own mother, the Duchess of Lüneburg-Celle; it is said that she was forbidden to write to either Georg or to Caroline, but Sophia Dorothea was certainly in correspondence with her son in 1709. More bizarre by far, the Electoral Prince and his bride were assigned the very apartments at the Leine Palace where Sophia Dorothea had been clandestinely visited by her murdered lover. Owing to the sudden death from a chill of Georg's maternal grandfather, the Duke of Lüneburg-Celle, the wedding of Georg and Caroline was a quiet affair, conducted in the chapel at Herrenhausen on 2 September 1705.[5] A number of inquisitive English were present. A ball preceded the wedding and a comedy followed it.

Some eight months later, Frederick Louis was conceived.

3

Abandoned

On 5 February 1707 the British envoy to Hanover, Emmanuel Scrope Howe, was reporting home: 'The Court having for some time past despaired of the Princess Electress being brought to bed, and most people apprehensive that her bigness, which had continued so long, was rather the effect of distemper than that she was with child, Her Highness was taken ill last Friday at dinner.' The result of her 'illness' was that she gave birth, it seems at seven o'clock on the evening of 3 February, at the Leine Palace in Hanover, to a healthy, chubby boy. But a cloak of mystery surrounded the birth of Frederick Louis, named Louis no doubt after his paternal grandfather and Frederick in memory of his mother's father. It was the Princess's lady-in-waiting, Countess d'Eke, who sent word to Howe of the birth, not even the Electoral Prince, and ten days passed before Howe was permitted to see the baby.

Although the first child to be born to Georg and Caroline would stand in direct succession to the English Crown, all protocol was abandoned, and not a single official witness was present. Had such an important birth taken place in England, the mother's bedroom would have been thronged with courtiers. So unusual were the circumstances of Frederick's birth that in years to come it was rumoured he was not Caroline's child, for how else could one account for his parents' detestation of him? Georg August did not help matters by referring to his son as the *Wechselbalg*, German for a changeling – and even as the Griff, a Creole term for a half-caste. His mother, too, thought nothing of referring to Frederick within the family as the Griff. But neither of these charmless nicknames provides evidence that Frederick was a foundling or illegitimate – which is just as well for the present British royal family and their right to the throne.

Insults were later to fly around St James's Palace like leaves in an autumn gale, and it would have been quite in character for

George II to have thought of a hurtful jibe like *Wechselbalg* without intending to convey that he had been party to a 'warming pan birth'. As for the appellation of half-caste, Frederick's natural complexion was yellowish. What was more natural, in the case of Georg August, whose father just happened to employ a pair of Turkish servants, than to pick on a personal misfortune and fling it back in the boy's face? It is hardly conceivable that he intended advertising himself as a cuckold. Caroline herself always referred to Frederick as her son. Even the fact that he was given names previously unknown to any English royal house has been adduced as a reason for casting doubt on his paternity, but any serious suggestion that Frederick was illegitimate is far-fetched, to say the least.

With hindsight we know how fecund Caroline was; after Frederick she gave birth to another seven live children. But royal brides were expected to give birth within a year of marriage, and it was quite natural that after seventeen months rumours about the need to import a changeling would be manufactured. Hence, in view of their conduct, George and Caroline had only themselves to blame if people imagined the worst. They did not even invite Howe to the child's christening, attended by Sophia and conducted in the Princess's bedroom. 'Unaccountable' was how Howe described this affront. When eventually the envoy *was* admitted to Caroline's apartments, he found 'the women all admiring the largeness and strength of the child'. Prince Georg took Howe on one side, 'and making great professions of duty to the Queen', as Howe wrote to London on 25 February,

> he desired me that I should represent all things favourably on his side, and *he* was not the cause that matters were arranged at the Princess's lying-in and the christening of the child with so little respect to the Queen, and so little regard to England. For my part I have taken no notice of it to any of them, but I think the whole proceeding has been very extraordinary. Wherever the fault is, I won't pretend to judge.

It is evident that Queen Anne, whose own relatively insignificant birth had been poorly attended, did not hold Georg August responsible for affronts to her dignity, for in 1709 Caroline gave birth to a girl, named Anne after the Queen, who stood as godmother, sending as a christening present a miniature of herself set in diamonds. Princess Anne was later created Princess Royal, and in 1733 made an unlikely marriage with the physically deformed Prince of Orange, a marriage that greatly irritated her brother Frederick, who thought he deserved to be married off first.[1] A second daughter, Princess Amelia, was born in 1710 while Caroline remained on German soil; a third, Princess Caroline, followed five years later, in England.

Herrenhausen, where Frederick was to grow up entirely alone, stood some two miles outside the medieval walls of Hanover, and was approached down a double avenue of lime trees. The royal family had lived there since 1666, and between 1696 and 1710 the Electress Sophia had taken charge of the gardens, 120 acres in all, ornamenting them with an orangery, a maze, fountains and an open-air theatre. The palace itself was not much more than a very large country house, surrounded by a moat; it was the park, 'curiously contrived and decked with perpetual verdure', and stabling for six hundred horses, which drew comment from English visitors. It was from Herrenhausen that the Elector controlled his property, in theory with the assistance of a prime minister, a foreign minister and a treasurer, but they were all at his beck and call, unable to make a single decision without reference to him. The Elector instituted criminal proceedings, sanctioned all expenditure over the equivalent of £12, appointed and dismissed his ministers and held the post of commander-in-chief. There was a paternalistic bond between the Hanoverians and their ruler akin to that of the English country squire and his tenants, but constitutional monarchy was undreamt of.

To Herrenhausen, while Frederick was playing in the park, came an increasing procession of English, particularly people who had fallen on hard times at home, politically or financially, and were hoping to ingratiate themselves with the Hanoverian royal family and recoup their losses when Queen Anne died. Among them were an ill-matched couple, Henrietta Howard and her husband Henry, a penniless younger son of the Earl of Suffolk, described by Frederick's future arch-enemy Lord Hervey as 'wrong-headed, ill-tempered, obstinate, drunken, extravagant and brutal'. Henrietta, the daughter of a baronet, had been worth £6,000 when she married Henry. Before long, she was worth a good deal less, her husband's addiction to the bottle consuming more than they could afford and contributing to an already violent character, so that offers of gainful employment were in short supply. They travelled to Hanover, Horace Walpole tells us, 'in the common waggon', but on arrival they gave an expensive dinner, and were soon received by both the Electress and the Electoral Princess, both of whom took a fancy to Mrs Howard who, compared with the Hanoverian ladies, was pretty and well read. She also had good manners and knew how to flatter royalty. Caroline appointed her to her household, as a *dame du palais*, an equivalent, perhaps, of an English maid of honour.[2] Before long she was tacitly recognized to be Georg August's mistress, an eminently sensible arrangement in the eyes of Sophia, who remarked that she would be able to improve her grandson's English.

It should not be imagined that because Georg took a mistress in his early twenties and so soon after his wedding that his marriage to Caroline was unhappy or that such an arrangement would have affected the children. Most royal unions were politically arranged   marriages of convenience, and for a prince to take a mistress was common practice. Charles II had at least seven mistresses and twice as many illegitimate children. Georg's father and grandfather both kept mistresses, and one of many silly criticisms of Frederick is that he did likewise. Most pragmatic royal wives connived. It relieved them of some of the physical terrors of child-bearing, and in the case of garrulous bores like George I and his son, at least some other poor woman took it in turn to listen to their tales of woe or of military valour. Again, if your husband had a recognized mistress, at least you knew where he was. You could set your clock by Georg August's visits to Mrs Howard, for whom, at Twickenham, he was to build a beautiful Palladian house called Marble Hill, later lived in by Mrs Fitzherbert, the illegal wife of Frederick's wayward grandson George IV. Far from developing into an all-consuming passion and thus a threat to the marriage, these visits became a part of daily domestic routine. A discreet and sensible mistress was as much a part of royal equipage as an equerry, and a necessary fillip to a prince's self-esteem. In the case of Georg August, it so happened that in his own peculiar way he was in love with his wife; and although he had a temper that would have driven a modern wife to distraction and probably the divorce court, as well as a streak of cruelty he found it almost impossible to curb or disguise, Caroline for her part remained devoted to him until the day she died.

We can assume that Frederick was at Herrenhausen (if not, at the nearby Leine Palace), although possibly already in bed, on the evening that his great-grandmother, the Electress Sophia, expired in the garden, and the sensational nature of the old lady's death would have been likely to impinge on his childhood memory. Two months later, on the evening of 5 August, the palace was in uproar again, with news of the death of Queen Anne and the accession of Frederick's grandfather, at the age of fifty-four, to the throne of Great Britain and Ireland. But Georg Ludwig's inheritance had not after all been a foregone conclusion. England remained divided in her loyalties until at the very last minute the Privy Council rescued the country from possible civil war. 'If you choose to listen to your cookmaids and footmen in the kitchen,' Daniel Defoe informed his more affluent readers, 'you shall hear them scolding and swearing and fighting among themselves, and when you think the noise is about beef and pudding, the dishwater or the kitchen staff, alas, you are mistaken; the feud is about who is for the Protestant Succession and who for the Pretender.'

A meeting of the Privy Council held as the Queen lay dying was initially packed with Jacobite supporters; even after a new Lord Treasurer, the Duke of Shrewsbury, had been appointed (it was the last act the Queen performed), and his predecessor, Lord Bolingbroke, in favour of the Old Pretender, had finally lost influence, lords lieutenant were instructed to seize arms and horses of Roman Catholics, ports were closed and several regiments moved in the direction of London. Before the Queen was dead a messenger was dispatched to Hanover warning the Elector of her condition, and this was followed up, the Queen still in the land of the living, by a letter signed by forty members of the Privy Council asking Georg Ludwig to embark immediately. In official circles most Jacobite support had by now melted away, but the Government was taking no chances. On the day of the Queen's death one distinguished cleric, Francis Atterbury, recently consecrated Bishop of Rochester, has been quoted as offering publicly to proclaim King James III, and was reluctantly dissuaded when Bolingbroke 'said that all our throats would be cut'. Bolingbroke, whose political philosophy was to have such an enormous influence on Frederick, was every inch a man of the world; when he received a curt note dismissing him from office he admitted it had shocked him 'for at least two minutes'. As for the Bishop's alleged indiscretion, the

Dictionary of National Biography, a valuable but by no means infallible work of reference, believes the tale 'rests on doubtful authority'. And as Atterbury, in his dual capacity as Dean of Westminster, officiated at the coronation of the new king, it seems the authorities did not rate him a very high risk at the time, although he and his secretary did eventually end up in the Tower.[3]

In the event, Georg Ludwig, Elector of Hanover, was proclaimed King George, the first king so named ever to reign in England, at St James's Palace, at four o'clock on the afternoon of the day Queen Anne died. Two days later two drafts of the Queen's will were discovered. Also revealed was the fact that she so feared death she had never signed them, and so she had died intestate. Although he could have claimed everything for the Crown, King George, rather surprisingly, agreed that a bequest of £2,000 to the poor should be honoured. He was not generally known for his generosity. A member of his comic-cut entourage, the Fat Hen, as Sophia unkindly called her, had been left behind in Hanover until she had paid off her debts, eventually catching up with the King in The Hague. The Fat Hen, who acquired ultimate respectability in 1722 when she was created Baroness Brentford and Countess of Darlington, was Baroness Sophia von Kielmannsegge (variously spelt Kielmansegge or Kielmensegge), almost certainly George's illegitimate half-sister as well as one of his mistresses.

Lord Bolingbroke was not the only person who feared for his life at this juncture in British politics. Melusina von der Schulenburg, the mother of George's three unacknowledged daughters and as tall and scraggy as Baroness von Kielmannsegge was obscenely fat, said she was sure they would all have their heads chopped off in the first fortnight. As if to balance the scandal of a possibly incestuous relationship with the Baroness, it has also been suggested that the King and his mother's former maid of honour, von der Schulenburg, were morganatically married. Canon law, in England at any rate, would certainly have forbidden remarriage for George while his divorced wife remained alive, and the rumour seems unlikely. Londoners were soon lampooning the pair of them as the Elephant and Castle, and von der Schulenburg, the Castle, did even better than the Elephant; she was set up at 43 Grosvenor Square, was elevated to the Irish peerage in 1716 as Duchess of Munster, distinguished herself, in 1718, by having Sir Christopher Wren dismissed as Surveyor-General, and was rewarded the following year by becoming Baroness Glastonbury, Countess of Faversham and Duchess of Kendal. Her fears of an unfriendly reception may have accounted for the leisurely nature of the King's departure from Hanover, a departure which for Frederick must have been traumatic. Not only was he compelled to take leave of his grandfather (in later life he was to describe him as his best friend), but of his parents, too; and to kiss his sisters goodbye. It was to be fourteen years before he saw his mother, father or sisters again, and by then he was twenty-one, his father was King of England and all of them were strangers to him.

There are a number of possible reasons why, at the age of seven, Frederick was abandoned to a solitary childhood in the care of his great-uncle Prince Ernst August, hereditary Bishop of Osnabrück and created, by his brother, Duke of York and Albany. Had he accompanied his parents to England, Hanover would have been denuded not only of its Elector but of both its heirs. But this raises the question why Frederick's parents were compelled to take up residence in England. The simple explanation must be that given a choice between the new Electoral Prince, as Frederick's father now became, remaining in Hanover, or the new Prince of Wales, as Frederick's father also became, residing in England, where the King could keep an eye on him and have him at his elbow to translate, the weight of the argument came down in favour of residence in England. That being so, there would have been no question of Caroline's remaining in Hanover – or the princesses. They were aged only four and five, far too young even by the rigorous standards of upbringing in those days to be separated from their mother. It seems that Frederick was considered as just an expendable pawn in a matter of protocol.

Accompanied by his son and heir, the King left Hanover on 31 August, lingered in The Hague a fortnight, and eventually sailed from Oranie Polder on 16 October, escorted by a squadron of twenty ships, arriving at Greenwich two days later, where he spent his first night on English soil as sovereign at the Queen's House. The scene of the King's arrival was later commemorated by Sir John Thornhill in a painted ceiling at the hospital, and on a visit to Hanover in 1719 Thornhill took the opportunity of sketching Frederick so that he could include him in the work. Frederick's mother and sisters followed behind, arriving on 15 October, with just five days to spare before the coronation, incongruously attended

by the Duchess of Portsmouth, a mistress of Charles II, Lady
Dorchester, mistress of James II, and Lady Orkney, William III's
mistress. 'Who would have thought,' commented Lady Orkney,
'that we three whores would have met here.'

King George was back in Hanover within two years, and he
paid six further visits to his electoral domains whenever he could
tear himself away from the arms of his dutiful English subjects;
Parliament strongly disapproved of his gallivanting about on the
Continent. And on his return trips to Herrenhausen, to attend to
his duties as Elector and to savour the docility of a subservient
people, Frederick would receive first-hand accounts of events in
England, political and domestic. But apart from his grandfather's
occasional visits and the company of his great-uncle he had no
contact throughout his boyhood or adolescence with any member
of his family. He might as well have been a single child and an
orphan, and when judging his conduct as a man it has to be
considered that someone so severely deprived might well have behaved in ways far more reprehensible than he did; conversely,
that in the circumstances it is surprising that Frederick matured
into such a kind, amusing and compassionate person.

As was only to be expected, the arrival in London of a new
royal house (the fact that King George was a great-grandson of
James I seemed too distant a connection to be relevant) was cause
for the most acute observation and comment. Since the restoration
of Charles II, well within living memory, the English had been
accustomed to a succession of recognizably British monarchs. The
new king did not even speak English. He brought with him eighteen
cooks, as much as to say he quite expected to be poisoned by
English food; also two Turkish servants, Mohamet and Mustapha,
who, to the disgust of English courtiers, whose job it was
ceremonially to dress and undress the King, were officially employed
as *valets de chambre*. And they had other duties besides. Mohamet
was appointed Keeper of the Closet, and paid the tailors' bills
and theatre subscriptions. He was a Christian convert, enriched
himself by selling offices, and was believed by the French ambassador
to exert considerable political influence on the King. When he
died in 1726 his nefarious duties were taken over by Mustapha.
The King had these faithful servants' portraits incorporated by
William Kent in a *trompe-l'oeil* on the King's Grand Staircase at
Kensington Palace.[4]

Worse still, he had brought with him German ministers, and a newly appointed private secretary, Jean de Robethon, a Huguenot refugee formerly in the employ of William III, described before long as a 'prying, impertinent, venomous creature, for ever crawling in some slimy intrigue'. It is unlikely that Robethon would have endeared himself to Frederick's parents when in 1718 he spread a rumour that the King was planning to bring his grandson to England to be educated at Cambridge. No doubt George felt safer in a strange land with men with names like Robethon, Andreas Gottlieb von Bernstorff and Hans Caspar von Bothmar around him, for he knew about the English politicians only by hearsay. If the English found George an enigma, England seemed to him an unfathomable place as well. He could not, for example, get over the fact that when he looked out of the windows of St James's Palace, he saw a park, in which tame deer still roamed, which belonged to him, yet when the ranger of the park sent him a pair of carp from the canal, which also happened to be his property, he was expected to give the man five guineas.

The most far-reaching and important aspect of George's accession was his decision to boycott most of the Tories, many of whom had been Jacobite sympathizers, and to favour the Whigs. His conduct at his first levee (a levee was a court at which only men were presented), held on the morning after his arrival, immediately revealed his hand, a hand prepared for him in advance by Bothmar and Robethon, both of whom knew far more about the political situation in England than the King. Hardly surprisingly, Bolingbroke was not even received, and the King scarcely deigned to notice Lord Oxford, 'of whom Your Majesty has heard me speak', a gentleman of the bedchamber, Lord Dorset, said to the King in an attempt to present the Earl. The Tory Lord Shrewsbury retained the office of Lord Treasurer for a few weeks, and was the last holder ever of that ancient office. The Earl of Nottingham, another Tory, but in favour of the Hanoverian succession, was also retained.

The rest of George's first administration were Whigs, although not every Whig of distinction was rewarded. George was graciously condescending towards Marlborough, but the great general was left in no doubt that his days of political influence were over. Lord Townshend was appointed secretary of the northern department and was thus deemed to be leader of the administration. For the time being his far more able brother-in-law, Robert Walpole, was content with the lucrative post of Paymaster. For reasons perhaps more to do with time-honoured tradition than loyalty, crowds gathered at Greenwich to cheer, and according to the *Weekly Journal*, 'His Majesty and the Prince were graciously pleased to expose themselves for some time at the windows of their palace to satisfy the impatient curiosity of the King's loving subjects.'[5]

Since a disastrous fire at the Palace of Westminster in 1698, St James's Palace had been the metropolitan palace of the sovereign (it still is), and it was to St James's that the King rode in procession on 20 September, seated in a glass coach beside Frederick's father, the King occasionally condescending to bow but not to smile, the Prince having been told to smile but not to bow. The Recorder of the City of London held up proceedings by making a long and tedious speech of welcome, not one word of which was intelligible to the King, and no doubt the Prince provided an adequate translation. Although the King was to exclude his son from affairs of state he demanded his presence at full meetings of the Cabinet for the purpose of providing a translation. It was at a meeting of the Privy Council the following day that the King invested his 'most dear son, a Prince whose eminent filial piety hath always endeared him to us', as Prince of Wales.[6] This eminent filial piety did not, however, encourage the King to sanction a suggestion made at dinner by the Duke of Marlborough, who offered to sell Marlborough House in the Mall to the Prince, on the grounds that it could easily be joined to St James's Palace by means of a gallery. The King preferred for the moment to keep his 'most dear son' under his own roof.[7]

The arrival of Frederick's mother in England was heralded by a bonanza of superlatives in the *Daily Courant*:

By the favourable wind since the embarkation of Madam the Princess of Wales it is not doubted that her Royal Highness, with the Princesses, her daughters, will soon safely arrive. The whole conversation of the town turns upon the charms, sweetness and good manners of this excellent princess, whose generous treatment of everybody, who has had the honour to approach her, is such that none have come from her without being obliged by some particular expression of her favour.

After the constraints of Hanover, where until so recently the Electoral

Prince, now Prince of Wales, had played second fiddle to both his father and his revered grandmother, George Augustus and his wife were looking forward to having fun. In England there would be no queen mother or even queen consort to deflect the spotlight from Caroline, and both she and her husband would find a far wider stage on which to strut. There were politicians, particularly disgruntled Whigs excluded from office by the King, waiting for a champion, and compared with Hanover, hordes of wealthy and elegant aristocracy longing to show off their newly embellished town houses and country mansions.

Caroline landed at Margate, where she was met by the Prince of Wales; it was early in the morning when they were reunited, and they slept at Rochester before completing the journey to St James's Palace. There their arrival was greeted with salutes fired from both the park and the Tower of London. Bonfires were lit, and the Prince and Princess were quick to capitalize on their instant popularity. Having monopolized the King's Drawing Room on her first evening, everyone deserting the basset and ombre tables when the Princess sat down to play piquet, Caroline, with the Prince, went for a walk next day in St James's Park, with two duchesses and the Countess of Nottingham in attendance. Crowds gathered, as no doubt the couple anticipated. It was incredible that Lady Nottingham was even on her feet, for over the years she was said to have given birth to no less than thirty children. Caroline was observed to talk to her a good deal, and it was no time at all before she had engaged her as governess to her own daughters.

Although the new Prince of Wales was five-eighths German, a quarter French and one-eighth Scottish, he was soon proclaiming in his Teutonic accent, and with ludicrous exaggeration, 'I have not a drop of blood in my veins vot is not English.' And according to a diary kept by Countess Cowper, a lady of the bedchamber to the Princess, he was busy announcing to all and sundry his belief that the English were 'the lovingest people in the world, and that if anybody would make their court to him, it must be by telling him that he was like an Englishman'. This was a tune he ceased to sing when he became king, never hesitating in later life to run down everything English and to praise everything Hanoverian. Meanwhile Caroline assured her newly acquired neighbours, in her usual down-to-earth way, that she would 'as

soon live in a dunghill as return to Hanover', sentiments unlikely
to find favour with her father-in-law, who regarded Hanover as
an oasis of peace and stability.

In making appointments to her household, Caroline rewarded
past loyalty and encouraged anti-Jacobites. Lady Cowper had 'for
four years past . . . kept a constant correspondence with the Princess,
now my mistress'. Another of Caroline's ladies, the Duchess of
Bolton, was a natural daughter of Charles II's favourite bastard,
the Duke of Monmouth, executed for treason by James II. And
Caroline retained her husband's mistress, Henrietta Howard, as a
woman of the bedchamber. No doubt it was thanks to Caroline's
good offices that Henry Howard was appointed a gentleman usher
to the King. From a younger generation still the Princess caused
an unaccustomed breath of fresh air to blow through the court
by her almost frivolous choice of maids of honour, a bevy of
light-hearted and extremely pretty girls the likes of whom had
not been seen tripping down the corridors of royal residences since
before the Commonwealth. One such was Sophia Howe, a granddaughter (although he was never married) of Prince Rupert, hence
Caroline's second cousin by marriage. It seems that Sophia could
never stop laughing or larking about, even in chapel, where one
day the Duchess of St Albans had occasion to tick her off. She
could not do a worse thing than giggle in church, the Duchess
told her. 'I beg Your Grace's pardon,' replied the irrepressible
Sophia, 'I can do a great many worse things.'

Services in the Chapel Royal at St James's became a focus for
ostentatious displays on the part of the Prince and Princess of
their allegiance to the Church of England, a convenient site for
assignations and the exchange of gossip, and an equally convenient
place for the King to fall asleep and snore. He was easily bored,
and he could not even follow the sermon. He was also
understandably upset when he attempted to make a spontaneous
but fruitless gesture of goodwill. He took the Prince and Princess
of Wales and their children to watch the Lord Mayor's Show and
was nonplussed when the owner of the house from whose balcony
the royal party enjoyed the procession declined the honour of
knighthood. He was a Quaker. English customs and protocol were
to provide any number of problems for the Hanoverians. Caroline
had debated at length with her ladies-in-waiting whether it would
be proper for her to kiss the Lady Mayoress when she went to

the Guildhall for a banquet, and was advised not to. The Lady Mayoress, however, had other ideas, and felt deeply affronted when the Princess declined to embrace her. On this occasion the King successfully made amends by bestowing on the Lord Mayor a baronetcy.

Soon Caroline began to tire of her efforts to ingratiate herself with the English, declared in language that came quite naturally to her that St James's Park 'stank of people', and took to driving to Kensington Palace so that she could walk undisturbed in the gardens there, 'gardens so immense that twenty or thirty gardeners work in them', according to a young Swiss visitor to England, César de Saussure. Writing home in 1726 he said: 'One evening, being surprised at seeing so many of these men going home from work, I enquired how many there were. One of them answered there had been fifty or sixty for the last fortnight.'[8] But even at Kensington the public were admitted by ticket, and as soon as it became known that the Princess of Wales could be viewed at a new location, crowds tramped across the surrounding fields to join her. According to the same M. de Saussure, pickpockets were 'legion', practising their profession 'in the streets, in churches, at the play, and especially in crowds'. He wrote from personal experience, having 'quite lately a valuable snuff-box ... stolen from me'.

Not even royalty were immune from the attentions of London's eighteenth-century footpads, and after he had become king, it seems that Caroline's husband went for a solitary stroll in Kensington Gardens and got mugged. That at any rate was the story told by William IV while walking in the gardens with Lord Duncannon, later 4th Earl of Bessborough and in 1834 appointed Home Secretary. When King William reached a certain spot he said to Duncannon, 'It was here, my Lord, that my great-grandfather, King George II, was robbed. He was in the habit of walking every morning alone round the garden, and one day a man jumped over the wall, approached the King, but with great respect, and told him he was in distress, and was compelled to ask him for his money, his watch, and the buckles in his shoes.' When the man had helped himself to what he wanted, George said there was a seal on the watch-chain of little value that he would like to retain. The man said, 'Your Majesty must be aware that we have already been here some time, and that it is not safe for me to stay longer, but if you will give me your word not to say anything of what has passed for twenty-four hours, I will place the seal at the same time to-morrow morning on that stone', and he pointed to a particular place. Both men kept their promise, the King retrieved his seal, and the robber made his escape over the wall. 'His Majesty,' the King told Lord Duncannon, 'never afterwards walked alone in Kensington Gardens.'[9] William IV was only five when his great-grandfather died, so no doubt he heard the story from his father, George III.

It was not only George II who seems to have fallen foul of his more robust subjects, but his wife also. Writing from Marlborough House on 23 September 1732, some four years after Frederick's arrival in England, Sarah Churchill, since 1722 Dowager Duchess of Marlborough, a lively letter-writer and invaluable gossip, told her granddaughter, Lady John Russell (whom she always addressed as Lady Russell):

Two or three days ago, Her sacred Majesty was in great danger of being ravished. She was walking from Kensington to London early in the morning and having a vast desire to appear more able in everything than other people, she walked so fast as to get before my Lord Chamberlain and the two princesses upon one of the causeways, quite out of sight. Whether this proceeded from their compliments to let her see how much stronger she was than they or from any other accident, I cannot say. But my Lord Grantham meeting a country clown asked him if he had met any person and how far they were off! To which he answered he had met a jolly crummy woman with whom he had been fighting some time to kiss her. I am surprised at the man's fancy! And my Lord Grantham was so frightened that he screamed out and said it was the Queen. Upon which the country fellow was out of his wits, fell upon his knees, cried and earnestly begged of my Lord Grantham to speak for him for he was sure he should be hanged for what he had done. But did not further explain what it was. And her Majesty does not own more than that he struggled with her, but that she got the better of him.

This story is not so extraordinary as it sounds. Both George and Caroline were great walkers. In September 1729, when George returned to England after his first visit to Hanover following his accession in 1727, Caroline set out from Kensington Palace with her children to meet the King, walking through Hyde Park and down Piccadilly to St James's Park where she encountered the King's procession, returning to Kensington in the King's coach.

Indoors, the custom of holding open court prevailed, and almost anyone who looked respectable was admitted to the Drawing Rooms, where, in the evening, they might witness the Princess of Wales and the Duchess of Montagu go 'halves at hazard' and win £600. Unless specifically invited, however, entrée to a ball might prove more difficult. In 1715 one Dudley Ryder was twice turned away from a court ball but eventually got in by tipping the doorman a shilling. The Prince of Wales's accomplishments as a dancer may have been the attraction. Of celebrations for his thirty-second birthday Lady Cowper wrote: 'I never saw the Court so splendidly fine. The evening concluded with a ball, which the Prince and Princess began. She danced in slippers very well; the Prince better than anybody.' A Drawing Room in 1715 was described as 'Extremely full and company dressed very fine, scarce any without gold or silk trimmings on their clothes.'

A decade later the observant César de Saussure attended a Sunday afternoon Drawing Room, held between two and three o'clock, when he saw the King 'immediately surrounded by a circle of persons all standing up there being no chairs in the room lest anyone should be guilty of seating themselves'. The King, he says, went to the end of the room and talked to the 'foreign ministers' for a few minutes, and then three ladies were presented, and the King 'kissed them all affectionately on the lips'. He explained: 'It is the custom in this country, and many ladies would be displeased should you fail to salute them thus; still some of the ladies who have travelled in foreign countries now offer their cheeks instead of their lips.' Saussure thought the evening Drawing Rooms, held on Mondays and Fridays 'from eight till ten or eleven in the evening', much more pleasant than those held on Sunday afternoons, 'for the apartments are magnificently lighted, and more ladies attend them, and the latter are always an adornment to society'.

César de Saussure, who had arrived in England at the age of twenty, and in 1740 was appointed secretary to Lord Cathcart, reported the Prince of Wales as 'taller than his father, his figure well-proportioned, and he is not as stout; his eyes are very prominent.

He looks serious and even grave, and is always richly dressed, being fond of fine clothes'. Caroline he described as having once been 'one of the most beautiful princesses in Europe, but has grown too stout'. She was witty and well read, gracious and amiable, 'besides being very charitable and kind; but the enemies of the House of Hanover complain that she is too economical'. Princess Anne, at the age of sixteen, he thought 'very pale, and would be good-looking were she not marked with smallpox'. Princess Amelia (at fifteen) he thought 'a handsome blond with charming features', and Princess Caroline, although only ten, he found 'very tall and stout, and looks like a woman. She is good-looking, with very dark hair'.[10]

Oddly enough, for she had the reputation of being a prude, it was Lady Cowper who recommended to Caroline that she should see a play called *The Wanton Wife* ('certainly not more obscene than all comedies are'),[11] and so partial was Caroline to the theatre that she stood as godmother to the daughter of an opera singer. She loved attending christenings, but gave a wide berth to weddings and funerals.

Life, however, was not simply a round of parties. Despite the smooth accession of King George, the Hanoverian honeymoon was swiftly drawing to a close. The English were not averse to the sale of honours and sinecures so long as only Englishmen were concerned, but when the King's avaricious German mistresses became involved it was time to wonder whether the Act of Settlement had been such a good idea after all.

No matter what the composition of the Commons or the House of Lords, the King was at liberty to appoint whatever ministers he pleased, and rather than placate the Tories by creating some sort of coalition, he had excluded Jacobite Tories from office entirely. Hence discontent on several fronts was mounting. Jacobite sentiments were openly expressed, and the distinct possibility of a rebellion was set in motion when early in 1715 a general election was held, during the course of which the King unwisely issued a proclamation urging voters to return only those parliamentary candidates in favour of the Protestant succession. The Whigs triumphed and immediately sought to impeach three Tory peers who had been at liberty since the death of Queen Anne. They posed no serious threat, but one of them, Lord Bolingbroke, sensing he now had little to lose, slipped out of the theatre on the evening of 6 April, and disguised as a valet escaped to France. There he made for the court of the Pretender, to be joined by the Duke of Ormonde, who had been sacked by the King as Captain-General. Not too well briefed on the true strength of his support in England, and in particular mistaking the liberty the English took in insulting their monarch for a desire actually to exchange him for another, Prince James decided – after dithering for some time – that his hour had come.

Bolingbroke, whose Parisian mistress was busy passing his plans to the English ambassador, advised the Prince to invade England. Instead, James sailed for Scotland, and firmly believing in the Divine Right of Kings he thought it unnecessary actually to appeal for support directly to the people. But on 6 September 1715 the Earl of Mar did declare for James, and eight days later Mar took the town of Perth. But like the Prince, he too was given to fatal indecisiveness, and failed to march on to Edinburgh. French support, on which Prince James had always pinned his hopes, failed to materialize, for by an act of extreme misfortune, on 1 September Louis XIV expired, and the new regent, the son of Sophia's niece Elizabeth-Charlotte, was in favour of a reconciliation with the Hanoverians. With hindsight, the Jacobite rebellion of 1715–16 can be seen to have been doomed from the start. But with large areas of Scotland nominally under the control of the Earl of Mar, the Hanoverian commander in the north, the handsome young Duke of Argyll, wrote to London insisting 'on considerable reinforcements, for without it, or a miracle, not only this country will be utterly destroyed but the rest of his Majesty's dominions put in extremist danger'.

'Extremist danger' had already been detected in Oxford, in London itself and in parts of the Midlands and the West Country, where the Duke of Ormonde was planning to invade. Twenty-one new regiments were raised, the Channel Fleet was manned and habeas corpus was suspended. Five members of the House of Commons and two peers, known Jacobite sympathizers, were detained. At the beginning of November the Earl of Mar crossed the border into England. However sanguine the King may have felt about the eventual outcome of Prince James's designs on his throne (and James himself had not yet trespassed on British soil), the least he could have been expected to do was dispatch his son to the scene of action, if not as commander-in-chief at least at the head of a

respectable contingent of men. This he flatly refused to do, setting
a most unfortunate precedent for the next reign, and throughout
the entire emergency the Prince of Wales was compelled to kick
his heels at St James's Palace. His biographer has left an amusing
summary of events:

> While the Pretender cut such an unheroic figure, it might have
> been thought that his rival, 'Young Hanover Brave', might have
> been given the chance to do rather better. But nothing of the
> sort occurred. Instead, the King took the rebellion as a chance
> to humiliate his son. The Prince may not have been a military
> genius, but he had shown himself at Oudenarde perfectly capable
> of performing an officer's basic duty, that of riding in front of
> his men and getting shot at first. It would, of course, never do
> for the heir to a precarious throne to be cut down by a bare-
> bummed Highlander; but some field command could surely have
> been found in which he could lose neither his own life nor too
> many of his men's, and the dividends in popularity would have
> been enormous. Instead he spent the months of crisis in inglorious
> ease at St James's.[12]

Prince James eventually got around to landing at Peterhead in
Aberdeenshire on 22 December. By this time an Anglo-Scottish
force of Jacobite rebels had been defeated with ease at Preston,
and in Scotland, at Sheriffmuir, five miles north of Stirling, an
indecisive battle was fought between the Earl of Mar and the
Duke of Argyll, at the conclusion of which many of Mar's troops
decided to go home. By the time the twenty-seven-year-old Prince
James arrived on the scene his cause was already hopeless. 'When
we saw the man whom they called our king, we found ourselves
not at all animated by his presence,' an anonymous writer declared. Indeed, they saw 'nothing that looked like spirit', and 'our
men began to despise him'.

James entered Dundee on 6 January 1716 and planned to be
crowned on the 23rd, at the Palace of Scone, but with news that
Argyll's forces had been reinforced he turned tail and re-embarked
for France. He had been on Scottish soil for just six inglorious
weeks. King George and his descendants survived not through
superiority of arms (Argyll remained pessimistic to the end) but
through sheer incompetence and lack of dynamic leadership from

Mar and James. The Pretender was now disowned by the French regent, lived for a time at Avignon, and eventually went into permanent exile in Italy.

The London crowds who had welcomed King George in 1714 and had flaunted Jacobite white roses in 1715 now turned out in force to jeer at the captured insurgents. On 9 February a number of prisoners were put on trial, and present to witness the proceedings was the Prince of Wales. He 'came home much touched with compassion', according to Lady Cowper. Considerable clemency was shown. Seven peers were brought to trial but only two, the twenty-six-year-old Earl of Derwentwater, a grandson of Charles II, and Viscount Kenmure, were beheaded. It is not impossible that behind the scenes the Prince and Princess of Wales had both cautioned restraint.

The King had kept his head throughout some anxious months, but he seemed incapable of gaining personal popularity. There was nothing the Londoners liked better than to cheer or to boo. They now decided to boo, for what use was a king who did not dine in state and who slunk off to the theatre in a sedan-chair? The only possible explanation for one of George's most hare-brained schemes can have been a desire to curb the popularity of his heir, who was forever showing himself off to the people. How much, the King asked Lord Townshend, would it cost to plough up St James's Park and grow turnips there? 'Only three crowns, Sir,' Townshend assured him. Whether the Secretary of State meant the crowns of England, Scotland and Ireland, or those of his master, the Prince of Wales and Frederick, the King took his point and left the park unharrowed.

Dull and unimaginative in so many ways, nevertheless George I was not quite such an 'honest blockhead' as some people imagine. At Kensington Palace, which he particularly liked, for it reminded him of Herrenhausen, he extended the modernizations already undertaken by Wren for William III, altering the south-west pavilion built on to the original property, Nottingham House, to provide a reception-room for visitors. And George called in William Kent to decorate the new state rooms, the most spectacular of which, the Cupola Room, was designed to reflect the wisdom and virtues of the new Hanoverian monarch. Kent may have intended to flatter, but it was George who acted as patron.

There is a theory that George I made no attempt to understand

England or the English because at heart he entertained doubts about his rights, and it is interesting that he declined to touch for the king's evil, just as William III, whose strict claim to the throne was also doubtful, had declined. That decision dismayed the poor. As for the aristocracy, they could scarcely credit the King's choice of mistresses. The least objectionable of them, however, they had not met, for being a Catholic she had had the sagacity to stay in Hanover. She was yet another Countess von Platen (the family more or less bred courtesans), and unlike the Elephant and Castle she was regarded as beautiful. The King now decided to pay her a visit – for was it not his duty to see that all was well with the Electorate and that his grandson was behaving himself? A visit to Hanover would enable him also to get away from a country he did not love and which did not care very much for him.

4

'They Are All Mad'

George I went home in July 1716. He had to inform Parliament of his plans, and because he would be away at least six months he proposed setting up a Council of Regency, as a method of curbing the influence of his son, to whom, when they met in the evening in the Prince's apartments, he no longer even spoke. He was told there was no precedent for a regency being put into commission other than to act for a monarch who was a minor. But not so ignorant of English history as has been supposed, the King suggested a compromise; he dug up a virtually meaningless medieval title for the Prince of Wales, Guardian of the Realm and Lieutenant. The beauty of it was that it carried few plenipotentiary powers.

There were two reasons why Frederick's father was taught this particular lesson in how a father might behave towards his son. The first was quite simply the King's jealousy of his son's popularity. The Elephant and Castle were incapable of entertaining as a queen consort might have done. There was little amusement at court, with the King popping out to play cards in private, virtually no patronage of the arts and no intellectual life whatever. George Augustus and Caroline, on the other hand, engaged Handel as music master to their daughters and enjoyed the company of writers. At least Caroline did. It would be an exaggeration to describe the Prince of Wales as well read (he was scarcely literate), but the Princess of Wales created in her own apartments at St James's Palace something of that atmosphere of a literary and philosophical salon in which she had been bred in Berlin. Caroline had no need to study Bacon for effect, and the fact that she did bury her head in the thirteenth-century works of Oxford's 'wonderful doctor' places her capacities, as well as her interests, in an intellectual league rare for royalty to inhabit. With no competition from the King's apartments it was no wonder that the young, the ambitious and the world of fashion all flocked to Caroline's Drawing Rooms, where apart from anything else English could be spoken and understood. It was greatly appreciated that the Princess had chosen only English women as members of her household, and she had learnt how to behave, embracing her ladies when they came into and out of waiting, and, as far as Lady Cowper was concerned, 'saying the kindest things'.

The Prince's popularity was not the only problem. Antagonism between the King and the Prince of Wales had also been caused because of George Augustus and Caroline's dislike of his German retinue, whose members consumed a considerable portion of the privy purse. 'Monsieur Robethon was a rogue', in the opinion of the Princess, and 'Baron Bothmar another'. Unfortunately Caroline spoke quite openly about her feelings, and the chatterboxes who attended her, especially her flighty maids of honour, one of whom, the buxom Mary Bellenden, the Prince of Wales tried to seduce, did not hesitate to repeat her indiscretions. In the claustrophobic environment of the court they soon got back to the Hanoverians, and of course to the King. Lady Cowper coined a phrase that has been used countless times since, by women offended by the conduct of other members of their sex; she described the Elephant and Castle as 'no better than they should be'. George Augustus let it be known he believed Madam von der Schulenburg had slept with every man in Hanover, Schulenburg complained to the Princess, and the Princess denied (probably without much conviction) that her husband would ever have dreamt of saying such a thing. It was from family bickering as much as anything that the King was anxious to escape.

However, there were reasons of state as well as jealousy that had made King George reluctant to acknowledge his son's position in the order of precedence and to leave him behind as regent. Power and influence were divided between the sovereign, Parliament, the ministry appointed by the sovereign, the Cabinet committee and the full Cabinet. In the reign of Queen Anne the Cabinet committee consisted of about eight principal ministers; the task of the full Cabinet was merely to ratify decisions already taken. Whereas William III, who enjoyed making policy, had presided over the Cabinet committee, Queen Anne declined to do so, for she was almost always in poor health and had no aptitude for chairmanship. But after dinner on Sundays (dinner being taken in the middle of the day) she did preside over the full Cabinet, thus being kept fully informed once a week of major decisions while being spared lengthy discussions and the details of administration. This was the situation inherited and continued by George I. Most of his ministers spoke French, and those like Walpole who did not, were alleged to resort to Latin when conversing with the King, so it was not George I's inability to speak English, as is often supposed, that dictated his decision not to attend meetings of the Cabinet committee but his basic lack of appetite for getting bogged down in matters that frankly did not interest him. As the King did not attend the Cabinet committee, naturally the Prince of Wales did not either; he merely accompanied his father at meetings of the full Cabinet, only about eight of which King George attended anyway, ceasing to put in an appearance at all after 1718. Even if he did not express his fears in so many words, what the King must now surely have suspected was that if George Augustus was appointed regent he might very easily join in meetings of the Cabinet committee, and thus have an opportunity of shaping foreign and domestic policy. But he did not mind his attendance at full Cabinet meetings in his absence and hearing details of decisions already taken.[1]

As if the humiliation of not being appointed regent was not enough for the Prince of Wales to have to swallow (a humiliation George Augustus would not hesitate to inflict in years to come on Frederick), the King had another trick up his sleeve. As the Duke of Marlborough had suffered a stroke it was necessary to appoint a new Captain-General. A serious candidate for the post was the Duke of Argyll, chamberlain to the Prince. Not only did the King appoint General Charles Cadogan, who had fought at Oudenarde but was a lifelong rival of Argyll, but he insisted the Prince should dismiss Argyll from his household. When George Augustus protested, the King threatened to bring his brother, the Duke of York, over from Hanover and make *him* Guardian of the Realm. The Prince was obliged to pocket his pride and to lose a perfectly satisfactory servant, telling Baron Bernstorff, one of his father's chief Hanoverian ministers, he was resolved to sacrifice everything 'to please and live well with the King'. The King left another of his Hanoverian advisers, von Bothmar, in London to spy on his son, taking with him to Hanover James Stanhope (created Earl Stanhope in 1718), who spoke German and was *au fait* with Hanoverian foreign policy, and Jean de Robethon, the arch intriguer, who had been given £300 a year by the Prince and was thus expected to spy on the King. Robethon told Lady Cowper that George Augustus 'only wanted power to displace everybody the King liked, and dissolve Parliament'. On receipt of this information, the Countess noted: 'They are all mad.'

On 3 July, while otherwise engaged in a row with his son over the Duke of Argyll, the King nominated his grandson Prince Frederick, still only nine years old, a Royal Knight of the Garter.[2] Frederick's installation in St George's Chapel, Windsor, was to be delayed two years, and then it was carried out (on 30 April 1718) by proxy, but the King was planning to invest his grandson in Hanover on Christmas Eve. In the wake of the King's journey to Herrenhausen for his reunion with Frederick and the Duke of York, there travelled an amusing if not always an entirely impartial observer of the contemporary scene, Lady Mary Wortley Montagu, an inveterate continental explorer. She was a daughter of the Duke of Kingston. Her husband, Edward Wortley Montagu, was for two years ambassador to Constantinople. Already intrigued by the new Hanoverian court in London, Lady Mary was naturally curious to set eyes on the boy who was second in line to the throne, and she may even have been asked by Caroline to report. Frederick's governor assured Lady Mary that his royal pupil was a genius, and felt sufficiently confident of his sycophantic judgement to leave the Prince alone with Lady Mary so that Frederick might not feel inhibited in talking to her. She had a long conversation with the Prince, and told the Countess of Bristol he had 'all the accomplishments which it is possible to have at his age, with an air of sprightliness and understanding, and something so very engaging and easy in his behaviour that he needs not the advantage of his rank to appear charming'. In other words, he was a perfectly normal little boy; and when Lady Bristol made the Prince's acquaintance on his eventual arrival in England her expectations, stirred up by Lady Mary, were not disappointed. Nevertheless Lady Mary was surprised 'by the quickness and politeness that appeared in everything that he said, joined to a person perfectly agreeable'. She found he had 'the fine fair hair of the Princess'.[3] And, indeed, some of the portraits painted of the Prince as a boy confirm his fair complexion, evidently exchanged in puberty for the sallow complexion with which he was born, as they do the bulging eyes he had inherited from his paternal Guelph ancestors. Other painters, no doubt inspired by hopes of later adult commissions, chose to emphasize his boyish good looks.

Left largely to his own devices, however, and waited upon by gentlemen of the bedchamber, fencing and dancing masters, doctors, fiddlers and a resident organist, footmen, at least a dozen cooks, innumerable coachmen and postilions but only one washerwoman (three other washerwomen had accompanied the King to England), Frederick had already discovered the pleasures of drink and cards, and hardly surprisingly, in the absence of both the Elector and the Electoral Prince, he had taken a fancy to dressing up, for without parental discipline, guidance or love he had begun to create his own fantasy world, holding levees at which he received courtiers, ministers and visitors to Hanover, ostensibly on behalf of his grandfather. This is why he needed the Garter with which to adorn himself. A sense of his own importance could only have been enhanced when in 1717 the King created him Duke of Gloucester, an injudicious choice of title, surely, and an ill omen as things turned out. On the very day his grandfather died, 11 June 1727, Frederick was also created Duke of Edinburgh (and just for good measure, Marquess of Ely, Earl of Eltham, Viscount Launceston and Baron Snowdon). As the King was on his way to Hanover at the time, he must have left instructions for this second dukedom to be gazetted before leaving England.

Another visitor to Herrenhausen in 1716 was one of Lady Bristol's sons, the Hon. John Hervey. On the face of it, he was there to pay his respects to the King; in reality, to take a rather closer look at Frederick, upon the 'blooming beauties of whose person and character' he was soon reporting to his father, a wealthy Suffolk country gentleman who had been raised to the peerage as Baron Hervey of Ickworth by Queen Anne and advanced to the earldom of Bristol on the accession of George I. John Hervey was the eldest son of the 1st Earl of Bristol by his second marriage, and his machinations as a minor eighteenth-century politician (he served for two years as Lord Privy Seal under Walpole) would not be remembered today were it not for the memoirs he wrote – and the memoirs would not have been written had he not ingratiated himself with Queen Caroline. On the death of this older half-brother he succeeded to his father's courtesy title, and he is known to history as Lord Hervey, although in fact in June 1733 he was summoned

to the House of Lords in his father's barony as Lord Hervey of
Ickworth. But he never succeeded as Earl of Bristol, for dying in
1743, when he was only forty-six, he predeceased his father.[4]

When he arrived at Hanover to inspect the nine-year-old Prince
Frederick, Hervey was an effeminate-looking young man of twenty,
fresh from study in Paris, and Frederick was probably pleased to
be taken notice of by someone a good deal closer to his own age
than his great-uncle or the ordinary run of courtier. A genuine
friendship between Frederick and Hervey soon developed, but from
the start Hervey's motive in cultivating the lonely boy's affection
was anything but disinterested. He was in receipt of strict paternal
instructions, Lord Bristol having told him: '. . . when you see and
are sure ye foundation in Prince Frederick's favour . . . is laid as
indelibly as you know how I would have it, and I know you are
capable of contriveing, you may think of returning homewards'.
The King was already fifty-six, with, at that time, only a short
life expectancy remaining. It was not too fanciful to imagine that
before long Frederick's father would be king, and it had occurred
to Lord Bristol that if Frederick were to suggest to his parents
that his new young friend from England would make an entertaining
addition to their household, his prospects would begin to shine –
which they did. By 1717 Hervey was already a gentleman of the
bedchamber to the Prince of Wales.

While King George was indulging his grandson in Hanover, his
son was left in England in a state of resentment, frustration and
humiliation. From foreign affairs, in which the King took a particular
interest, the Prince of Wales had been excluded entirely. If
appointments within the Cabinet, the Treasury, the Board of
Admiralty or among colonial governorships were to fall vacant,
he was not permitted to fill them. He might not even sanction
promotions above the rank of ensign in the Brigade of Guards.
Yet he was not idle, and he made the very best of a bad job,
determined to prepare himself for the day when he would be king
– and in a position to take his revenge not upon his father but
his own son. 'The King was no sooner gone than the Prince took
a turn of being kind and civil to everyone,' according to Lady
Cowper, 'and applied himself to be well with the King's Ministers
and to understand the state of the nation.' He deserted St James's
Palace for Hampton Court, commandeered Queen Anne's apartments
and commissioned James Thornhill to repaint the bedroom ceiling,

having a portrait of his missing son incorporated in the cornice. Frederick hangs above the window, opposite his grandfather's portrait, which is positioned immediately above the bed; on either side are likenesses of George Augustus and Caroline. Frederick looks charming in a blue costume and a red cloak trimmed with ermine, and Thornhill's magnificent ceiling remains one of the essential items for any visitor to Hampton Court to view.

George took to dining in public, and the *haut monde* streamed out of London to share the romantic setting of Cardinal Wolsey's riverside palace. Caroline was again pregnant, but in September, anxious to make as much of his father's absence as he could, the Prince of Wales dragged her off on a provincial tour, taking in Tunbridge Wells, where he tipped the dipper at the well 5 guineas. The Prince was determined to exert authority and became 'very inquisitive about the revenue', Robert Walpole reported to Stanhope in Hanover, 'calls daily for papers, which may tend to very particular informations; and I am not sure they are not more for other people's perusal than his own. By some things that daily drop from him, he seems to be preparing to keep an interest of his own in Parliament independent of the King's' – in other words, to form an Opposition. Ministers were in an exceedingly difficult situation, as Walpole fully realized, for if they denied the Prince any requests they would be offending their future sovereign. 'As to our behaviour to His Highness,'[5] he went on to Stanhope,

> we take care not to be wanting in duty and respect, nor to give any offence or handle to such as are ready to take any opportunity to render business impracticable, and we hope we demean ourselves so that neither they who would misrepresent us to the King for making our court too much to the Prince, nor they who would hurt us with the Prince for doing it too little, can have any fair advantage over us, but this is a game not to be managed without difficulty.

Games were what Walpole was particularly good at playing, and he had every reason to try to keep in with both the King and his heir. His office was largely a lucrative sinecure, and he was devoted to money. Until the Hanoverian succession, Walpole was a comparatively poor man. Born into the Norfolk squirearchy, he was the third of a family of nineteen children, and although educated at Eton and King's College, Cambridge, he retained the rough-and-ready manners expected of a hard-drinking, hard-riding county worthy, which is what he became when he inherited his father's estate at Houghton on the death of his two older brothers. When he entered Parliament in 1701 he did so for Castle Rising, but a year later he was elected for King's Lynn, a seat he retained for forty years. Within three years of George I's accession Walpole was a rich man, and he intended to remain one, for his tastes ran to every kind of expense and extravagance, from hounds and shooting to building, eating, drinking and buying china, furniture and pictures. Between 1722 and 1735 William Kent, who was later to work for Frederick, virtually lived at Houghton Hall, and by the time he had finished he had produced for Walpole what remains 'the most complete and sumptuous Palladian house in England'.[6] The paintings Walpole accumulated were so important they eventually formed the nucleus of the Hermitage Collection in Russia, being sold in 1791 by Walpole's wastrel grandson to Catherine the Great.[7] With his ruddy cheeks, bushy eyebrows and double chin, Robert Walpole was a big man in every way. He employed no less than fifty gardeners just to do the weeding. He spent £1,219. 3s. 11d. on hangings for a state bed. His wine bill commonly ran to £1,500 a year. In 1733 he returned to his wine merchant a cool 552 *dozen* empties.

With the onset of autumn the Prince and Princess of Wales were rowed away from Hampton Court and returned to St James's. That was on 28 October. A week later Caroline went into labour. The Council was summoned and a German midwife, 'whose countenance prognosticated ill', according to Lady Cowper, was hired. Delivery was delayed, the Princess had 'a shivering fit', and 'everybody but the Princess and the Germans were now in a great fright'. Arguments raged between the nationalities as to which doctor should be called. The midwife claimed the English women had threatened to hang her if the Princess miscarried, and the Prince joined in the helpful hubbub by threatening to throw out of the window anyone who meddled. Lord Townshend 'met the midwife in the outward room, and ran and shook and squeezed her by the hand, and made kind faces at her: for she understood no language but German'. The Princess, meanwhile, 'continued in a languishing condition', and was eventually delivered 'of a dead Prince'.

The King was still overseas when this predictable outcome occurred, and what Frederick's thoughts were when eventually he was told, we do not know. Had the baby survived birth he would have been brought up in England with his sisters, and would have been twelve years old and, like the rest of the family, a stranger to his brother in 1728, when Frederick finally arrived in England, but he might have proved a more congenial brother than the brat born five years later, upon whom Caroline, having by that time lost two baby boys, was to lavish all her affection.

Leaving his wife behind to recuperate, the Prince of Wales, realizing his father would be home in a matter of weeks, made one last bid for popularity by engineering a progress through Kent, Sussex and Hampshire, receiving loyal addresses from Jacobites, dispensing with passports to France and generally thinking up ways to incite paternal wrath – which was not long in descending on his head. When the King landed, at the end of 1716, it was to find his son and heir basking in greater popular esteem than ever; so, taking a leaf out of the Prince's book, in the summer of 1717 he removed to Hampton Court, where he took to dining each day in company. In August he shouldered a gun, and managed to bring down a brace of partridge. He even braced himself for a visit to his least favourite residence, Windsor Castle, and went stag-hunting in the Great Park. Hearing that the Prince intended to honour the October Newmarket race meeting with his presence, the King decided he too could be as English as the English, and dashed to the racecourse ahead of him.

This childish game of leapfrog continued for a year, but with two men as temperamentally unstable as George I and the Prince of Wales, a final clash was almost inevitable. It came on the occasion of the birth of another boy to Caroline, on 2 November 1717, the first live birth of a Hanoverian prince on British soil. Into the bedroom at St James's Palace crowded the Archbishop of Canterbury and at least a dozen peeresses.[8] Every semblance of proper conduct was observed, in marked contrast to the lack of oversight when Frederick was born. The Prince of Wales sent John Hervey to inform the King of the birth, the child being third in line of succession to the throne, and the King dispatched the Duke of Portland with a message of congratulations to the parents.

The Prince had two godfathers in mind, his father and his uncle, the Duke of York. The King consented to stand, but insisted that the Duke of Newcastle, who had spent his life ingratiating himself first with Sophia of Hanover and then with King George, and who had recently been appointed Lord Chamberlain, should take the place of his brother. Newcastle was a particular enemy of the Prince and Princess (no one liked him, in point of fact), and the King's action can only have been a deliberate attempt to create friction. The child was baptized George William. Even before the Archbishop of Canterbury had read the final prayers the King left the room, leaving the powder-keg he had planted to be ignited without any further assistance from him.

As soon as the service was over the Prince, his temper short at the best of times and now no longer under control, darted round the bed, shook his fist at the Duke of Newcastle, and said, 'You are a rascal, but I shall find you', a remark considered tantamount to a challenge to a duel. (The Duke later insisted that the Prince had actually said, 'I shall fight you.') Newcastle duly complained to the King, and without troubling to hear his son's side of the story the King ordered the arrest of the Prince of Wales. Farce, soon to turn to tragedy, had well and truly set in. Caroline said that if her husband was under arrest she too must be arrested. They both remained overnight in her bedroom. In the morning, when Henrietta Howard arrived to perform her duties as lady-in-waiting, she found the palace under siege. 'What was my astonishment,' she recounted later, 'when going to the Princess's apartment the yeomen in the guard chamber pointed their halberds at my breast, and told me I must not pass. I urged that it was my duty to attend the Princess, but they said, "No matter, I must not pass that way."'

News of the drama nearly set London alight. Persuaded that to send his son and daughter-in-law to the Tower was not a good idea, the King simply gave orders that, without delaying even to pack, the pair of them were to leave St James's. It was pointed out that the Princess was still recovering from childbirth, so her benevolent father-in-law relented to the extent that if she promised not to communicate with her husband she might remain at the palace with her children. He did not know Caroline very well. Torn between her new-born son and her daughters, of whom she was reasonably fond, and her husband, upon whom her political future depended, she sent word to the King that if the Prince were to leave, she would leave also. Hence in the chill of a November

evening the heir to the throne and his wife, accompanied by the
Princess's maids of honour, most of them in tears except Mary
Bellenden who tried to keep everybody's spirits up by singing 'Over
the Hills and Far Away', scampered up St James's to Arlington
Street, where they were provided with temporary accommodation
by the Earl of Grantham, the Prince's chamberlain.[9] Not surprisingly,
on her arrival Caroline fainted.[10]

Somewhat late in the day, the King now demanded an explanation
from the Prince for his conduct at the christening, and sent a
deputation of three dukes to extract it. They returned empty-handed.
Caroline, realizing that things were getting seriously out of hand,
and recalling the fate still being endured at Ahlden by her banished
mother-in-law, advised the Prince to calm down, whereupon he
sent a reasonably submissive letter to his irate parent:

> Your Majesty will have the goodness not to look upon what I
> said, to the duke in particular, as a want of respect to your
> Majesty. However, if I have been so unhappy as to offend your
> Majesty contrary to my intention, I ask your pardon, and beg
> your Majesty will be persuaded that I am, with the greatest
> respect, your Majesty's most humble dutiful son and servant.

But that did not constitute sufficient humble pie for the King's
taste. He said he had received enough professions of the Prince
and Princess's sincerity in the past to make him vomit, and this
time the Prince must sign a document agreeing never to have in
his service 'any person or persons distasteful to the King'. He was
also to surrender to the King the guardianship of his children.
Pushed too far, George Augustus and Caroline refused to sign.
They were informed they would not be admitted on Sunday to
the chapel at St James's Palace, so with commendable initiative
they repaired to St James's Church in Piccadilly, there to receive
Holy Communion and gather public sympathy.

The King's ministers were advising caution, but without a doubt
George must have been egged on by his mistresses, intent on getting
their own back on the Princess for her many disparaging remarks
about them. What the King would have liked to do was bring his
son back on bended knees, grovelling for money, by making
Parliament renounce the £100,000 a year agreed as his portion of
the civil list. Stymied in this ambition, he began to thrash around

with ever-increasing stupidity. Ambassadors were told that if they called on the couple they need not expect to be received by the Sovereign, and peers and Privy Councillors were likewise warned away from George and Caroline. Sentries were instructed no longer to salute; husbands and wives in separate royal households were to leave one or the other. Mrs Howard, whose husband was employed by the King, declined to forsake the Princess so she separated from her husband – which in her case may not have been too great a sacrifice. Eventually what the King achieved by his outrageous conduct (apart from laying down a pattern of behaviour to be reiterated almost in its entirety in the next reign) was the death of his new grandson.

The King had insisted that all the children, including the baby prince, remain at St James's Palace. Denied attention from his mother, George William began to pine. So the King reluctantly allowed the Princess to visit her baby. But when he found her presence at St James's too distasteful to endure, he packed the baby off to Kensington Palace, where it was perceived to be desperately ill. To Kensington the Prince and Princess hurried, and they were with Frederick's little brother when at eight o'clock on the evening of 6 February 1718 he died, just three months old. He was buried at night (royal funerals were traditionally conducted after dark) in the Henry VII Chapel at Westminster Abbey, and the drama of the expulsion from court, together with its tragic consequences, gripped Europe, even engaging the attention of the supreme chronicler of his time, the Duc de Saint-Simon. 'For a long time,' he wrote in his memoirs, 'a species of war had been declared between the King of England and his son, the Prince of Wales, which had caused much scandal; and which had enlisted the Court on one side, and made much stir in the Parliament. George had more than once broken out with indecency against his son; he had long since driven him from the palace, and would not see him. He had so cut down his income that he could scarcely subsist.'

And Saint-Simon went on to offer an explanation for the antagonism between George I and George II with extraordinary echoes of one possible reason for the later detestation of George II for Frederick. 'The father never could endure this son, because he did not believe him to be his own. He had more than suspected the Duchess, his wife, to be in relations with Count Königsmarck.'

And for good measure the Duke supplied his own quixotic version of Königsmarck's death. George, he says, surprised the Count one morning leaving Sophia Dorothea's chamber, and 'threw him into a hot oven'.[11]

When news of the baby prince's death reached the Dowager Duchesse d'Orléans, she wrote to one of her many correspondents:

> The poor Princess is greatly to be pitied. There must be something else at the bottom of all this, when everything is given a double meaning. They say that the King is himself in love with the Princess. I do not believe this, for I consider that the King has in no ways a lover-like nature; he only loves himself. He is a bad man, he never had any consideration for the mother who loved him so tenderly, yet without her he would never have become King of England.[12]

While waiting to inherit the throne bequeathed to his mother by the English Parliament, it seems highly probable that George, indifferent though he may have been to the English language, may have whiled away some idle hours at Herrenhausen leafing through the pages of English history. He would have found there was no need even to go back as far as the imprisoning by Mary Tudor of her sister Elizabeth to discover precedents for family harassment. As recently as 1685 the future Queen Anne had become a focus for Protestant opposition to her father's desire to return England to the Catholic fold, and during the reign of William and Mary, Anne went into political opposition. When she and Prince George withdrew from court to live at Syon House, the Middlesex home of the Duke of Somerset, her guards were withdrawn. 'Ye guards in St James's Park did not stand to theire arms nether when the Prince went nor came,' the Princess complained to Sarah Churchill. And when Anne refused instructions from her sister Queen Mary to dismiss Sarah from her household, the Queen issued orders that no one who visited Anne was to appear at court.

As to the Duchess's hint of incestuous affection for Caroline on the part of the King, this need not be dismissed too lightly. While mocked for his taste in mistresses, the King may well have felt a twinge of jealousy because of his son's essentially happy marriage to an attractive and intelligent woman, and incest, or at any rate fantasies of incest, is often the last resort of a man unable to cope with what are loosely regarded as normal relationships. If the rumours were true that the newly ennobled Duchess of Munster (she was not yet Duchess of Kendal) was the King's half-sister as well as his mistress, his penchant for incest was a fact.

George Augustus and Caroline could not remain in Lord Grantham's house for long, so they set up home in an area of London known as Leicester Fields, moving intially into Savile House, which proved too small, and finally settling on the house next door, Leicester House, built in 1630 by the 2nd Earl of Leicester, linking the two houses together by means of a covered passage (this was removed in 1727). Although the 4th Earl of Leicester had spent £2,000 on repairs to the house at the turn of the century, the Prince of Wales now spent a further £2,760 on alterations. The 6th Earl had let the house to John Leveson-Gower, 2nd Lord Gower (he later became 1st Earl Gower), and it was in fact from Lord Gower that George now took a lease, at a rent of £500 a year, paying his first quarter's rent on 25 March 1718.

Leicester House stood on the north side of what is now Leicester Square. The area was not yet fashionable (brothels and footpads abounded) but it was soon to become so. Leicester House had a rather dull formal garden at the rear but a useful large forecourt through which a procession of carriages were soon to make their way, for in Leicester Fields the Prince of Wales was now to establish what in effect was a rival court to his father's. Disaffected Whig politicians who were out of office anyway had little to lose and possibly much to gain by being friendly to the heir to the throne, and despite the King's rather pathetic attempts to enliven life at St James's Palace, his entertainments were no match for the balls and masquerades laid on by Caroline. Before long even Townshend and Walpole could not resist calling at Leicester House, joking to the Princess that in England people were fond of forbidden fruit. One of the most colourful visitors was an implacable enemy of the Hanoverians, who attended Leicester House merely to annoy the King, the vain, eccentric and immensely rich Duchess of Buckingham, a daughter of James II by his mistress Katherine Sedley, Countess of Dorchester. It was the Duchess's husband who built Buckingham House (later purchased by George III) on the site of the present Buckingham Palace.

The King seemed to be on a hiding to nowhere. Advised that the Prince of Wales had a perfect right to appoint members of his own household, he next attempted to use Frederick as a pawn, suggesting that the Prince of Wales should contribute £40,000 a year to pay for the boy's education. George Augustus said he would be delighted to do so if the King would kindly make arrangements for his son to come to England to be educated. George Augustus could not possibly have raised that sort of money, and Frederick remained in Hanover.

Alexander Pope, whose friendship Prince Frederick was to cultivate, told Lady Mary Wortley Montagu he had found Hampton Court deserted save for the King 'who was giving audience all alone to the birds under the garden wall'. This was hardly surprising; the Prince and Princess of Wales had been banned from Hampton Court, just as they had from Kensington Palace and Windsor Castle. As a retreat from Leicester House they took possession in the summer of 1718 of Richmond Lodge, just to the south of the present Kew Gardens. It was formerly the home of the exiled Jacobite Duke of Ormonde, who had leased it from William III. His estate had been forfeited for high treason, and despite the King's best endeavours to prevent him, the Prince obtained the property from the Commissioners of the Confiscated Estates Court for £6,000. The house was at this time described as 'a pleasant residence for a country gentleman', and here the Prince became a member of the newly established hunting fraternity, the Princess's maids of honour being compelled to follow the hounds as well. It was at Richmond that John Hervey fell in love with the most beautiful of the maids, Mary Lepel, and they were married in 1720, an event that inspired Lord Stanhope of Shelford, better known to history as Lord Chesterfield (he inherited his father's earldom in 1726), to a ribald pun:

> Heaven keep our good King from a rising!
> But that rising who's fitter to quell
> Than some lady with beauty surprising;
> And who should that be but Lepel?

Chesterfield had been appointed a gentleman of the bedchamber to the Prince of Wales in 1715. His mildly obscene verses were not perhaps his most polished brand of humour; Dr Johnson, who seldom flung excessive praise at his peers, described Chesterfield as 'a wit among lords and a lord among wits'. His declared aim was to make every man he met like him and every woman love him, and in 1733 he married a woman of forty, Petronilla von der Schulenburg, created in 1722 Countess of Walsingham, whom he did not love one scrap. She was the daughter of George I by the Duchess of Kendal, and the marriage was purely one of political and financial convenience; they even lived separately, in next-door houses.

By now Caroline was well into her stride as a political intriguer, boasting of her conquests ('We have all the country gentlemen of the Tories with us'), enlisting further recruits ('Pray see what can be done with Carteret, I am afraid of him'), and daring even to challenge Lord Chesterfield, when she discovered he had taken to mimicking her. 'You have more wit, my Lord, than I,' she told him, 'but I have a bitter tongue, and always repay my debts with exorbitant interest.' Most importantly for the future, a strong alliance was forming between Caroline and Walpole, the latter, according to Lady Cowper, making it plain to the Prince that neither he nor Caroline would object if His Royal Highness cared to sleep with Mrs Walpole. Walpole had already realized it was Caroline who would eventually rule her husband, that she was quite prepared to turn a pragmatic eye towards his schoolboy philanderings, and that it was by encouraging George Augustus to think himself no end of a lad that his innate stupidity could be kept in check. Any suggestion that Caroline and Walpole were sexually attracted misses the point.[13]

Once more the King fled from family squabbles, most of them of his own making, and spent the summer of 1719 in Hanover, returning to England in November – again without his grandson. Caroline is supposed to have pleaded to have her son at home with her, but the delay in Frederick's being summoned home after his grandfather's death makes nonsense of such fairy-tales. During this absence of the King a Council of Regency was set up, without even a place on it for the Prince of Wales, and no greater insult could have been dreamt up. George Augustus and Caroline were even forbidden to hold levees or Drawing Rooms while the King was abroad, such duties being delegated to Frederick's infant sisters. No wonder Lady Cowper thought the family mad.

But Walpole felt it was time to put a stop to so much unseemly behaviour, and after much argument about whether the Prince should again reside at St James's (he said he did not wish to do so, and until he succeeded to the throne he retained Leicester House, where his last three children were all born), and whether, in the event of another visit to Hanover by the King, the Prince should be appointed regent, an artificial reconciliation was contrived. (Just such an artificial reconciliation between George II and Frederick was one day to be cooked up, and the repeated patterns of conduct between George I and his son and George II and *his* son make one wonder whether George II had any character of his own at all, independent of the baleful influence of his father.) The King received the Prince at St James's Palace on 23 April 1720, when the Prince told his father 'it had been a great grief to him to have been in his displeasure so long . . . and that he hoped the rest of his life would be such as the King would never have cause to complain of'. The King kept muttering, in French, 'Your conduct, your conduct', and, if Lady Cowper is to be believed (and communication between royal parents and children, until Prince Frederick's time, was on such a formal footing she almost certainly can be), addressed the Prince in the second person plural.

There was nothing that could be described as communication between the King and the Prince of Wales, but on the way back to Leicester House the Prince found himself escorted by Yeoman Warders, and by early evening guards were back on duty, 'the square full of coaches; the rooms full of company; everything gay and laughing; nothing but kissing and wishing of joy'. The Prince, it seems, kissed Lady Cowper 'five or six times, and with his usual heartiness which he means sincerely'. Notwithstanding, the King declined that night to see the Princess, and next day, at chapel, 'When the King came out, the Prince stood by him. The King spoke to most people except the Prince: they two only looked grave and out of humour.'[14]

The King was one of those people quite unable to exhibit affection, even towards men, in an age when many men (Frederick was to be one of them) embraced their friends and acquaintances as a matter of course. But he did now relent with regard to the children, permitting their parents free access to them. It was at this time that both Anne, now eleven, and Caroline, five, caught smallpox; the Prince, who whatever his faults never lacked courage, helped to nurse them, and the entire family survived.

5

'Von Big Lie'

As everything seemed quite calm, in June 1720 King George again set sail for the Continent. Running two courts, he now had debts of £600,000. But he had left bigger financial worries than these in London. Not only the royal family but the entire nation, it seemed, had parted company with their senses, and within four months the King's visit to Hanover was cut short by an urgent request from the Government to return. The South Sea Bubble had burst.

In 1711 a company had been set up by Queen Anne's Treasurer, Robert Harley, Earl of Oxford and Mortimer, called the South Sea Company. In theory it existed to take over a portion of the national debt at a fixed interest and to use its credit to finance capital expansion, with the exclusive right of trading in the South Seas. Interest was secured through tax on such commodities as wine, and creditors were assured of a prosperous trade along the Spanish coasts of America. Despite serious setbacks – the Treaty of Utrecht of 1713 limited trade, and the first South Sea Company ship did not sail until 1717 – the Company was believed to be on a par with the Bank of England, founded in 1694; by the end of 1719 the Bank and the Company were competing to purchase and diminish irredeemable annuities amounting to £800,000 per annum, and the Company won, paying the Government £7½ million. A bill called the South Sea Bill was passed, and the Company opened large subscriptions which were swiftly filled. There was no trade, but for some extraordinary reason everyone saw investment in the South Sea Company as an infallible way to make a fortune. Shares quoted in January 1720 at 130 per cent had risen four months later to 1,000 per cent. The exiled Duchess of Ormonde, writing to Swift on 18 August, had the matter more or less in perspective: 'You will remember when the South Sea was said to be Lord Oxford's bride. Now the King has adopted it and calls it

his beloved child, though perhaps you may say that if he loves it
no better than his son it may not be saying much.'

Speculation in anything and everything now became the rage,
and no sooner had the King left England than the Prince of Wales
lent his name as governor to a Welsh copper company, withdrawing
only after the company had been threatened with prosecution and
the Prince was £40,000 better off. The return of the King was not
only necessary in order that Parliament might be recalled; he was
a large stockholder, having invested £60,000 from the civil list.
An initial profit of £46,400 seemed to justify the venture, but the
King was so greedy that he determined to reinvest this enormous
windfall, presumably convinced that money really did grow on
trees. The Chancellor of the Exchequer, John Aislabie, managed
to 'endeavour to divert His Majesty from this resolution, for that
the stock was carried up to an exorbitant height by the madness
of people, and that it was impossible it could stand, but must
fall'. The King told him he had 'the character of a timorous man',
and 'positively commanded me to lay it out in the purchase of
stock and subscriptions'. Needless to say, the King's mistresses
had been gambling on the Stock Exchange with reckless abandon,
and as they were not known for losing money, more frequently
for making it, others followed their example. New companies began
to come into existence daily, some said hourly, and anybody waving
stocks and shares over his or her head could be sure of having
them snapped up. As speculators made instant fortunes, so yet
more speculators were drawn to the mythical honey-pot. Jewish
stockbrokers were suddenly accepted in fashionable society;
companies were registered to manufacture 'salt fresh water', to
make oil from sunflower seeds (not an impossible objective, as it
transpired two hundred years later), to import jackasses, build
hospitals for bastards, fatten up pigs, and to invent 'a wheel with
a perpetual motion'. Over a hundred 'bubbles' beside the South
Sea Company itself floated over London overnight, including one,
alleged by those who believe it existed, to have been set up for
'an undertaking which shall in due time be revealed'. Its somewhat
nebulous prospectus was said to have attracted a thousand
subscribers in a morning.

Another almost certainly apocryphal story went the rounds, of a
well-dressed man being asked how long he had been a gentleman
and replying, 'Only a week, madam.' But like so many apocryphal

stories, those relating to the South Sea Bubble perfectly epitomized the current situation. A friend told Henrietta Howard she was 'almost South Sea mad', and for lack of funds had been 'forced to let slip' an opportunity which was never likely to happen again. Indeed it was not. When the South Sea Company began taking proceedings against illegal companies, these bogus companies collapsed, general confidence drained away, and shares in the South Sea Company itself began to fall. Before the crash, Walpole, untainted by corruption, as it happened, and saved by a fortuitous delay (the post), had made a large profit, selling when the Company's stock was quoted at 1,000 per cent; by the end of September it stood at 150 per cent. Everyone began to panic. Those Hanoverians left behind by the King were so frightened they suggested to the Prince of Wales that they should all flee to Hanover together. Between them, they were coming close to losing the crown for Frederick.

It was amidst scenes of bedlam that the King landed, at Margate, on 9 November. A month later a debate in the House of Lords became so heated that the Secretary of State, Lord Stanhope, had a fit and died next day. He was well out of it. It transpired that £500,000 worth of fictitious South Sea stock had been invented to get the South Sea Bill through Parliament, two royal mistresses had creameed off £10,000 each, and other sums had been appropriated by their daughters. At least one miscreant committed suicide, Aislabie was sent to the Tower, and the First Lord of the Treasury resigned.

But the South Sea Bubble was the making of Walpole. He succeeded the Earl of Sunderland as First Lord of the Treasury and Aislabie as Chancellor of the Exchequer. Sunderland remained in office as Groom of the Stole, with control over Secret Service money, but when he died in April 1722 Walpole emerged as the most powerful man in the House of Commons, in effect England's first prime minister – and he remained so for twenty-one years.[1] Medicine was to benefit too, for a miserable old miser by the name of Thomas Guy made £20,000 out of the South Sea Bubble and founded Guy's Hospital.[2]

On 15 April 1721 another brother for Frederick, William Augustus, was born at Leicester House. When he was four he was given the newly revived Order of the Bath, and when he was five he was created Duke of Cumberland. Thanks to the soubriquet attached to him by the City, he has gained eternal notoriety as the Butcher of Culloden. It was upon this initially bookish little boy that Caroline was to pin her maternal love, such as it was, missing no opportunity, once Frederick had landed in England, of expressing her infinite preference for William. Their sisters, too, doted on William, the last two girls, Mary and Louisa, making their appearances, also at Leicester House, on 22 February 1722 and 7 December 1724 respectively.[3] (The year of Mary's birth was also the year in which, although Caroline had already had the disease, the Princess of Wales had Caroline and Amelia inoculated against smallpox, a controversial and courageous thing to do. Frederick was inoculated a year later.) Caroline's nine confinements had been spread over a period of only seventeen years; her last, the birth of Louisa, was to have fatal consequences.

The year before William's arrival the Jacobites had been cock-a-hoop at news received from Rome of the birth of a son, Charles Edward, to the wife of the Pretender. It was this young Prince's attempt to regain the throne in the Stuart cause in 1745 that the Duke of Cumberland was to avenge so savagely. Alas for many innocent lives, the Stuarts were not overburdened with brains; in 1722 the Old Pretender seriously suggested that if King George would restore him to the throne of England he would make him King of Hanover and guarantee him safe passage to Herrenhausen. News was leaked by the Duc d'Orléans to the English ambassador of a plot to land five thousand mercenaries led by the Duke of Ormonde, and Walpole had Bishop Atterbury, now sixty years of age, arrested and imprisoned in the Tower of London for seven months. He had certainly been in contact with the Jacobites in 1717; now, on scant evidence, he was condemned by the House of Lords, all but one of the bishops voting against him. (The total tally was eighty-three to forty-three against the Bishop.) Although universally regarded as the finest preacher of his day, recently bereaved and in poor health, he was deprived of all his ecclesiastical offices, and in 1723 he was banished for life.

The idea of separating the thrones of England and Hanover (although not necessarily in favour of the Jacobite Pretenders) had in fact occurred to King George himself. In theory, it made a certain amount of sense. The idea was to occur, even more strongly, to the Prince and Princess of Wales, and by the time Prince William was four they had firmly made up their minds that the main beneficiary from the division of the spoils should be their younger son. In 1725 Robert Walpole told the Lord Chancellor, Lord King, that 'the Prince and his wife had been for excluding Prince Frederick from the throne of England but that after the King and Prince should be Elector of Hanover and Prince William King of Great Britain'.[4] This would have kept Frederick in Hanover the whole of his life, waiting to succeed his father as elector, which in the event he would never have done; and as William never married, the English throne would presumably have gone, in 1765 (the year of William's death), to any children born to the Princess Royal, and after them to any children of Princess Mary or Princess Louisa. Subsequently it would have reverted to Frederick the Great and his sister, Wilhelmina. By 1725 Frederick was eighteen, and King George apparently said there was no question of rearranging the succession without Prince Frederick's consent.[5] The King was in Hanover in 1726, when presumably he discussed the matter with Frederick, who no doubt declined to forgo his rightful inheritance. Lord King and Robert Walpole would not have been the only people gossiping on the subject. As the years went by, George II's and Queen Caroline's fantasy of disinheriting their elder son grew stronger and stronger, and without a doubt their impotent anger and Frederick's perfectly understandable resentment were a prime cause of the monumental dissention in the family.

The land over which the Hanoverians were squabbling among themselves, and over which the Stuarts still dreamt of reigning, was a country of startling contrasts. While in many ways Frederick's English inheritance was still nearly as barbaric as it had been in the Middle Ages, its cities were soon to be more perfectly designed and its buildings more beautifully proportioned than ever before or since (Hanover Square in London, for example, was constructed in 1717). Yet its open sewers remained a network of disease, and William the Conqueror's Tower of London was still a repository for prisoners of state. James Gibbs's St Martin-in-the-Fields was being built in the year of the South Sea Bubble; in 1719 a young printer by the name of John Matthews was being hanged, drawn and quartered. Kent, Adam and 'Capability' Brown coexisted in Georgian England with language at court so coarse that Caroline, no prude herself, felt obliged to complain to Walpole about the way he addressed her daughters. There was endemic drunkenness, goose-riding at fairs and rampant tuberculosis. Few starved to death but many lived in abject poverty, while the rich led lives of such indolent luxury it is a wonder they did not die of ennui. Walpole is frequently lauded for leaving England in peace and financial prosperity, but social welfare was a concept beyond his, or most of his contemporaries', mental boundaries. Many of the rural Anglican clergy were so preoccupied with building spacious rectories and riding to hounds that the moral and religious concerns of the nation began to fall into the altogether more worthy hands of Methodists. Bullying at public schools might as well have been on the curriculum, it was so prevalant; indeed, violence, both physical and verbal, was more or less the normal currency of everyday life. By no stretch of the imagination could the English aristocracy Frederick was shortly to meet for the first time be described as civilized, merely elegantly housed and dressed.

On the Continent, marriage plans conceived many years ago by the King's daughter, another Sophia Dorothea, who had married the Prince of Wales's detested playmate, now King William I of Prussia, had begun to do rather more than simmer. They involved Prince Frederick, whom Sophia wished as a husband for her daughter, Frederick's cousin Wilhelmina; they also involved Frederick's sister Amelia, whom Sophia wanted as wife for her third son, the future Frederick the Great, whose two older brothers had died. As it turned out, Amelia had a lucky escape; Frederick was homosexual. In 1730 he tried to escape to England, not to wed Amelia but to get away from his tyrannical father. He was court-martialled and compelled to watch the execution of his accomplice, believed also to have been his lover. Three years later he was reluctantly married to Elizabeth Christina of Brunswick-Wolfenbüttel and succeeded to the throne in 1740. Part of this cosy family plan, for a marriage between Amelia and Frederick of Prussia, was more or less approved by the sovereigns of England and Prussia, the latter being as mad as a hatter, his mind permanently poisoned by murderous intent. Marriage between Frederick of England and Wilhelmina, on the other hand, was strongly opposed by the Prince of Wales, who detested both of Wilhelmina's parents. But the views of the Prince of Wales mattered not a scrap to King George, who was warned by Lady Darlington, quite untruthfully, that Wilhelmina was as bad as she was ugly, and, according to the young Princess herself, 'that I was so violent that my violence often caused me to have epileptic fits'.[6]

Frederick Louis was represented to Wilhelmina by her mother

as 'a good-natured prince, kind-hearted but very foolish'. The scheming Queen added: 'If you will have sense enough to tolerate his mistresses, you will be able to do what you like with him.' This remark should not be taken to infer that as a boy Frederick possessed a harem, merely that it was a reasonable assumption that as mistresses were a tendency in the Hanoverian family, Frederick would eventually take one too. He acquired his first at seventeen.

In 1723 the King paid a visit to Berlin to form an opinion about his granddaughter for himself. This he did, on his arrival on the evening of 7 October, in a trice. The twelve-year-old Wilhelmina curtsied to her grandfather, who, again according to the Princess's own account, 'embraced me, and said nothing further than, "She is very tall. How old is she?"' They went to the Queen's room where King George picked up a candle, held it under Wilhelmina's nose and examined her from top to toe. 'I can never describe the state of agitation I was in,' she recalled. 'I turned red and pale by turns; and all the time he never uttered one word.'

Wilhelmina spoke fluent English, which was more than her grandfather did, and was an extremely intelligent girl. 'Serious and melancholy' was how she found the King of England, and throughout the entire visit, which got off to a very frightening start, she found it impossible to talk to him, even in their native German. After two hours of eating and drinking, Lord Townshend, who had accompanied the King to Berlin as Minister in Attendance, concluded the King was not well, and he asked Wilhelmina to ask her mother to end the party. It was about to come to an abrupt end anyway. King George denied that he was tired or unwell, and promptly fell down in some sort of apoplectic fit, a prelude to his death, in similar circumstances, four years later. 'His wig lay on one side,' Wilhelmina remembered, 'and his hat on the other, and they had to lay him down on the floor, where he remained a whole hour before regaining consciousness. Everyone thought he had had a paralytic stroke.' He recovered, however, and on regaining his composure he refused to go to bed before escorting his daughter to her own apartments.

Plans for the double marriage were later discussed, but any final decisions were left in abeyance. When, three years later, the King and Queen of Prussia paid a return visit to King George at Hanover, the Queen continued to press for a settlement, but still the King stalled, saying the parties were too young; in 1726 Frederick

Louis was nineteen, his sister Amelia sixteen. The King had no intention of discussing arrangements for Frederick's marriage with the Prince of Wales but he did recall it was customary to mention the matter to Parliament, and so he managed to avoid giving any formal consent. But with discussion about his future at such a high level, Frederick probably felt flattered that anyone should think him worthy of so much attention, and without ever having met Wilhelmina he seems to have warmed to the idea of marriage, indeed almost to have considered himself engaged. Having been totally excluded from domestic affairs in England, he probably felt of some account for the first time in his life.

In London his mother, far from being excluded from affairs, was acting almost as though she were already queen. Her birthday in 1724 was celebrated by a visit to Leicester House from the 'Stewards of the Societies of Ancient Britons', and the court assembled to pay their respects was said by the *Weekly Journal* to have been 'the most splendid and numerous that has been known, the concourse being so great that many of the nobility could not obtain admittance and were obliged to return without seeing the Prince and Princess'. Both archbishops, the Lord Chancellor and assorted ambassadors plied their way to Leicester House for the occasion, a salute was fired in St James's Park, and in the evening there was 'a magnificent ball' at the palace. In 1726, when he was just five years old, Frederick's brother William was out and about with his parents, being shown off to the crowds who turned out to watch the Lord Mayor's Show.

From all these junketings Frederick remained excluded, and naturally curiosity regarding the character and demeanour of the seemingly exiled heir apparent to the Prince of Wales began to mount. And when, in 1727, Frederick's grandfather once again set off for Hanover, it was widely believed, and certainly hoped by Frederick, that he would sanction marriage to Wilhelmina. The King left England – for the last time, as it transpired – on 3 June, but not before Walpole's ten-year-old son Horace had been taken by Lady Walpole to see him, a feat engineered by the Duchess of Kendal – who may well have anticipated a tip for her services; two years earlier it had been possible for Lord Bolingbroke to pay one of his periodic return visits to England only by bribing the Duchess. 'The person of the King is as perfect in my memory,' Horace Walpole was to write in adult life, 'as if I saw him but yesterday. It was that of an elderly man, rather pale, and exactly like to his pictures and coins; not tall, of an aspect rather good and august, with a dark tye wig, a plain coat, waistcoat and breeches of snuff-coloured cloth, with stockings of the same colour, and a blue riband over all.'[7] As far as the Duchess was concerned, she appeared to the child 'a very tall, lean, ill-favoured old lady'. Ushering Horace into the King's presence two nights before he left England, whether she received a present at the time or not, proved a lucrative action; on the King's death, Horace's father procured for her an annual pension of £17,500.

The King's crossing from Greenwich to Holland took a tedious four days, and this may have contributed to his impatience, once disembarked, to press on to Hanover. The Duchess of Kendal felt so ill that she stayed behind to rest. On 9 June the King reached the frontier town of Delden, where he called on the improbable-sounding Count de Twillet for supper.[8] The meal was enormous, and included a possibly fatal number of water-melons. Instead of resting all night, like any sensible man of sixty-seven, King George insisted that he and his entourage should take to the road again at seven in the morning. An hour later he collapsed. On showing signs of partial recovery he refused to abandon the journey, and now seems to have become a bit deranged. 'To Osnabrück! To Osnabrück!' the dying man kept yelling, the castle at Osnabrück being the home, some miles to the west of Herrenhausen, where his brother the Prince Bishop lived. The coachman, disinclined to disobey royal orders, whipped the horses forward. By the time the King reached the fraternal fortress, at ten o'clock that night, he was unconscious. He was carried to the room in which he had been born, and there, on 11 June, he died.

Apart from his great-uncle, Frederick would have been the first member of the family to learn that his father was at last King of England. His grandfather's visits had meant a lot to him, and he had no one to whom to express his feelings. So on 27 June, from Herrenhausen, he wrote to his eldest sister, Princess Anne, whom he had not seen since she was five:

I am sure that you share the grief I have felt since the death of our dear grandfather. I should be lacking in filial duty and the most ungrateful of men if it had not caused me great sorrow, for he treated me with especial affection and friendship. I was

so overcome by sadness when they told me the news that I
could not leave my bed for two days and fainted twice. My
only consolation in this sad affliction is the knowledge of my
dear parents' goodness. I flatter myself that I shall always conduct
myself in a manner deserving of their esteem and friendship for
me. I pray you, dear sister, as you are by them, to remember
me often to Their Majesties.

It took three days for news of the King's death to be conveyed
to England, by means of a letter from Lord Townshend to Walpole,
who was at dinner in Chelsea when it arrived. He immediately
rode to Richmond – according to Horace Walpole (Robert Walpole's
fourth son and eventually 4th Earl of Orford), killing two horses
in his eagerness to be the first to fall on his fat knees and inform
George Augustus that he was now George II, but Horace was
much given to embroidery. At the lodge, where he arrived about
three o'clock in the afternoon, Robert Walpole was informed that
the Prince of Wales (as his household still imagined him to be)
was resting, which he always did after dinner. Walpole insisted
the Prince must be called, and George came into the room to
learn that he was King, while doing up his breeches. Ignoring
the sovereign's state of undress, Walpole kissed his hand and
informed him his father was dead. No doubt suspecting a subtle
plot to see how he might react in such circumstances, the new
monarch exclaimed, 'Dat is von big lie.' It was an appropriately
comical commencement to a turbulent and in many ways farcical
reign.

The first thing George II did was dismiss the man who had
brought him news of his accession, telling him to go to Chiswick
to take orders from the Treasurer, Sir Spencer Compton, who
was also Speaker of the House of Commons. In the opinion of
Lord Hervey, Compton was 'a plodding, heavy fellow, with great
application but no talents' whose only pleasures were money and
eating. Walpole behaved extremely well, or prudently anyway,
even assisting Compton to draft a speech for the new king to
deliver at his first council, a council meeting at which the Archbishop
of Canterbury produced a copy of the late king's will, which George
II thrust into his pocket, and almost certainly tore up later. While
rummaging through her father-in-law's papers, Caroline had already
discovered a suggestion sent to George I by the Earl of Berkeley,

First Lord of the Admiralty, that George Augustus be kidnapped and shipped to America, and perhaps for that reason George thought it wisest to digest his father's last will and testament in private. But just why George destroyed the will, and what it contained, are matters for conjecture. It is believed that George I deposited copies of his will with his cousin and German neighbour the Duke of Wolfenbüttel, and with the Electoral Emperor, and that the document contained a proposal that after Frederick's death the English Crown should descend to Frederick's first son, the Crown of Hanover to his second son, and that in default of heirs to Frederick, Hanover should go to the Duke. The last thing George II wanted was for Frederick to inherit the English Crown at all. It seems he managed to retrieve both copies of the will, but who became disinherited we do not know for sure; possibly Frederick and the Queen of Prussia, and possibly also the Duchess of Kendal – but if this is so, Caroline had a nerve, writing to the Duchess on 25 June to assure her she was her friend and that she loved her. Almost certainly mentioned in the will was the Countess of Walsingham; when she married Lord Chesterfield she told him her royal father had bequeathed her £40,000, and that eventually she had been paid £20,000 in an out-of-court settlement.

The family rather went in for destroying wills. George I had torn up his wife's will, and George II had always suspected, probably with good reason, that he and his sister had thereby been swindled. The Duke of Celle, George II's grandfather, is also believed to have left money to the new king, which got diverted to George I. It was not long before Frederick was accusing his father of tearing up the Duke of York's will, by which he and the Queen of Prussia both believed they were due to benefit, and indeed it is highly likely the Duke of York would have made Frederick a major beneficiary.

On becoming king, George must have removed immediately from Richmond Lodge to Leicester House, which he continued to inhabit until Christmas, for it was outside Leicester House that he was proclaimed king, and inside that 'all the nobility in town . . . had the honour to kiss their Majesties hands'. George had no plans to attend his father's funeral in Hanover, but having learnt in detail of the matrimonial arrangements George I had virtually sanctioned for Frederick, he decreed that these should be shelved until he himself made a visit to Herrenhausen.

Frederick almost certainly realized that with the death of his grandfather his prospects of marrying Wilhelmina of Prussia were slipping away, and egged on initially by Wilhelmina's mother, who clearly fancied her daughter as Queen of England, and goaded too by his undirected youthful high spirits and impetous nature, he seems to have convinced himself, without ever having met his cousin, that he was in love – so in love that only the adventure of a secret wedding would prove to the world that his was no politically motivated liaison. But did the Queen panic, fearing perhaps the wrath of her unstable husband and the very real possibility of a diplomatic rift with her brother, the new King of England? It is said it was she who let slip these crazy plans to the English ambassador in Berlin. Certainly he learnt of them from someone, and naturally he thought it was his duty to inform King George that his son and heir was about to marry without his or Parliament's consent.

From that point plans for a marriage between Frederick and Wilhelmina gradually fizzled out, and in 1730 they were formally broken off. George II's objection to Frederick's marriage to Wilhelmina has been cited as the major cause of friction between father and son, but this seems most unlikely; Frederick's discovery that his father wished to deprive him of the throne would have been a matter of far greater bitterness and concern.

Not only had George II no plans to attend his father's funeral (George I was buried at Herrenhausen on 30 August, at a service at which the King was represented by the Duke of York rather than by Frederick); he had no plans to invite his elder son to his coronation either, which meant that Frederick was denied the opportunity to swear allegiance. It was discovered that George I had lavished all Queen Anne's jewellery on his mistresses, and Caroline had to borrow jewels to wear at the ceremony, which took place on 11 October 1727, and was emblazoned by Handel's new anthem *Zadok the Priest*, sung at every coronation ever since. A decade earlier Handel had made memorable a river fête for George I with his *Water Music*; in 1743 he was to commemorate George II's heroic feats on the field of battle with his great *Dettingen Te Deum*. Were ever such a philistine pair as George I and his son so honoured by genius?

Parliament had met before the coronation (on 27 June) to settle the civil list, an occasion that was to be the cause of one of Frederick's most dramatic bones of contention with his father. Perhaps relying on the excuse that Prince Frederick still resided abroad, £700,000 a year was settled on the King together with £100,000 a year for his heir. Frederick's allowance, however, was to be paid direct to the King, and the King was to hand it over to the Prince at his own discretion, a sure recipe for disaster. This was not the end of the upturn in George's fortunes, engineered by the crafty Walpole, who seems to have played with Parliament as with putty. He told the Commons that the King had 'the expense of a wife and a great many children' (seven, in fact), as if, the caustic Hervey commented, 'no King of England before had ever been married, or to a pregnant wife'.[9] Walpole pleaded, too, an increase in the cost of living, and he persuaded Parliament that should the money voted for the King prove in excess of his requirements, it need no longer be invested in a sinking fund but the interest should accrue to the King. Thus, it was estimated, the King was assured of an average income of about £900,000 a year. To put that vast sum in perspective, it is worth recalling that 210 years later George II's great-great-great-great-great-grandson, George VI, was voted only £410,000. When Compton suggested £60,000 would be right for the Queen, Walpole made out a case for £100,000. She walked away, too, with Somerset House and Richmond Lodge. Shortly after the votes had been taken, Compton confessed he was not up to the rigours of leading a government, and retired to the Upper House as Lord Wilmington. Having secured the King and Queen's financial independence and peace of mind, Walpole was reinstated, being appointed, on 24 July 1727, First Lord of the Treasury and Chancellor of the Exchequer. (Wilmington was to return to office, however, in 1742 as First Lord of the Treasury.)

There were many at the time, and there have been many since, who believed that Caroline governed the country, for Caroline governed the King. But it was Walpole who came to govern the country, exercising his influence over George II through Queen Caroline. The three of them were to operate at a time of unbridled political lampooning, and a ditty with George II's distinct limitations in mind was soon circulating, even at court. It made reference, too, to the fate of George's mother:

You may strut, dapper George, but 'twill all be in vain;
We know 'tis Queen Caroline, not you, that reign.
You govern no more than Don Philip of Spain....

Then if you would have us fall down and adore you,
Lock up your fat spouse, as your dad did before you.

Although much political and social patronage was wrested from
the hands of the first two Hanoverian monarchs, the amount of
patronage remaining in the gift of the King was huge, and whoever
governed the King had access to power, influence and money.
Parliament still consisted of the occupants of those rotten boroughs
that kept urban communities subservient to the landed gentry and
provided the basis for Walpole's corrupt control of the Commons;
the relative handful of enfranchised citizens expected to be flattered and bribed; sinecure offices were freely distributed as a reward for services rendered or were blatantly put up for sale. When
Horace Walpole was still a boy his father made him Clerk of the
Estreats, whatever they were, and Comptroller of the Pipe, exotic
but otherwise meaningless posts he held for life, yet providing an
income of £300 a year. When he was nineteen his father gave
him another sinecure financed from the public purse worth £900
a year. The political complexion of Parliament was often hard to
discern, for 'parties' were more easily recognized on account of
the people they supported than the policies they pursued. If the
King wanted a certain piece of legislation enacted, those in favour
of that proposal constituted in effect the King's party; once they
ceased to support the King, they were registered as the Opposition.
On certain issues, Tories and Whigs might close ranks, on other
issues they might fall out among themselves. It can be a great
oversimplification to equate eighteenth-century Tories with the
twentieth-century Conservative Party, or eighteenth-century Whigs
with twentieth-century Liberals, whose party was not even founded
until 1828, especially when one bears in mind that both George I
and George II were Whigs – at any rate, that they chose Whigs
for their ministers. They chose Whig ministers because they felt
more confident of support from the Whigs than from the Tories –
Tories, however, forming a majority in the country. Neither monarch
had a liberal sentiment in his body, as we would understand such
sentiments today. It is true that Dissension and Whiggery tended

to run hand in hand, but those Whigs who did the bidding of
George II were, like the King, profoundly conservative in outlook
and temperament.

Very broadly, during the seventeenth century the Tories had
made their stand in defence of Church and King, but the seeds of
their long decline in influence were sown by the Glorious Revolution
of 1688, when it was mainly Whig politicians who were responsible
for the importation of a foreign king, William III. The Tories'
future electoral fortunes were not enhanced by internal wrangles
and poor organization, and throughout Queen Anne's reign they
hastened their eclipse by their opposition to the Hanoverian succession. Unlike the Tories, who were hopelessly divided in their
loyalties, the Whigs had supported the Hanoverians almost
unanimously, and once George I arrived they were bound to reap
their reward, coming increasingly to be regarded as a kind of
establishment party. Most of the wealthiest peers were Whigs,
and by and large it was Whigs who ran the country's commerce
and banking.

'You have, I am sure, heard of the appellations "Tories" and
"Whigs" as being nicknames given to the two principal parties in
England,' a contemporary letter-writer reported home in 1729.

I should be much embarrassed were you to ask me to give you
the etymology for these names, but I believe the two parties
first appeared under the reign of Charles II, and that these names
were given them satirically and opprobriously, but this is no
longer so. The Tories uphold all the prerogatives of the Sovereign, and declare that his or her subjects must submit without
resistance, even though his or her power be arbitrary. The opposite party, or Whigs, accuse their opponents of wishing to
upset the recognised form of government and the liberties of
the nation by endeavouring to establish despotism, thus making the King a tyrant and his subjects slaves. . . .

These two parties are so opposed to each other that nothing
but a real miracle could cause them to become united. Many
causes contribute to this animosity, and none more than the
antipathy that exists between the Anglicans and the Presbyterians,
together with other Nonconformists. The latter are Whigs, and
so great is their fear lest a Roman Catholic monarch powerful
enough to annihilate the tolerance recognised by the laws should

ascend the throne, that they uphold the Whigs with all their
might. Zealous Anglicans, on the other hand, are Tories. . . .[10]

The King may not always have been able to determine the result
of a general election, and hence the composition of the House of
Commons, but the beauty of the system, from his point of view,
was that come what might he remained free to appoint and dismiss
his Ministers, most of whom were peers and did not require election to Parliament anyway. Walpole's great contribution to the
evolution of the British constitution was to remain leader of the
Government for two decades while remaining a commoner, even
though it was not until 1902 that the convention was finally established that the prime minister must be answerable to the House
of Commons; but Walpole had paved the way, in his role, as
Harold Wilson has put it, as 'Leader of the House on behalf of
the Sovereign'.[11] What was also established by 1742, the year of
Walpole's downfall, was that no prime minister could hope to
retain office, no matter how much the King might desire his services,
once he had lost the support of the Commons.

Lady Mary Wortley Montagu has provided her own satirical
explanation as to how offices were distributed under the Hanoverians:

> The Ministry is like a play at Court. There's a little door to get
> in and a great crowd without, shoving and thrusting who shall
> be the foremost; people who knock others with their elbows,
> disregard a little kick of the shins, and still thrust heartily for-
> ward, are sure of a good place. Your modest man stands be-
> hind in the crowd, is shoved about by everybody, his clothes
> tore, almost squeezed to death, and sees a thousand get in be-
> fore him that do not make so good a figure as himself. I do not
> say it is impossible for an imprudent man not to rise in the
> world; but a modest merit, with a large share of imprudence, is
> more probable to be advanced than the greatest qualification
> without it.

The temptation for men with ability who were not offered office
to switch allegiance and go into opposition was one that even
Walpole could not at one time resist. Dismissed early in his career
in 1710, when the Tories came in, he had thrown himself so
heartily into opposition that for a brief spell he discovered what

life was like in the Tower. The reason Walpole remained in office so long was because he became indispensable to the King, and the reason he was indispensable to the King was because he exercised such mastery over the House of Commons. At the very commencement of George II's reign, Walpole, having been ungratefully dismissed without ceremony, had the presence of mind to ask for a private audience, at which he assured the King he could persuade Parliament to vote him more money than Sir Spencer Compton could; and it had been at the conclusion of that audience that Sir Spencer was politely persuaded he would be happier in the House of Lords, with the lucrative post of Paymaster to the Forces, and Walpole again took over.

Walpole was openly referred to as 'our Premier', and one reason his years in office saw the emergence of an embryonic prime minister was because George II, with his preference for matters military, his vile temper and his lack of imagination, was only too happy to be spared the boring details of government. He was equally happy to imagine all along that decisions being taken were his. They were in fact Walpole's, filtered to the King through Caroline. John Gay, a friend of Lord Bolingbroke, was well aware what was going on, and in 1728, when *The Beggar's Opera* was first produced, everyone realized that the disreputable Peachum was Walpole. (Frederick attended a performance on 2 January 1729.) When George II was in opposition to his father, Gay's satire on corruption at court would have assured him of a warm welcome at Leicester House. Now that George and Caroline operated the fountain of honour they found criticism hard to take, and former friends like Dean Swift were discarded. Indeed, Swift returned to Ireland in 1728 never to set foot in England again, dying in 1745 an embittered man, for he was convinced that Caroline had blocked his preferment to a bishopric.[12]

It was not until eighteen months after coming to the throne that George II was finally persuaded to send for Frederick. According to Lord Hervey, 'His ministers told him that if the Prince's coming were longer delayed an address from Parliament and the voice of the whole nation would certainly oblige His Majesty to send for him and consequently that he would be necessitated to do that with an ill grace which he might now do with a good one.' Hervey says that when Frederick first arrived 'he was in great favour with his father, but it lasted not long'. The favour shown by

George II to his son has to be put in perspective. Frederick was very nearly twenty-two; his parents had not clapped eyes on him since he was seven. Frederick's first experience of the land over which he had been born to reign was no more propitious than the nature of the family circle he was about to enter. The King sent to Hanover a representative of no consequence to escort the Prince to England, and the journey, in mid-winter, was a nightmare. He landed on 7 December 1728. Next day the *Daily Post* reported: 'Yesterday His Royal Highness Prince Frederick came to Whitechapel about seven in the evening, and proceeded thence privately in a hackney coach to St James's. His Royal Highness alighted at the Friary [Friary Court is today on the itinerary of thousands of tourists] and walked down to the Queen's backstairs, and was there conducted to Their Majestys' apartment.'

George and Caroline had had great fun exciting popularity for themselves when George I was in Hanover; they had no intention of encouraging their son to play similar tricks. The hackney coach and the back-stairs say it all. Not only had Frederick walked into a kind of fairyland, where parents he could scarcely have recognized and certainly did not know were King and Queen, he had done so as some sort of inferior being, a second-class prince who was not even to be admitted by the front door, or escorted by outriders. He spoke indifferent English, he knew no English courtiers or politicians, save Hervey slightly, and although long past an age when an heir to a throne would normally have expected to have been given his own establishment, he had not a single servant or stick of furniture to call his own. Hence it was not long before Benjamin Goodison, only twenty-eight years old when Frederick arrived in England, was appointed his cabinet-maker. For the Prince's library at St James's, Goodison produced two 'large mahogany bookcases with glass doors, brass pilaster mouldings and large brass handles'. Over a period of seventeen years Goodison made almost all Frederick's furniture, scarcely an item of which has survived.

On his arrival at St James's Frederick was like an adopted child. His family, if they can be considered as such, consisted of a brother and three sisters he had never seen before and two other sisters who had grown up without him. They had all formed relationships from which he had been totally excluded. The only relative he had ever really known, his great-uncle the Duke of York, chose the year 1728 to die, and it is not too far-fetched to imagine that in the absence of any other permanent male in his life, York had assumed the role of a father-figure. Now Frederick was confronted with his real father, who was also his sovereign. The most incomprehensible aspect of this weird reunion at St James's Palace on the evening of 7 December 1728 is how Caroline was able, if at all, to square her conscience. It may well be that the almost unfathomable depths of her pending hatred for Frederick were the consequence of a guilt she was never able to face.

6

Homes and Gardens

Because the upbringing of royal children was somewhat stern, at times even Spartan, intended to prepare them from a tender age for the discipline of court etiquette, it would be a mistake to think that they and their parents were without normal feelings of affection and need, and many royal offspring received much love at a time when most of the children of the aristocracy lived quite divorced from parental care; royal boys, in particular, were spared the horrors of public schools. But even allowing for the most unenlightened concepts of eighteenth-century family life, Frederick's boyhood and adolescence had been passed in a state of emotional deprivation of exceptional severity. Small wonder that in the position he found himself on his arrival in England Frederick was open to flattery, pleased to acquire almost any friends, and became pliable material for anyone intent on causing trouble for parents who had so misused him. His experience of life had been as a stand-in in Hanover, and it is extraordinary how soon he found his feet in England. Within two years Lord Hervey was asking him to stand as godfather to his third son, 'a thumping Boy' as Hervey described the child to his friend Lady Murray. Born on 1 August 1730, the thumping boy was baptized Frederick in honour of the Prince and became the eccentric Bishop of Derry and 4th Earl of Bristol.[1]

The christening took place, on 3 September, at Hervey's house in Great Burlington Street, with a celebratory supper afterwards. The other godparents were the Duke of Richmond, and Henrietta, 2nd Duchess of Marlborough, who had succeeded her father by special remainder in 1722. Frederick could easily have sent a proxy but attended the christening in person. Afterwards Hervey reported to his great confidant, Stephen Fox, brother of the politician Henry Fox and a young man with whom many people had good reason to believe he was in love, 'Every Body was gay, easy, and seemed pleased, but particularly the Prince & Duchess of Marlborough, who are so taken with one another that I am not sure it will not end in a Flirtation.' Henrietta Marlborough was twenty-six years older than Frederick, and it was her niece Diana Spencer the Prince was to come within a whisker of marrying. Any flirtation, if it did occur, would not necessarily have been consummated.

Much love-making at the time remained verbal and platonic. Hervey's letters to Fox were undoubtedly love-letters, but they do not prove a physical relationship. Hervey and the Prince also indulged in a good deal of heightened banter, for the Prince was refreshingly relaxed in his relationships, and Hervey, who was greatly attracted to young men, seems to have been a little in love with the Prince as well as head over heels in love with Fox. He was once rash enough to tell Fox he wished he could love Frederick as well as he loved Fox, a suggestion that caused an anguished response, and was hastily followed up by Hervey with apologies and renewed professions of adoration.

Frederick was well aware of the homoerotic relationship between Fox and Hervey, who spent as much time in each other's company as Hervey's duties as a husband and courtier allowed. The Prince also knew that Hervey had once self-deprecatingly referred to himself as a chicken, because of his preference for following the hunt in a closed coach rather than an open and rain-swept chaise. Hence, having received a letter from Hervey in 1729, Frederick replied: 'My Dear Hervey, I receiv'd Sunday evening your Letter from Salisbury, & I am mighty sensible that fatigue at one Side, & pleasures, Balls, and fine Ladys at another side did not make you forget Orestes, the warm Orestes, to his Dear Pylades.' Orestes and his cousin Pylades, the son and nephew of Agamemnon respectively, who grew up as companions, were as much a byword for male friendship as were David and Jonathan. He enclosed 'a foolish Scottish Ballad' and signed off 'Adieu, my dear Chicken. Take care for you burn the ballad or I'll kill you. Frederick P.'

Hervey's reply to this was followed by another letter from Frederick telling him: 'These two days we have had no remarcable things at Court except that Mylord Chicken went into Sommerset Shire.' (Frederick's English spelling was to remain as idiosyncratic as his mother's.) Political gossip and a mildly indiscreet satirical sketch of the oft-derided Duke of Newcastle followed. He concluded: 'I have many little droleries still to tell you but the time

presses, so I end, but being a fraid that this letter should be opened
if I sent it directly to you, so I make a direction to Mr Fox, as if
it was written to You by a Lady, to make you be teazed a little
about it. Adieu my Dear, Frederick P.'

These letters are important because of the evidence they provide of an initial warm intimacy between Hervey and the Prince.
On one occasion in 1731 Frederick had Hervey at his home in
Kew where they went on playing ninepins so long that dinner
was delayed until five o'clock, only just giving Hervey time to
make a reluctant ride to Hampton Court to play cards with the
King. But by mid-December 1731 Hervey was suddenly raging
against the Prince in letters to Stephen Fox, and it was at this
time that Hervey received two pricks to his vanity. Frederick was
to take as his mistress a former mistress of Hervey's; and it was
this shared mistress who was to introduce to the Prince a not
very worthy man who immediately took over Hervey's role as
Frederick's principal political adviser.

Most importantly for the future, Hervey's pique was reinforced
by the loss of a friendship that clearly had meant a great deal to
him. In an age when social and economic pressures to marry were
stronger than they are today, men whose sexual inclination was
predominantly homosexual almost invariably subjugated those pref-
erences sufficiently to marry and have children. Hervey produced
a brood of eight, and Stephen Fox was eventually himself to marry
– but not before Hervey had actually suggested they should live
together, a situation almost unheard of at the time.

In 1736 Hervey became infatuated with a twenty-four-year-old
Italian, Francesco Algarotti, and his need to repress overt homosexual conduct by engaging in homoerotic relations of a platonic
nature was so strong that in forming a close attachment to Frederick
he may have bitten off more than he could chew. When the relationship soured over a mistress and a political adviser, Hervey
was quite unable to shrug the matter off but lived out his bitterness
on paper. A sizeable section of Hervey's memoirs, dealing with
events between May 1730 and the summer of 1732, were destroyed
by Hervey's grandson, the 1st Marquess of Bristol. It is generally
assumed that they dealt with the rift in friendship between Hervey
and the Prince, and reflected badly on Hervey; and that rift has
to be borne in mind when one reads Hervey's evaluation of the
Prince's character on his arrival in England, for it was not writ-

ten at the time but some two years after they had fallen out.

The Prince's character at his first coming over, though little more respectable, seemed much more amiable than it was upon his opening himself and being better known. For though there appeared nothing in him to be admired, yet there seemed nothing in him to be hated – neither nothing great nor nothing vicious. His behaviour was something that gained one's good wishes, though it gave one no esteem for him. For his best qualities, while they prepossessed one the most in his favour, always gave one a degree of contempt for him at the same time, his carriage, whilst it seemed engaging to those who did not examine it, appearing mean to those who did; for though his manners had the show of benevolence from a good deal of natural or habitual civility, yet his cajoling everybody, and almost in an equal degree, made those things which might have been thought favours, if more judiciously or sparingly bestowed, lose all their weight. He carried this affection of general benevolence so far that he often condescended below the character of a Prince, and so people attributed this familiarity to popular and not particular motives, so it only lessened their respect without increasing their good will, and instead of giving them good impressions of his humanity, only gave them ill ones of his sincerity.

There was more in similar vein, but Hervey sums up the problems accurately enough when he writes: ' . . . his case, in short, was this: he had a father that abhorred him, a mother that despised and neglected him, a sister that betrayed him, a brother set up to pique, and a set of servants [he meant the Prince's household] that neither were of use to him, nor were capable of being of use to him, nor desirous of being so'.

On top of the Prince's income of £10,000 a year from the Duchy of Cornwall the King proposed making him an allowance of £24,000 a year, which meant the Prince's total income would be considerably less than the £100,000 a year intended by Parliament for the new Prince of Wales. (The title was bestowed on Frederick on 9 January 1729.)[2] We have Hervey's assessment of Frederick's reaction: 'The Prince, on this occasion, as on all like occasions afterwards, between anger and timidity went just such lengths with those who were against the Court as served to irritate his father and not far enough to attach them to his service.'

One reason the King retained £76,000 of the Prince's portion of the civil list was because he had no intention of allowing him to set up a separate home of his own. Nor had the King any intention of allowing Frederick to appoint his own household; all his servants were hired, paid for and if need be fired by the King. Although his first secretary, the Reverend Charles Hedges, was English, his Keeper of the Privy Purse, for example, was a Hanoverian. If the King had wished to drive his son into the arms of disgruntled politicians he could not have gone about it more adroitly, which was extremely foolish of him, for when Frederick first arrived in England he thought of himself very much as a member of the Establishment, and indeed was treated as such, receiving the Duke of Lorraine, for instance, in his own apartments when he arrived on a state visit, and giving a ball in his honour. In 1730 he expressed to a courtier of impeccable credentials, Viscount Perceval (he was created Earl of Egmont in 1733), his disapproval of disaffection, telling him he hoped 'time would reconcile all to be friends of the Government'. The previous year he had been discussing with Lord Perceval ways to make the House of Hanover more popular, especially among the young.[3] A young man four years younger even than himself whom Frederick much admired was Perceval's clever son, and in 1748, the year that he succeeded to the earldom of Egmont, Frederick appointed him a lord of the bedchamber.

But for all his early adherence to the proprieties, Frederick did not hesitate to slip out to meet Lord Bolingbroke in secret. Although permitted to make visits to England, Henry Bolingbroke remained in disgrace, and was forbidden to attend the House of Lords, so Frederick's act was a fairly audacious one; provocative, at any rate. Somehow, while rising from his chair to bow to the Prince, Bolingbroke contrived to slip and fall. It was entirely in character for Frederick to assist him to his feet; in doing so he was equally swift with a *bon mot*: 'I trust, my Lord, this may be an omen for me succeeding in raising your fortunes.' Bolingbroke, it should be remembered, was a Jacobite! But as Robert Walpole's nineteenth-century biographer, William Coxe, Archdeacon of Wiltshire, has explained: 'The Prince was fascinated by [Bolingbroke's] conversation and manners.'

There are plenty of contemporary estimates of the Prince's character to set beside Lord Hervey's. 'I believe you would like the Prince,' Anne Irwin wrote to her father, Charles Howard, 3rd Earl of Carlisle, who at the turn of the century had had the imagination to commission the finest country house of its time, Castle Howard, near York, from a playwright, John Vanbrugh, who had never built a house before. 'There is a frankness and affability in his way very different from his rank and very engaging.' Lady Irwin was to become a lady-in-waiting to Frederick's future wife. Although she did not find Frederick in the least handsome, Lord Hervey's mother thought him 'the most agreeable young man it is possible to imagine'. She noted his person was 'little, but well made and genteel', and that there was 'a liveliness in his eyes that is indescribable and the most obliging address that can be conceived'. Those who presumed to take liberties saw another side to the Prince's lively nature, however. Someone who may not have realized who he was went up to the Prince at a masque and started abusing him, whereupon the Prince gave the man a box on the ear.

So far as we know, Frederick never travelled outside the Electorate of Hanover, and his knowledge of life when he arrived in England was limited, by any standards. He was in effect extremely naïve. In 1734,[4] in London, he resorted to a prostitute, and managed to have his watch and money stolen. Gambling was the principal indoor occupation at court, as it was throughout society in the eighteenth century, but like many insecure and immature young men Frederick took to risking far more than he could afford, and thought nothing of losing £1,000 in a night. Soon he had his own circle of friends, and it is hardly surprising that he sought company and some sort of entertaining social life away from the court, where his parents were busy indulging his priggish younger brother and permitting him every kind of freedom and licence. In 1732 the future Lord Egmont, a rather pompous philanthropist and genealogist who succeeded in being on good terms with both the King and the Prince, drew a sympathetic but not uncritical pen-portrait of Frederick which has the ring of truth. He liked nothing better, it seems, than to 'pass the evening with six or seven others over a glass of wine and hear them talk of a variety of things'. Egmont confirmed the Prince's love of cards, and explained that he played to win 'that he may supply his pleasures and generosity, which last are great but so ill placed that he often wants

wherewith to do a well-placed kindness, by giving to unworthy
objects'. He thought the Prince could 'talk gravely according to
his company, but is sometimes more childish than becomes his
age. He thinks he knows business [he meant politics] but attends
to none; likes to be flattered. He is good-natured; and if [on becoming
king] he meets with a good Ministry, may satisfy his people'. He
added something Lord Hervey would never had admitted, that
Frederick was 'extremely dutiful to his parents, who do not return
it in love, and seem to neglect him by letting him do as he will,
but they keep him short of money'.[5]

If the King thought that by keeping his elder son short of money
he would thus be able to keep him at home he had overlooked
the fact that princes were seldom expected to live within their
means; there were always people more than willing to lend them
money or give them credit. One such, in Frederick's case, was
George Bubb Dodington, a wealthy landowner with two
parliamentary seats in his pocket, which he originally placed at
Walpole's disposal. In 1726 he had addressed complimentary poems
to the less than literary Walpole, and when Walpole refused him
the peerage for which he yearned, Dodington became a tiresome
opponent.[6] Any views he expressed in the House of Commons
were generally believed to reflect those of the Prince, whose chief
political adviser he became in 1731. He it was who usurped Hervey's
former prerogative. He was said to endure being paraded as an
Aunt Sally for the Prince's rather feeble practical jokes, so much
did he relish basking in the royal limelight. Dodington was so
rich he thought nothing of spending £140,000 embellishing his
Vanbrugh mansion in Dorset, and he surely regarded his role as
court jester as well as his financial loans to Frederick as a good
investment. In the view of Peter Quennell, Dodington had 'the
weaknesses of a very rich man and the vices of a *parvenu*'.[7]

So although Frederick had left debts behind him in Hanover in
the aftermath of his hasty exit (he was to die without paying
them off and bequeathed them to his son), before long he had his
eye on a property at Kew, known then as Kew House but often
since referred to as The White House. It stood beside the Thames
just to the west of Kew Green, and only a mile from his mother's
Surrey residence, Richmond Lodge, indicative of the fact that relations
between mother and son were as cordial as could be expected in
1730, the year Frederick took a long lease on The White House.

Even more indicative of the fact that he and his sisters were then on good terms was the fact that The White House was virtually adjacent to another royal residence, the so-called Dutch House, officially known as Kew Palace, leased by Queen Caroline before Frederick arrived in England; by 1728 the princesses were in residence, and for a time Frederick also leased the Dutch House. His cipher can be seen on some of the brass locks. The Dutch House, built in 1631 in Flemish bond brick by a Dutch merchant, Samuel Fortrey, is the only royal home at Kew to have survived, and can be viewed by visitors to Kew Gardens. It is sturdy and rather dull, with three distinctive gables on the main fronts, and has hardly been altered since it was built. An eighteenth-century portico over the front door has been removed; otherwise Frederick would have no difficulty recognizing it today.

In 1732 Frederick took up the cello, and made such progress on the instrument that the following year he had Philippe Mercier, his principal court painter from 1729 until 1736, paint – or arrange to have painted – three versions of a work known as *The Music Party*. Two versions of this conversation piece, one in the National Portrait Gallery, the other at Cliveden, in the possession of the National Trust, depict Frederick and his three older sisters out of doors, with the Dutch House as a backdrop. Frederick is busy scraping away at his cello, his efforts seeming to appeal very little to Princess Amelia; Frederick has his back to her, and she is resting her head on her hand with a book in her lap, looking decidedly bored. On the left of the picture Anne is seated at a harpsichord and Caroline stands behind her, strumming away at a Milanese mandolin.[8] The third version of this painting, in the Royal Collection and presently hung at Windsor Castle, in which a pet dog makes its appearance, is set in the Banqueting House at Hampton Court, with a view of the palace through the window. Mercier included two gilt mirrors in this interior scene, and the mirrors are still at Hampton Court. They are probably among those made for Frederick in 1733 by Benjamin Goodison. A former Surveyor of the Queen's Works of Art, Sir Oliver Miller, has identified this painting (not on view to the public) as undoubtedly by Mercier, whereas it is possible that the two with the Dutch House in the background were slightly later copies entrusted to other painters. The Prince's accounts for 1732–5 contain payments to Mercier for pictures, but Sir Oliver has stated 'there is no evidence that they were all from his brush'.[9] Mercier was a French Huguenot, born in 1689, and was clearly an adaptable sort of fellow; as well as painter to Frederick he served as librarian and as a page of the bedchamber.

It is doubtful whether Prince Frederick ever achieved what we would regard today as professional standards as a musician, but professional standards in his day were often not particularly high, and there is no reason to think he did not become a perfectly competent cellist. Almost everyone in society sang, or played an instrument of some sort, and so-called amateur standards were so high that Frederick's grandson George IV played the cello with Haydn. It was typical of Lord Hervey to leave a disparaging account of the Prince's accomplishments. In 1734 he said he had seen Frederick 'once or twice a week during this whole summer at Kensington seated at an open window of his apartment with his violoncello between his legs, singing French and Italian songs to his own playing for an hour or two together, whilst his audience was composed of all the underling servants and rabble of the palace'. Why the Dutch House was chosen as one of the settings for *The Music Party* is not entirely clear, although Princess Anne was certainly in residence in 1733. In 1781 Frederick's eldest son, King George III, purchased the property, and it was here, in 1818, that his wife, Queen Charlotte, was to die. When Frederick's White House was demolished in 1802 all the pictures, china and furniture Frederick had purchased were transferred to the Dutch House.

The White House was the first home of his own Frederick had ever possessed, and between 1731 and 1735 he had William Kent, when he could be spared from Walpole's Houghton Hall, encase the 'old timber house', as the diarist and traveller John Evelyn had described it in 1678, in the new and fashionable Palladian fabric. The house acquired its new name after Kent had whitewashed the plain brick and stone façade. One benefit of the remodelling of the interior was to rid the house of rats, and by the time Kent had provided the Prince with a pretty substantial country house, Frederick had laid out £8,000. There were three courtyards, the central one being approached from Kew Green. A vestibule led to the Central Hall, two storeys high, lit by windows from an upper storey and hung with portraits of William and Mary; and of Frederick himself, in the hunting field, painted by John Wootton. Off a passage leading to the garden was a suite of semi-state apartments, a drawing-room hung with tapestry and family portraits, a gallery and waiting-rooms. Frederick did not marry until 1736 but he and his architect saw no reason not to plan ahead, and there was a separate drawing-room prepared for use by women of the bedchamber. The Prince's bedroom and dressing-room, together with apartments prepared in expectation of the birth of children, were situated on the first floor. Much of the interior decoration was designed by Kent – the chimneypiece and furniture for the gallery, for example, as well as the ceiling and furniture in the drawing-room intended for the use of the Prince's wife. So attached did his wife, Augusta, become to The White House that she retained use of the property until her death in 1772. Among those the Prince entertained at The White House was Alexander Pope, since 1712, with *The Rape of the Lock* (and on account of his translations of Homer), the most formidable literary figure of his day. (Together with Shakespeare and Milton he was the only English writer to feature on the future curriculum of George IV.)

In lighter vein Pope was much given to deriding people at court, particularly Lord Hervey. For Frederick he provided both a dog and a couplet for the canine collar: 'I am his Highness' dog at Kew; / Pray tell me, Sir, whose dog are you?'

With his great-grandmother's horticultural efforts at Herrenhaüsen as an example, Frederick was eventually to take as much interest in the garden as the house. For many years the garden at Kew had been reputed to provide the best fruit of any garden in England; there was an open lawn in front of the house, with dense plantings of trees to the south, and a square parterre – an ornamental garden with paths between the beds – divided into four sections. In 1735 Frederick was ordering urns and terms – square pedestals, usually with a bust at the top depicting the Roman god Terminus. Kent had two large urns sent over from Bristol, while the painter John Jones submitted a bill for painting '24 figures in the garden 3 times done'. But major redesigning of the garden at Kew seems to have been delayed until shortly before Frederick's death, when the Prince got down to serious work outdoors in person, roping in family and friends to lend a hand. 'Worked in the new walk at Kew,' the Prince's Treasurer noted in his diary in 1750. And the next day: 'All of us, men, women and children, worked at the same place – a cold supper.' The Prince's taste in garden ornamentation was eclectic. At Kew he erected a Chinese-style garden temple, the House of Confucius, not merely a chinoiserie-style garden folly 'but a building specifically dedicated to the life and work of Confucius, whose doctrines of political morality were well known and much admired in eighteenth-century Europe'.[10]

Frederick's deliberate hotchpotch of garden buildings may have been a result of the influence upon him of the gardens at Stowe, in Buckinghamshire, where ancient and modern were juxtaposed by Lord Cobham, whose portrait hung at The White House. Plans to build a Moorish-style Alhambra at Kew were put into operation by Frederick's widow, who took great pains and pleasure in enlarging the gardens in the lonely and largely unfulfilled years after the Prince's death. Indeed, much that she achieved stands as a fitting memorial to Frederick. Six years after the Prince's death she appointed William Chambers as her architect, and it was he who built for her the 163-foot-high Chinese pagoda at Kew. In 1761 he also built the Orangery, now a restaurant, as fine a piece of design as Wren's earlier Orangery at Kensington Palace. For two nights of every week in the summer George III and his wife slept at The White House, where family life imitated the informal style initiated by Frederick, to the extent, so Fanny Burney recorded in 1786, that the King 'has not even an equerry with him, nor the Queen any lady to attend her when she goes her airings'.

Even before The White House was habitable Frederick got William Kent to design for him a stupendously ornate barge in which to be rowed from London to view the work in progress, and Kent's meticulous drawings are preserved at the Royal Institute of British Architects in London. Sixty-seven feet long, it was decorated with carvings of shells, mermaids and dolphins. There was of course a cabin in which to recline, and the prow was adorned with the Prince of Wales's feathers and a replica of the Garter star. The great Grinling Gibbons had been succeeded in 1721 as Master Carver to the Crown by James Richards, and it was he who was employed, between 1731 and 1732, to embellish the first of the three barges Frederick was eventually to order. It was manned by a dozen oarsmen and a bargemaster, the crew being decked out in uniforms 'laced in the fashion of the Yeomen of the Guards, only not quite so long.'

The first time Frederick showed off his new barge, which can be seen at the National Maritime Museum in Greenwich,[11] was one evening in July 1732 when he took his mother, his brother and all five sisters to inspect the cleaning of some pictures at

Somerset House. After 'taking a turn in the Great Hall' at Chelsea Hospital, the family party 'walk'd to the Water-side and went on board the Prince of Wales's fine Barge, lately built under the direction of Lord Baltimore, and being attended by the Officers and Ladies in Waiting of the Court in another Barge, and a Set of Musick in the third Barge, they proceeded to Somerset House'.[12] Frederick's state barge, in which he later attended concerts on the Thames, had to compete in splendour with those in everyday use by the Lord Mayor and the City companies, and relatively short of money though he may have been, he was learning to display himself in the way expected of a prince. At the age of twenty-five, after less than four years in England, it must have gratified him to be able to organize such a spectacular river trip for his sisters, whose lives were far from jolly and who were themselves kept pitifully short of money by their father.

Sixteen years after this first outing Horace Walpole spied Frederick, attired in 'a new sky-blue watered tabby coat, with gold button-holes, and a magnificent gold waistcoat fringed', entertaining a diplomatic party on the Thames. 'They went into one of the Prince of Wales's barges,' he reported to a friend, 'had another barge filled with violins and hautboys, and an open boat with drums and trumpets.'[13] Frederick's first and most splendid barge remained in commission for over a hundred years; the last person to use it was the Prince Consort when he was rowed in 1849 to the opening of a new coal wharf. Exactly a century before, in May 1749, Frederick had watched from the third of his barges to be built – this one in the Venetian style – while scullers competed for a silver cup worth 75 guineas presented by himself. The previous spring 'His Royal Highness the Prince of Wales had been pleased to give a Silver Cup, of Twenty-five Guineas Value, to be rowed for by six Oars on the 24th of May next, being Prince George's Birth-Day, from Whitehall to Putney-Bridge.'[14] For silver punch-bowls as prizes for sailing races at sea, the Prince would pay 50 guineas; horse races were also patronized by him.

By 1732 Frederick had decided that a rented house at Kew and a barge on the Thames were all very well but the heir to the throne deserved a town house too, a place set quite apart from the formal apartments allocated for his use at St James's Palace. He alighted on Carlton House, in Pall Mall, where he planned initially to entertain rather than live. The property Frederick purchased should not be too closely identified with the house his profligate grandson the Prince Regent later got Henry Holland to transform into a glittering palace. It was a relatively modest town house in Frederick's day, built in 1709 for the Secretary of State, Henry Boyle, and acquired its name when Boyle was raised to the peerage as Lord Carlton (sometimes spelt Carleton, and the house was spelt Carleton House as late as 1807). Carlton died in 1725. His heir was that great patron of Palladian architecture, his nephew Richard Boyle, 3rd Earl of Burlington, responsible for Burlington House in Piccadilly and the exquisite Chiswick House. In *The Country Life Book of Royal Palaces, Castles and Homes*[15] we are told that two years after Lord Carlton's death, Burlington 'parted with Carlton House to Frederick, Prince of Wales', but in 1727 Frederick was still living in Hanover. In point of fact, Frederick purchased Carlton House, in 1732, from Lord Burlington's mother, to whom the Earl had made over the house that year. 'The Prince bought his house in Pall Mall of Lord Chesterfield,' Lord Hervey records, but it was only that Chesterfield negotiated the sale on behalf of the Dowager Countess. The price, Hervey says, was £6,000, which sum the Prince did not possess and he had to borrow the money from Dodington. As Dodington had a town house of his own hard by, he would have regarded the loan of a mere £6,000 as money well spent in enticing the Prince to become his next-door neighbour. On inspecting Henry Holland's work in 1785, Horace Walpole told the Countess of Ossory that Carlton House would be the most perfect palace in Europe, but not a stone of George IV's or his grandfather's house is left standing. It straddled what is now the site between the lower end of Regent Street and the Duke of York's Steps, and in part would have stood where today the Athenaeum can be found.

Frederick was evidently well pleased with the work William Kent had done for him at Kew, for in August 1732 he appointed him his architect, and by January 1733 Kent was involved in restoration work on Carlton House. By March that year Frederick was already able to entertain in the house. Kent was the most versatile and influential decorator, builder, interior designer and landscape gardener of his time, and at Carlton House he transformed twelve acres of gardens by means of dense planting interspersed with small open spaces, thereby contriving to make the gardens seem much bigger than they were while successfully shielding them from public gaze by walls and trees. In 1735 the gardens were adorned with a temple, a miniature version, in effect, of Chiswick House.

By this time Frederick had spent £5,418, and alterations and additions continued throughout his lifetime. As with The White House at Kew, his widow was to retain Carlton House after his death, for it developed, particularly after she and Frederick had been expelled from court, into far more than a mere place in which to entertain; it became a principal home. How influential upon contemporary taste the gardens were to become can be gauged from a letter written in 1734 by Sir Thomas Robinson to Lord Carlisle, in which he says: 'There is a new taste in gardening just arisen, which has been practiced with so great success at the Prince's garden in Town... after Mr Kent's notion of gardening, viz. to lay them out, and work without level or line. By this means I really think the 12 acres the Prince's garden consists of is more diversified and of greater variety than anything of that compass I ever saw.' There can be no doubt the informal 'new taste in gardening just arisen' matched closely the relaxed, informal nature of the Prince himself; not for him the rigid formality of a landscape gardener like Louis XIV's André Le Nôtre.

Within five months of Frederick's arrival in England his father had decided to pay his first return visit to Hanover – his first since leaving the Electorate in 1714 on the accession of George I. He was to return to Hanover a dozen times, and instead of appointing his heir as regent in his absence he did exactly what his own father had done, bypassed his son and appointed in his place the Queen. Having already had £76,000 of his parliamentary pension withheld, an action he regarded as nothing less than daylight robbery, Frederick now had this second proof of his father's regard for him to contend with. In order to appoint Caroline regent, a position she held four times, with the 'Style and Title of Guardian of the Kingdom of Great Britain, and His Majesty's Lieutenant within the same during His Majesty's absence', George had to get an act passed by Parliament. Frederick was present at Kensington Palace on 22 May 1729, together with the Archbishop of Canterbury, the Lord Chancellor, the Lord Privy Seal, the Lord Steward, the Lord Chamberlain, eight dukes, a dozen earls, three viscounts, a baron, the Speaker of the House of Commons, the Chancellor of the Exchequer and the Master of the Rolls, when the King's

Commission 'was this day by Her Majesty's command opened
and read in His Majesty's Most Honourable Privy Council'.
Afterwards Frederick 'and all the Lords and others of the Council
who were present had the honour to kiss Her Majesty's hand'.

On this first occasion of his mother assuming the Regency,
Frederick seems to have concealed his feelings and to have mingled
quite happily with his family, as indeed he had from the start;
within five days of his arrival in England he had been to the
theatre with his three older sisters to see a piece called *The Constant Couple*. Peter Wentworth, who had started his career at
court as an equerry to Prince George of Denmark and was at this
time an equerry to the Queen and a groom of the bedchamber to
the eight-year-old Duke of Cumberland, was writing to his brother
the Earl of Strafford from Kensington Palace, on 25 July 1729, to
say the Prince had told his mother he, Wentworth, was 'one of
the most diligent servants he ever saw'. By August that year Frederick
and his brother and sisters were all identically clad in hunting
clothes of 'blue, trimmed with gold, and faced and lined with
red'. On 20 August the Queen 'and all the Royal Family' dined
at Claremont, a house in Surrey bought from Sir John Vanbrugh
by the Duke of Newcastle, formerly Earl of Clare – hence Claremont.
It was pulled down by Clive of India, who built an entirely new
house, now a girls' boarding-school. It was at Claremont, in 1817,
that Frederick's great-granddaughter, Princess Charlotte, heiress
presumptive to the future George IV, died in childbirth. 'The Prince
of Wales came to us as soon as his, and our, dinner was over,'
Wentworth told Lord Strafford, 'and drank a bumper of rack-
punch to the Queen's health, which you may be sure I devotedly
pledged, and he was going on with another, but her Majesty sent
us word that she was going to walk in the garden, so that broke
up the company. We walked till candle-light, being entertained
with very fine French horns, then returned to the great hall, and
everybody agreed never was anything finer lit.'[16]

A good many bumpers had been pledged by Frederick at a
dinner party at Richmond in July, when Peter Wentworth witnessed the undisguised flirtation of Princess Amelia with the elderly
Duke of Grafton, Lord Chamberlain and a grandson of Charles
II. The Queen seems to have turned a blind eye to her daughter's
conduct, for in August she and Prince Frederick invited themselves
to the Duke's hunting-lodge near Richmond. 'He fended off for a

great while,' according to Wentworth, 'saying his house was not
fit to receive them, and 'twas so old he was afraid 'twould fall
upon their heads. But his Royal Highness, who is very quick at
good inventions, told him he would bring tents and pitch them in
the garden, so his Grace's excuse did not come off; the thing
must be Saturday.'[17]

Just as Amelia, a rather horsy type, entertained a hopeless attachment to the Duke of Grafton, so Princess Caroline was plagued
by a quite inexplicable passion for Lord Hervey. But she ended
her life in retirement, an invalid spinster. Equally unfulfilled, Amelia
became a disagreeable, ill-mannered, cantankerous and, in contrast
to her mother, who for all her faults was famously generous, a
penny-pinching old maid.

Peter Wentworth, who was often in attendance on Frederick,
has provided a glimpse of court 'entertainment' in 1730. 'The
quadrille table is well known,' he reported to his brother on 10
August that year, 'and there is a large table surrounded by my
master (the Prince of Wales), the Princesses, the Duke of Cumberland,
the bedchamber ladies, Lord Lumley, and all the *belle-assemblée*,
at a most stupid game, to my mind, lottery ticket. £100 is sometimes
lost at this pastime.'[18] Then there was dancing. The *Daily Advertiser*
for 3 March 1731 reported: 'On Monday night His Royal Highness
the Prince of Wales and the Princess Royal opened a ball at Court
with a minuet, and afterwards they danced several set dances with
several of the quality till between four and five o'clock next
morning. . . . There never was seen so great an appearance, either
for number or magnificence as on the like occasion.' Soon after
his arrival in England Frederick had given a ball upon 'the Island
in St James's Park'; and at Richmond, before family relationships
had soured, he had laid on for 'the Queen and all his dear sisters . . . a
very pretty entertainment', a performance, in fact, of a theatrical
piece entitled *Hob in the Garden*.

But much more commonly – and especially when the King was
in England – life at court was almost as tedious as it had been
during the reign of George I. 'All things appear to move in the
same manner as usual, and all our actions are as mechanical as
the clock which directs them,' the Countess of Pomfret, a lady-in-
waiting to the Queen who was yearning perhaps for the beauties
and peace of her lovely new country house, Easton Neston, wrote
to a fellow long-suffering courtier, Viscountess Sundon, from

Hampton Court, where in July 1733 Hervey too was complaining to Lady Sundon, a woman of the bedchamber, of the boredom and routine: 'No mill-horse ever went in a more constant track, or a more unchanging circle, so that by the assistance of an almanack for the day of the week, and a watch for the hour of the day, you may inform yourself fully, without any other intelligence but your memory, of every transaction within the verge of the Court. Walking, chaises, levees, and audiences fill the morning; at night the King plays at commerce and backgammon, and the Queen at quadrille.'

For all the seeming early family accord, the King's slight in appointing the Queen as regent in 1729, and his withholding of most of Frederick's income, served as a preliminary signal for disaffected politicians to begin to gather round the Prince. Whether to back the monarch or the heir was always something of a gamble; the King might live for years, he might die at any moment. As Duke of Cornwall, any Prince of Wales had parliamentary seats, and other patronage, at his disposal; but the King of course had ministries in his gift, not to mention knighthoods, baronetcies and peerages, and a whole host of sinecure offices wrapped up with large incomes. If one was, in any case, out of favour with George II and out of office, life in the company of Prince Frederick promised to be more lively than at court, quite apart from the prospects it promised of preferment when he came to the throne. Many of those who gravitated to Frederick when he went seriously into opposition had learnt their skills as opponents of Walpole under the tuition of Lord Cobham, one of Marlborough's finest generals, and it was to Cobham's mansion, Stowe, that men like William Pitt, in 1737 appointed a groom of the bedchamber to Frederick, and Frederick's future secretary, George Lyttelton, were drawn initially.

The age in which these men were obliged to seek private patronage if they had not been born to the purple was essentially one of deep insecurity. As Frederick remarked in 1733 in a letter to Dodington, 'one can't in this wicked age be sure of anything, or anybody'. Before his elevation to the peerage as Lord Hervey of Ickworth, Hervey was MP for Bury St Edmunds and originally opposed Walpole, but in 1730, by appointing him Vice-Chamberlain, Walpole neatly positioned Hervey at court to help govern the King through the Queen. The day after his appointment

(7 May) Hervey was also made a Privy Councillor. Since Hervey had served as a gentleman of the bedchamber to George II when he was Prince of Wales, his support for the King and Queen was almost inevitable, and the early formation of a party centred on Frederick was just as inevitably one cause of the rift between the Prince and his former close friend. That friendship had been very close indeed, which is why, when they drew apart, they did so, on Hervey's side at any rate, with so much bitterness. On one occasion, when Hervey was ill, he had reported to a friend that the Prince 'sat with me all yesterday, and has promised to do so again to-day'. Together Frederick and Hervey had collaborated on, or caused to have written, a second-rate Restoration comedy. John Wilkes, the actor manager, was amusingly scathing about its merits. 'If the last two acts,' he said, 'which I have not seen, are exceeding better than the first three, which I have, the play might last one night.' It lasted four. Set in Hampton Court and entitled *The Modish Couple*, it went into rehearsal at the Theatre Royal, Drury Lane, in December 1731 and opened on 10 January the following year. On the third night – traditionally the author's benefit night – Frederick made a point of appearing, making his bow to 'one of the finest Assemblies of Persons of Quality that has been seen'. On the fourth night it was booed off the stage.

It was Hervey's second son, Augustus, who became 3rd Earl of Bristol, who left instructions that his father's memoirs were not to be published during the lifetime of George III, and they did not appear until 1848, 105 years after Hervey's death. They need to be read while bearing in mind not only Hervey's natural spleen and almost pathological hatred of Frederick but the fact that Hervey was physically a very sick man, plagued with indigestion and an agonizing gall-bladder. His industry, therefore, is all the more remarkable, but his friendships were usually only skin-deep, tainted with disdain and cynicism. How far wide of the mark he could fly can be judged by his description of Lord Chesterfield: 'a ... stunted giant, with a person as disagreeable as it was possible for a human being to have without being deformed. A broad, rough-featured, ugly face with black teeth, and a head big enough for a Polyphemus'. If this is true, there must have been something wrong with Gainsborough's eyesight when he came to paint this brilliant man; but of course Chesterfield was an outspoken critic of Hervey's patron, Walpole. Probably the only person for whom Hervey ever

really cared was the Queen. W.H. Wilkins, in his life of Queen
Caroline, says that Hervey 'possessed some of the worst vices of
courtiers; he was double-faced, untrustworthy and ungrateful'. He
adds for good measure that he had 'a frivolous and effeminate
character'.[19] Like many homosexuals, Hervey was greatly attracted
to women, and they to him, and Hervey's wife was famed not
only for her beauty but her charm and high spirits. Another of
Chesterfield's efforts, on her behalf, went as follows:

> Bright venus yet never saw bedded
> So perfect a beau and a belle
> As when Hervey the handsome was wedded
> To the beautiful Molly Lepel.
>
> Had I Hanover, Bremen and Verdun,
> And likewise the Duchy of Zell!
> I'd part with them all for a farthing
> To have my dear Molly Lepel.

But in an effeminate age Hervey took to rouge and camp behaviour to such an extent that his contemporaries nicknamed him
Lord Fanny. Effeminacy in a man can lead to some most unat-
tractive traits, and would account for the spite and meanness of
which Hervey was widely accused. The Duke of Marlborough's
widow thought him 'the most wretched, profligate man that ever
was born, besides ridiculous; a painted face, and not a tooth in
his head'. Yet others thought he possessed great personal beauty.
Frederick was not the only friend with whom Hervey managed to
fall out. He and William Pulteney, leader of the Whig opposition,
whose name in 1731 George II personally struck from the list of
Privy Councillors because he had insulted the royal family, were
at one time great friends. But in 1730 Pulteney accused Hervey of
having libelled him. The row got out of hand, and in January the
following year the two of them fought a duel 'in Upper St James's
Park, behind Arlington Street'. According to an eye-witness, both
combatants were slightly wounded before being parted by their
respective seconds. Effeminate Hervey may have been, but he did
not lack courage, and he could be a very dangerous enemy.

7

'No Excise!'

One reason George II was reluctant to sanction Frederick's marriage – to anyone – was because the longer Frederick remained a bachelor the longer, so the King reckoned, he could be kept short of money, with no excuse for setting up a separate establishment and the ever-increasing chance of creating a rival court. It was George who had finally dashed Frederick's romantic notions of an alliance with Wilhelmina of Prussia. What more natural than for Frederick to bait his father with a far more improbable scheme, to marry a commoner. This was a plan that met with whole-hearted support from the still ambitious Dowager Duchess of Marlborough, for the commoner in question was her granddaughter, Lady Diana Spencer, the younger daughter of her own second daughter, Lady Anne Churchill, who had married Charles Spencer, 3rd Earl of Sunderland. Diana, referred to by her widowed father as 'poor dear little Dye', had been brought up by her grandmother, and became Sarah Marlborough's favourite grandchild. Nothing was too good for her, and the Duchess saw no reason why the most elegible bachelor in England should not become her husband.

Frederick could have done far worse. Lady Diana was a slim, intelligent and charming girl, well versed in social and political affairs and at ease in the atmosphere of great country houses. One of her suitors, before he made his marriage of convenience to Lady Walsingham, was Lord Chesterfield, who told Sarah: 'The person, the merit and the family of Lady Diana Spencer are objects so valuable that they must necessarily have . . . caused many such applications of this nature to Your Grace.' Unfortunately, the only person who apparently saw no reason why Lady Di, as Diana Spencer liked to be called, should not become Queen of England was Walpole, who wanted a European princess for Frederick, and warned Sarah Marlborough that there was in any case no hope of the King's approving the match. The marriage of the future

James II to Anne Hyde had caused a political storm, and the last monarch to sit on the throne beside English women, and commoners at that, Henry VIII, had not set a happy precedent. So denied her prince, Diana was wed, in October 1731, aged twenty-one, to Lord John Russell, heir presumptive to the dukedom of Bedford, which he soon inherited on the premature death of his brother, the 3rd Duke. But Diana only briefly enjoyed the splendours of Woburn Abbey, dying from consumption at the age of twenty-six. Thus at any rate Frederick had been saved from the tragedy of himself early becoming a widower.

Nevertheless at the time Walpole's actions were hardly likely to have endeared him to the Prince. And frustrated a second time in his desire to marry, Frederick took a mistress. With a somewhat reckless disregard for scandal, and perhaps wishing to cock a snook at those he saw at court determined to trip him up, he chose a maid of honour, Anne Vane, an accomplished artist and a daughter of Lord Barnard. Not only was Anne a member of his mother's household (she was appointed a maid of honour in 1726, when she was twenty-one), she was the former mistress of both Lord Hervey and Lord Harrington, the current Secretary of State. Writing to Lady John Russell from Scarborough on 26 July 1732, Sarah Marlborough remarked: 'I think it is very plain that there is some tincture more or less of madness in almost everybody that one knows.' And she offered as an instance of her theory the fact that 'I read in a letter to-day that Miss Vane goes a visiting in her chair with her son in her lap and two nurses in chairs to attend her.' The child in question was none other than her five- or perhaps six-week-old son by Frederick, Prince of Wales (the baby was born on 5 June), whose christening at Miss Vane's house in St James's Street by the Prince's chaplain, Dr Snowe, was recorded in the parish register of St James's, Westminster, on 17 June 1732.[1] Anne Vane was so pleased with the paternity of her child that the Dowager Lady Northampton thought no one else had ever been 'so proud of a big belly'. Because Anne Vane had also bestowed her favours on Hervey and Harrington her baby was sometimes foolishly referred to as 'the child of a triumvirate', but only one man can father a child, and this one was undoubtedly the Prince's. Only the Queen had cause to wish otherwise, for in her anxiety somehow or other to have William supplant Frederick she was determined to prove that Frederick was impotent.

The godparents to the boy were Lord Baltimore, a member of Frederick's household, and his uncle, the Hon. Henry Vane, and far from making any pretence as to the baby's parentage, Frederick had the child baptized Cornwall Fitz-Frederick. He was fond of his son and proud of his mistress, allowing her, after her dismissal from court, a substantial allowance of £1,600 a year, and setting her up in a house in Grosvenor Street. Lord Egmont, a strait-laced evangelical, records that Anne was soon being visited by 'a great number of people of fashion, men and ladies . . . to the just scandal of all sober and religious folks'[2] – as if no royal bastard had until then ever seen the light of day. Frederick insisted on due deference being paid to his mistress, treating her almost as the wife he had so recently been denied, and he was cross when his Keeper of the Privy Purse, the Hanoverian Colonel Schütz, hesitated to call for as long as he could, not in his case out of moral scruples but for fear of antagonizing the King and Queen.

Egmont, who so strongly disapproved of the liaison he was probably biased, says that Anne was a 'fat, and ill-shaped dwarf' with 'nothing good to recommend her . . . neither sense nor wit',[3] but Frederick seems to have been well content with his 'beautiful Vanella', as Miss Vane was known to everyone except Lord Egmont. Within a few months of the birth of Fitz-Frederick she had again conceived, and a girl, baptized Amelia *in extremis*, was born about midnight on 21 April 1733, but lived for only two hours. Was Frederick's choice of his sister's name a coincidence, an intended compliment or merely mischievous?

Before this sad occurrence, however, two other events connected with Miss Vane served to sever the friendship between Frederick and Lord Hervey. One of Frederick's crimes, in Hervey's eyes, had been his adoption of Dodington as chief political adviser in his place – and to compound the felony, Dodington had been introduced to Frederick by Miss Vane, Hervey's former paramour. Hervey's crime, in Frederick's eyes, was a letter the impetuous courtier had written to Miss Vane two months before her first confinement, remonstrating with her in terms of such virulent abuse it was calculated to cause outrage in anyone who read it. Hervey apparently told the innocent bearer of this stupid missive, his brother-in-law Bussy Mansel, that it merely contained advice about hiring a midwife; but when Miss Vane fainted on reading the letter, Mansel vowed vengeance on the wretched Hervey, and Frederick had to use his influence to prevent yet another duel. To Stephen Fox Lord Hervey was now writing of Frederick: 'That fool plagues my heart out. He is as false as he is silly.' And in a further fit of impotent rage, on 30 December 1731 Fox was informed that the Prince, Miss Vane and Dodington had been together 'all last night at that pretty idiot Lady Deloraine's lodgings'.

Marriage became a sore subject again in 1733, the year that Frederick's oldest sister, Princess Anne, the Princess Royal, became engaged to Prince William of Orange. Negotiations for the marriage had been opened by Lord Chesterfield, since 1728 an outstanding ambassador to The Hague. One reason Frederick, really quite desperate for an adequate income, had been attracted to the idea of a romantic elopement with Diana Spencer was because he had bargained a settlement of £100,000 a year from the Dowager Duchess of Marlborough in the event of his marrying her granddaughter, and he felt reasonably confident that when eventually he did marry, his father would be compelled to hand over his full entitlement. So it naturally irked him to see a sister, and a sister younger even than he, making off with a marriage settlement first. 'I hear there has lately been a great quarrel at court between the Prince, the King and the Queen,' Sarah Marlborough wrote to her granddaughter Diana, now Duchess of Bedford, on 29 June 1734. 'Nobody knows certainly what it is about, but some say that it was upon his desiring that he might be married to some German Princess. I suppose it was so. His reason was to get some settlement, which will not be easily obtained, besides that her majesty will never like to have any court but her own.'

The King had sent a message to both Houses of Parliament in 1733 to communicate the intended marriage of the Princess Royal to the Prince of Orange, 'a miserable match', in the opinion of Lord Hervey, 'both in point of man and fortune, his figure being deformed and his estate not clear £12,000 a year'. Hervey retained the general belief that the King approved the alliance because he was anxious that should the Princess Royal, third in line of succession, inherit the throne, she would be married to a staunch Protestant. But he made no secret of his own opinion; that a severe shortage of marriageable princes on the Continent meant that Anne had no choice but to 'go to bed to this piece of deformity in Holland, or die an ancient maid immured in her royal convent at St James's'.

Crown lands in St Kitts-Nevis had recently been sold for £93,000, and out of the proceeds Parliament agreed to settle £80,000 on the Princess. If the description by the cruel but fastidious Lord Hervey of Prince William of Orange is anything like an accurate one, it seems the Princess deserved every penny: 'The Prince of Orange's figure, besides his being almost a dwarf, was as much deformed as it was possible for a human creature to be; his face was not bad, his countenance was sensible, but his breath more offensive than it is possible for those who have not been offended by it to imagine.' However, if Hervey is again to be believed, perhaps the Prince had not himself acquired the most desirable bride. 'The Princess Royal's beauties,' Lord Hervey tells us, 'were a lively clean look and a very fine complexion, though she was marked a good deal by the small-pox. The faults of her person were that of being very ill made, though not crooked, and a great propensity to fat.' She was an accomplished harpsichordist, hence her pose in *The Music Party*, and a clever linguist, speaking fluent English, German, French and Italian, but 'the proudest of all her proud family; and her family the proudest of all their proud nation'.

It was precisely his snobbery, discourtesy to opponents and misplaced pride that made the King antagonize both the landed county families and the aristocracy, defects which Frederick so manifestly set out to counter in his own behaviour. In 1730 a courtier was complaining about 'the King's not speaking to the country gentry when they come to Court, which tries them and makes them declare they have no business to come here, since they are not regarded, and so they betake themselves to the discontented party'. And in the very year Lord Hervey was writing about the proudest family 'of all their proud nation' Lord Egmont noted: 'It were to be wished the King had more affability, and that the sincerity in showing his resentment where he is displeased with his subject's conduct did not prejudice His Majesty's affairs after this manner. For the nobility of England are proud, and presently take fire at any slight the Crown casts upon them; besides there are conjunctions of time when Kings should take some pains to please.'[4]

As for Frederick's reaction to the engagement of his sister, Lord Hervey noted: 'As those who had now the ear of the Prince lost no opportunity to irritate and blow him up against his father, so this marriage gave them occasion to make His Royal Highness think it very hard that the first establishment provided by Parliament for one of the royal progeny should be for any but the heir-apparent to the Crown. He was so very uneasy that to everybody his looks told he was so, and to many his words.' Hervey went on to recount that the coldness between the Prince and his parents at this time 'increased so much that it furnished conversation to the whole town', the King no longer speaking to his son at all, the Queen 'very slightly'. When the Prince of Orange arrived in November, to stay at Somerset House, Frederick must have recalled, with some belated pleasure, the mean arrangements made for his own arrival in England, for according to Hervey the King sent 'only one miserable leading coach with only a pair of horses and a pair of footmen'. Because the King regarded William as a mere nobody who was going to be raised in the world by receiving the hand of his oldest daughter, he 'suffered no sort of public honours to be paid to the Prince on his arrival, and behaved himself with scarce common civility towards him'. Guns at the Tower of London remained silent; guards failed to turn out. When Lord Hervey reported Frederick's conduct towards his future brother-in-law, his dry wit came into its own: 'The Prince of Wales forced himself to be tolerably civil to the Prince of Orange, though he was hurt at the distinctions paid him by the nation. Yet the Prince of Wales had at least this satisfaction in obliging himself to do what he thought right on this occasion, that he was sure what he was doing was disagreeable to his father.'

It seems that whenever Frederick spoke to Anne 'it was as with as little decency as affection. His mother was not much more in favour than his sister. He said they were both so interested, so false, so designing and so worthless that it was as impossible to love or value them as it was to trust them without being betrayed, or believe them without being deceived'. The wedding of Princess Anne having been postponed because the Prince of Orange fell ill, it was eventually fixed for 14 March 1734, the arrangements being entrusted to Lord Hervey. Four thousand people attended, the Prince gave his bride jewels 'of immense value', and the King, too, 'spared no expense'. As for the ceremonial bedding of the couple, Hervey says that when the Prince 'was undressed, and came in his nightgown and nightcap into the room to go to bed, the appearance he made was as indescribable as the astonished countenances of everybody who beheld him. From the make of his brocaded gown, and the make of his back, he looked behind as if he had no head, and before as if he had no neck and no legs'. Next morning, speaking to Hervey in French, the Queen asked him: 'et n'aviez-vous pas bien pitié de la pauvre Anne?' (Caroline generally spoke French with Cumberland, Anne and Caroline, and wrote letters to Frederick in French, but for all the claims made for her education, the only language in which she was ever fluent, and in which she usually conversed with the King, remained German. Her French was largely phonetic, and her English spelling idiosyncratic, to say the least: St Jemes, hampthancout, Lord harway, the Duke of graffthan, Richement and Kinsinthon may suffice as examples.)

Throughout the visit of the Prince of Orange to England, Frederick had harked on to his sister about her 'daring to be married before him', and by the time of the wedding, brother and sister were scarcely speaking to one another. To his mother, Frederick now spoke only in public, and apparently he told his sisters 'the reason of his coming so seldom to the Queen was Lord Hervey's always being there'. Hervey's organizing of the nuptials would hardly have drawn the two former friends any closer.

With family relations sinking to such a low ebb, Frederick was becoming more and more dependent for friendship and support outside the inner confines of the court. Now that he adhered to the Julian calendar (as noted in Chapter 1), he celebrated his birthday on 23 January, and on 23 January 1733 Lady Irwin was writing to her father to say: 'The entertainment my Lord Tankerville gave upon the Prince's birthday was one of the finest things that has been known upon that occasion; the company was the foreign ministers and our great men; the service was upon a long table; 96 dishes; beans, peas, and all the rarities that could be thought on was there.' In January the following year a court ball to celebrate the Prince's birthday was cancelled, because, it was alleged, the Queen was suffering an attack of gout; the more probable reason was to prevent any public demonstration of sympathy for the Prince. On New Year's Day 1734 George Dodington had persuaded Frederick to attend the King's levee, as he had not attended a levee for some months. Hervey was so prejudiced against the Prince that he believed the Prince hoped the King would snub him so that everyone should see how badly he was treated. He was also so conceited he believed it was his duty to contrive a reconciliation, and that by advising the Queen beforehand to tell the King to make a point of speaking to his son he, Lord Hervey, had been responsible for the great success of the occasion. Hervey's real purpose in speaking to the Queen would have been to foil Prince Frederick's plot.

Hervey also claimed to have told the Queen it was generally agreed the Prince was kept too short of funds, and that 'whilst he was so straitened in his circumstances it was impossible he should ever be quiet'.

'Good God!' the Queen exclaimed, 'that people will always be judging and deciding upon what they know nothing of.' She demanded to be told who these 'wise people' were. 'Pray,' she said to Hervey, 'when you hear them, my Lord, talk their nonsense again, tell them that the Prince costs the King £50,000 a year, which, till he is married, I believe any reasonable body will think a sufficient allowance for him. But, poor creature, with not a bad heart, he is induced by knaves and fools that blow him up to do things that are as unlike an honest man as a wise one. I wonder what length those monsters wish to carry him?' The Queen was being disingenuous. Even if Frederick was by this time receiving £50,000, it was not coming from the King's private resources but from the £100,000 always intended by Parliament for the Prince, £50,000 of which the King was still stuffing into his own pocket. When Hervey suggested it would be easier for everybody if the Prince had his allowance in a lump sum and his own establishment, the Queen apparently had no answer. 'The truth was,' Hervey wrote, 'they both hated their son to that immoderate degree that they would rather put themselves to inconveniences than make him easy.' With Frederick's debts mounting, his creditors becoming importunate, and with his treasury empty, 'the clandestine correspondence between him and the Opposition continued in full force, he hoping to make some use of their despair, and they of his distress'.

No wonder Frederick was anxious to go his own way. As an instance of the King and Queen entertaining two visitors, Lord Lifford and his sister Lady Charlotte de Roucy,[5] Hervey says the King 'walked about and talked to the brother of armies, or to the sister of genealogies, whilst the Queen knitted and yawned, till from yawning she came to nodding, and from nodding to snoring'. The parents with whom the Prince of Wales was saddled were a father who was an illiterate philistine and a mother whose appreciation of good conversation, history, literature, philosophy and metaphysics was subjugated to her love of power, and who suffered the necessity, in order to exercise power, of pretending for hours at a stretch to listen to and approve of her husband's stubborn opinions. According to Lord Hervey, the Queen's power was 'unrivalled and unbounded'. As soon as George II became king 'the whole world began to find out that her will was the sole spring on which every movement in the Court turned'.

The royal family took music extremely seriously, which is why they found no difficulty whatsoever in falling out among themselves over the patronage of the greatest musical exponent in England in their day, George Frideric Handel. Music, indeed, was the one creative activity in which George II took a practical interest, paying Handel a pension of £1,000 a year, and in 1743 attending the first London performance of *Messiah*. Handel's operas were originally performed at London's principal home of opera and ballet, the King's Theatre in the Haymarket, but they moved to Covent Garden two years after the impresario John Rich had opened a new theatre on the site of a convent (hence the name Covent Garden) in 1732. *The Beggar's Opera*, which Rich had produced at a theatre in Lincoln's Inn Fields of which he was manager, was said to have made Gay rich and Rich gay, but it can safely be assumed that John Rich had profited too from this enormously popular production (it was an early revival of *The Beggar's Opera* that provided his new Covent Garden theatre with financial stability). At Lincoln's Inn Fields an Italian opera season – and not a very good one – was established as a rival to that of the Haymarket (and later Covent Garden), and as the King and Queen, and the Princess Royal, patronized the great German, Prince Frederick and his friends repaired, as ostentatiously as they knew how, to Lincoln's Inn. As a result, Lord Hervey reports that the King and Queen 'sat freezing constantly' at Handel's 'empty Haymarket Opera'. He said the affair 'grew as serious as that of the Greens and the Blues under Justinian at Constantinople'. Voting against the court in Parliament was hardly regarded as a more venial sin than speaking against Handel or going to the Lincoln's Inn opera. But so many of the nobility wished to keep the Prince of Wales company that Princess Anne said she expected in a little while to see half the House of Lords playing in the orchestra in their robes and coronets.

Not every member of the aristocracy fell for Prince Frederick's invitations to boycott Handel, however. Lady Betty Germain, who was a daughter of the 2nd Earl of Berkeley, a former lady-in-waiting to Queen Anne and widow of the eccentric Sir George Germain of Drayton House in Northamptonshire (Sir George believed a certain Sir Matthew Germain had written St Matthew's Gospel), was a great friend of Lionel Sackville, created Duke of Dorset in 1720 by George I and appointed by George II Lord Lieutenant of Ireland. She lived in St James's Square but stayed so often with the Duke and Duchess at Knole that the bedroom she always used is still identified as hers. She wrote to the Duke, saying: 'The delight of everybody's heart seems to be set upon the King's sitting by himself at the Hay Market House; . . . and t'other day at Dodington's the Prince was as eager and press'd me as earnestly to go to Lincoln's inn field's Opera as if it had been a thing of great moment to the nation, but by good luck I had company at home.' It was typical of Frederick's generous nature as well as of his somewhat retarded adolescent desire to tease his parents that, while doing all he could to hijack Handel's patrons, he was making financial payments to the composer himself: £250 in 1734 as a contribution to the cost of staging operas at the Haymarket; £52. 10s. towards 'Handel's entertainment' in 1741; and on 29 April 1743 'To George Frederick Handel Esq per warrent oratorios £73 10s'.

The Dowager Duchess of Marlborough recounted for the benefit of the Duchess of Bedford an absurd story relating to the King's behaviour at Covent Garden, some time in 1735. 'I never in my life heard so strange a thing as happened at the opera not long before the King left England,' she wrote. (He was due to visit Hanover.) It appears the King spotted a Member of Parliament in a box wearing a hat, and sent an equerry over to ask the gentleman to remove it. The MP declined, saying he was ill, and could not remove his hat for fear of catching cold. 'Several very curious messages followed, but all in vain.' The King became so exasperated that he sent a guard across to remove the offending headgear, again without success. It was generally trivial matters, as the Princess Royal remarked to Lord Hervey, that drove the King into his worst humours; having his periwig ill-powdered by a page, for instance, or finding a housemaid had placed a chair where it did not normally stand.

Hence one can see how easily an essentially humourless marti-

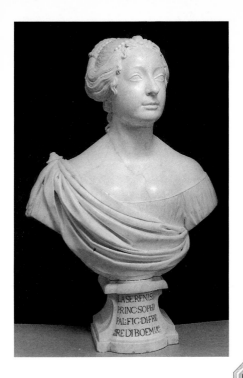

1. Princess Sophia, Electress of Hanover (1630–1714). A charming marble bust of the mother of George I, granddaughter of James I. (By an assistant of Francois Dieussart?, National Portrait Gallery, London)

2. (*above*) George I (1660–1727), father of George II and grandfather of Frederick Louis. Frederick regarded him as his greatest friend. (Detail from a drawing by George Vertue, 1803)

3. (*left*) George II (1683–1760), father of Frederick Louis; his lifetime's ambition was to have Frederick disinherited in favour of 'Butcher' Cumberland. (From the painting by J. Faber)

4. (*left*) Caroline of Brandenburg-Ansbach (1683–1737), wife of George II and mother of Frederick Louis. (After Godfrey Kneller, 1716, National Portrait Gallery, London)

5. (*below*) Frederick Louis, Prince of Wales (1707–51), elder surviving son of George II. (Detail from the portrait by Bartholomew Dandridge, 1732, National Portrait Gallery, London)

6. (*above*) *The Music Party*. From L to R: Anne (Princess Royal); Princess Caroline; Frederick, Prince of Wales; Princess Amelia. (Detail from a painting attr. to Philippe Mercier, 1733, National Portrait Gallery, London)

7. (*below*) Prince Frederick with his brother and all five sisters. Mary and Louise, the two youngest, are on the left; the Princess Royal, seated; Caroline and Amelia are on the right. (Detail from a rare depiction of this family group by William Aikman, the Devonshire Collection, Chatsworth)

9. (*below*) Sir Robert Walpole, England's first prime minister, whose downfall in 1742 Frederick was instrumental in bringing about. (This portrait of Walpole is a detail from a grandiose engraving executed in 1748, three years after his death, by George Vertue)

8. (*above*) William Pitt the Elder, 1st Earl of Chatham. Frederick appointed him a Groom of the Bedchamber in 1733. (Detail from a contemporary engraving)

10. The young George III (1738–1820), with his brother the Duke of York and their tutor, Francis Ayscough. (Richard Wilson, *ca* 1749, National Portrait Gallery, London)

net like George II would be riled by the mischievous machinations of a son who enjoyed nothing more than a good lark; and
one can see how much more easily George would have been thrown
into a fit once he realized that, despite all his attempts to curtail
his activities, Frederick was prepared to take an active part in
politics, and even to side with the rabble when they felt they had
a justifiable grievance. Frederick had spotted an opportunity to
flex his political muscles in 1733, when Walpole decided it was
time to tackle what had almost become a national pastime,
smuggling. Smugglers were regarded as heroes, like highwaymen.
They were said to import at least 3 million pounds of tea a year,
and operating in gangs a hundred strong they ran ashore, in a
variety of guises, wine, brandy, tobacco and lace. Walpole himself
patronized smugglers, but realizing that smuggling was costing
the Exchequer at least £1 million a year he decided to relieve the
Customs officers of their responsibilities (they may have been only
too thankful, as a number of Customs officers had been murdered
by smugglers) and hand over their duties to the more efficient
Excise Department. He wished also to placate Tory landowners,
who were complaining that they had to finance too much national
taxation, by reducing the land tax from 4 shillings in the pound
to 1 shilling. The Excise were now to control the importation of
wine and tobacco – with the right to enter and search shops and
taverns. This plan was pounced on as a heaven-sent opportunity
by Walpole's enemies to turn on him, on the pretence that the
recovery of Excise duty on wine and tobacco would lead to the
loss of every sort of liberty, even to the suspension of Magna
Carta. The King believed that if smuggling could be curtailed,
surely the civil list could be increased, and as always, he equated
opposition to his servant Walpole as outright disloyalty to the
Crown.

It was Dodington who urged the Prince to come out against
Walpole by showing support for the enraged London merchants.
Walpole was in danger of losing control of the House of Commons, and so seriously did the King take Frederick's influence
over Walpole's enemies that he swallowed his pride and told
Frederick that if he called off his friends he might have £80,000 a
year, a wife and his own establishment.

Not for the last time in his life, Frederick declined to be bribed,
kept his nerve and coolly retorted that these provisions were his

by right in any case. 'No Excise! No Excise!' the easily assembled crowds continued to bellow at coaches full of women they thought lived in or near St James's Palace. 'Good people,' the terrified but quick-witted women called back, 'though we live at St James's end of town we are as much against Excise as you.'

Her partiality for taking a dominant role in public affairs well and truly ignited, Caroline received the Earl of Stair, a former ambassador to Paris and now Vice-Admiral of Scotland, and listened with growing impatience to home truths she could scarcely credit. 'In no age, in no country, was any Minister so universally odious as the man you support,' Lord Stair dared to tell the Queen, who said he made her feel faint. When Lord Scarborough told her he would answer for his regiment against the Pretender but not against the enemies of Excise, she began to feel qualms as well. The King hurled defiance in all directions, far too stubborn to imagine himself anything but a beleaguered hero, determined if need be to go down fighting – but he had no seat in Parliament in jeopardy at the next election. On the bill's first reading the Government obtained a majority of sixty-one. By the third reading that majority had fallen to seventeen, and with the country on the verge of riot Walpole admitted defeat. But Frederick and his friends enjoyed only a limited victory; out of malice the King dismissed half a dozen courtiers and deprived two peers of their regiments. And by dint of massive bribes and the confiscation of Opposition literature Walpole went on next year to achieve a resounding majority at the polls. But into Frederick's arms, with hopes of his future patronage, had been driven the Lord Steward, Lord Chesterfield, Lord Stair, the Dukes of Montrose and Bolton, Lord Clinton and Lord Burlington. Interestingly enough, the King escaped popular censure; it was the Queen and Walpole who were burnt in effigy.

Following their marriage, Princess Anne and her husband had been in no hurry to embark for Holland, and when they did, they were immediately becalmed at Greenwich. Hervey reports that the King gave Anne a thousand kisses and a shower of tears, but not one guinea; that the Queen never ceased crying for three days, but that after three weeks 'Her Royal Highness seemed as much forgotten as if she had been buried three years.' Frederick had sent a message to say he had stayed away for fear of upsetting his sister too much, a nice piece of nonsense, and typical of

Frederick's tongue-in-cheek style of humour, which cut no ice with Prince William.

A few weeks later, with marriage still very much on his mind, and presumably hoping the King had forgotten or forgiven his blatant opposition to Walpole over Excise, the Prince of Wales requested a private audience with his father, and was received at Kensington Palace, in the King's closet, at the conclusion of a levee. But the King preferred not to see his son alone, and asked Walpole to be present, which was fortunate for us, for Walpole passed on an account of the audience to Lord Hervey. The Prince first of all asked, without success, to serve against the French on the Rhine. The fact that Frederick had had no military experience was neither here nor there; George would never have taken the risk that Frederick might cover himself in glory and return home a hero. Frederick's other request was for permission to marry, and he thought it prudent to add that he regretted earning His Majesty's displeasure. The King told him 'that his behaviour in general was very childish and silly' (no doubt he had his solitary visits to the opera in mind), and that it was his 'undutiful conduct' towards his mother that offended him most. As for getting married, matches had been proposed and 'it was not his fault these had not taken effect'. It was hardly Frederick's either, and the King was being just as disingenuous as the Queen had been over his allowance; Frederick had been offered, in the first place, a Danish princess, Charlotte, who was deformed and mentally retarded, and had then turned down the daughter of the Duke of Württemberg. She was only thirteen.

Addressing him as Fritz, the Queen next day told Prince Frederick that people were trying to make a fool of him; were using him, in effect, as a tool with which to distress the King. She advised her son to write a submissive letter to the King, and told him she would deliver it herself 'and do everything she could to set matters right'. It had been Caroline, of course, who had advised George II when Prince of Wales to write a submissive letter to *his* father. Well versed in the art, the Queen now set about correcting and rewriting Frederick's letter, which she duly handed over to the King. George merely commented that he would judge the sincerity of Frederick's words by the tenor of his future actions.

How are *we* to judge Frederick's words and actions? In order to do so at all one has to tread with care through a minefield of second- and even third-hand reports. On taking his leave of the Queen in 1730, on one of her rare visits to Windsor Castle, the Prince's governor, M. Neibourg, is supposed to have told the Queen that the Prince had 'the most vicious nature and the most false heart that ever man had, nor are his vices the vices of a gentleman, but the mean base tricks of a knavish footman'. This damning indictment of the then twenty-three-year-old heir to the throne was apparently relayed four years later by the Queen to Sir Robert Walpole, who passed it on to Lord Hervey. Its pedigree is somewhat tainted, surely. Only Walpole could be regarded as remotely dis-interested when it came to running down the Prince, and that is a charitable view; by 1734 he would have been aware that oppo-sition to many of his policies and practices was coalescing round Frederick, who had done so much to help wreck his Excise Bill. The Prince's parents quite simply detested him, and Hervey wanted to keep in with the King and Queen. He was particularly busy at this time ingratiating himself with Caroline by telling her how he used to remind the Prince of the unfortunate consequences of his father's quarrels with his grandfather, and how he was forever urging Frederick to moderate his conduct; and how Frederick seemed to see the force of his arguments. It is difficult to rescue some-one's reputation from the clutches of a contemporary prepared to write, as was Hervey of the Prince: 'What regard indeed could anybody have for a man who like His Royal Highness had no truth in his words, no justice in his inclinations, no integrity in his commerce, no sincerity in his professions, no stability in his attachments, no sense in his conversation, no dignity in his be-haviour, and no judgement in his conduct?' But at the time that Hervey was penning his unredeemed criticisms of the Prince he was, on his own admission, 'in greater favour with the Queen, and consequently with the King, than ever'. He was with the Queen every morning while she had breakfast. She gave him a hunter, and when she followed the chase Hervey rode beside her. 'Lord Hervey,' he wrote of himself, 'made prodigious court to [the Queen], and really loved and admired her.' In addition to the gift of a new horse the Queen raised his salary to £1,000 a year, 'which was,' Hervey could not resist explaining, 'a new sub-ject of complaint to the Prince'.

The Prince had plenty to complain about. His sister the Princess of Orange paid a visit to England, and on her departure she left the Queen and Princess Caroline 'drinking chocolate, drowned in tears, and choked with sighs'. The door opened, and the Queen inquired, 'Is the King here already?' When Lord Hervey told her it was the Prince of Wales about to enter the room, the Queen, 'detesting the exchange of the son for the daughter, burst out anew into tears, and cried out, "Oh! my God, this is too much"'. However, 'She was soon relieved from this irksome company by the arrival of the King, who, finding this unusual and disagreeable guest in the gallery, broke up the breakfast, and took the Queen out to walk.' Hervey continued: 'Whenever the Prince was in a room with the King, it put one in mind of stories one has heard of ghosts that appear to part of the company and are invisible to the rest; and in this manner, wherever the Prince stood, though the King passed him ever so often or ever so near, it always seemed as if the King thought the place the Prince filled a void space.'

Against the advice of his ministers, in 1735 George II insisted on paying another visit to Hanover, where he fixed himself up with a new mistress, Amelia-Sophia von Walmoden, young, attractive and married to Baron von Walmoden. The King sent copious details of the affair to the Queen, and found time also to inspect Princess Augusta, daughter of Frederick, Duke of Saxe-Gotha. Without troubling to consult Prince Frederick, he decided Augusta would do very well for a daughter-in-law, and wrote to the Queen telling her to inform the Prince of Wales that a bride was on the way. He added that Frederick would be well advised to part with Anne Vane. A mistress kept discreetly was one thing; in so open a manner as Frederick flaunted Miss Vane and their child, quite another. But events had overtaken the King, for Frederick was already preparing to dispose of Anne Vane in order, so some people imagined at the time, and have done since, to replace her with a cosy mother-figure. Although not in reality yet middle aged, Lady Archibald Hamilton, whose much older husband was uncle to the Duke of Hamilton, was the mother of ten children. She had never been pretty, according to Lord Hervey, 'and had lost at least as much of that small share of beauty she once possessed as it is usual for women to do at five-and-thirty'.

Although Frederick does not seem to have required any prompting from his father to dismiss Miss Vane (although when he did so he used as an excuse the fact that he was about to be married), and the start of his long friendship with Lady Archibald overlapped with the departure of Miss Vane and the arrival of Princess Augusta, there is little evidence that Lady Archibald was the Prince's mistress. The Queen thought she was, but she was capable of thinking only the worst where Frederick was concerned. Hervey's account of events certainly does not add up to evidence of an affair. He says the Prince was often at the Hamiltons' house, 'where he seemed as welcome to the master as the mistress', and met her also at her sister's. In the morning, it seems, the couple walked for hours tête-à-tête in St James's Park, and whenever Lady Archibald made an appearance at the Drawing Room, 'which was pretty frequently', the Prince's behaviour 'was so remarkable that his nose and her ear were inseparable'.

While perhaps flirting with Lady Archibald, who was to join his wife's household and remain a lifelong friend, Frederick funked facing Anne Vane, and sent a lord of the bedchamber, her son's godfather Lord Baltimore, to the house where Miss Vane now lived in Wimbledon, to explain to her that he was on the point of getting married. He regretted they must part, but if she would be so good as to remove herself to the Continent for two or three years he would continue to pay her allowance of £1,600 a year. If, on the other hand, she declined to leave England, she would not receive another farthing. Professing shock at receiving the Prince's callous message from someone she had regarded as a friend, Miss Vane declined to leave England, and recovered her composure sufficiently to take up again with Lord Hervey. This was to cause Hervey an almighty fright, for one night, while his wife was in France and he was taking the opportunity of sleeping with Miss Vane in his apartments at St James's Palace, she had a fit. Hervey says she had been subject to fits for several years, and it sounds as though she was epileptic, as Hervey certainly was. After a quarter of an hour 'she fell into convulsions ... her convulsions grew stronger and at last she fell into a swoon that lasted so long [Lord Hervey] thought her absolutely dead'. Terrified he would be found with a corpse in his room, Hervey did not dare call for assistance, 'nor even call a servant into the room, for not one was trusted with the secret'. Eventually Miss Vane recovered consciousness, and Hervey smuggled her out and found a sedan-chair for her in Pall Mall.

She was soon sufficiently recovered to get Lord Hervey to draft a letter for her to send to the Prince of Wales, a task he relished, for he wanted to keep Miss Vane in England 'and was not a little pleased to have an opportunity of fretting the Prince'. She began by remonstrating with Frederick for sending 'an ambassador', and went on to complain that while she perfectly understood the Prince's desire to marry, there was no necessity to banish her abroad, and in this assertion she was surely right; it is difficult to imagine what Frederick was thinking of. She went on to claim, in this instance perhaps with some exaggeration, that she had sacrificed her time, her youth, her character, the world, her family 'and everything that a woman can sacrifice to a man she loves'. She said her health made it impossible to be separated from doctors she could trust, and that her child was the only consolation she had left. 'I cannot leave him,' she told the Prince, 'nor shall anything but death ever make me quit the country he is in.'

Lord Hervey made sure Miss Vane copied out the letter in her own hand before she left his apartments, afraid in case a copy in his own handwriting should be discovered, and a *valet de chambre* was entrusted to deliver it to the Prince. According to Hervey, although he does not tell us how he knew, as soon as the Prince received it 'he flew into a violent passion', showed the letter to his household and servants, and swore vengeance on Miss Vane if she did not reveal who had drafted the letter for her. But when the Prince was under far worse stress than this, his habit was always to remain perfectly calm, and while his judgement may sometimes, and rightly, be called into question, there is nothing in his conduct to lend credence to Hervey's gleeful account on this occasion. Hervey goes on to record that when Miss Vane told everyone of Lord Baltimore's visit, the Prince, 'finding everybody condemned the brutality of this rough message, determined to deny he had ever sent it', and even managed to persuade Baltimore to say that he had not been the messenger.

Miss Vane still had a lot to lose, and was advised by friends to write a second, conciliatory, letter to Frederick. The upshot was that the Prince agreed she should retain her house in Grosvenor Street and her allowance for life, that she need not go abroad and that she could keep her son, for whom Frederick had already made generous provision by appointing him, aged two and a half, Lord Warden of the Stanneries and Steward of the Duchy of Cornwall. These arrangements were to last a very short time, however. Leaving the child in the care of relatives, Miss Vane

repaired to Bath to try to recover her health. On 23 February her
son died, according to Hervey 'of convulsion fits'. A month later,
on 27 March, Miss Vane died too. Hervey was told by the Queen,
and by Princess Caroline, that they thought the Prince more afflicted by the loss of his son 'than they had ever seen him on any
occasion, or thought him capable of being'. On 26 February the
boy was buried in Westminster Abbey, at the east end of Henry
VII's Chapel in the Jacobite Duke of Ormonde's vault, under the
name Cornwall Fitz-Frederick Esq.[6]

Relations between Frederick and his father can hardly have been
improved when the King's birthday, on 30 October, was celebrated
by 'a very thin appearance', and the reason given for the poor
apparel of those who did turn out was that they 'kept their fine
clothes for the Prince's wedding'. Drawing Rooms and levees were
a chore to the King at the best of times (he could not bear the
company of men, according to Lord Hervey, which meant in effect
he wanted to be left alone to be flattered and petted by his mistresses), and he thought the least his English courtiers could do,
as he had rushed back from Hanover for his birthday, suffering
from piles and a fever for several days after his return, was show
some respect. One reason they failed to do so was because, having
forgotten his absurd boast on first arriving in England, that he
had not a drop of blood that was not English, the King now
never let an opportunity pass to disparage everything English. English
food, English horses, English jockeys, actors, manners and diversions
were all inferior to those to be enjoyed in Hanover. It was no
wonder Frederick found easy popularity by being pleasant to the
English, and pleasant about them. He was the first member of the
royal family to play cricket. He would drape his arm round
someone's shoulder. He loved party games, meals out of doors,
excursions on the river, bull-baiting, visits to fortune-tellers and
nipping into taverns for a noggin of gin. His popularity was such
that in 1736 Frederick was made a Freeman of the City of London
and admitted to the Worshipful Company of Saddlers. Hervey
goes so far as to assert that George II actually hated the English,
looked upon them as republicans, and grudged them their riches
as well as their liberty. He had 'an abominable temper' and could
be insufferably rude and cruel to his wife. Such a man could only
ever have been an indifferent father, and if he found in his elder
son and heir traits of decency and humanity, this would have

been sure to prejudice and annoy him. Nothing irks an irascible father more than to see an unruffled offspring standing nonchalantly by when he himself is in full spate.

'One very often sees fathers and sons very little alike,' the King observed one evening while chatting with the Queen. 'A wise father has very often a fool for his son. One sees a father a very brave man, and his son a scoundrel; a father very honest and his son a great knave; a father a man of truth and his son a great liar; in short, a father that has all sorts of good qualities and a son that is good for nothing.' The father he had in mind was of course himself; the son, Frederick. Then, with his own father as the paternal model, he rambled on with equally unconscious comic effect, saying that of course sometimes it was just the reverse, 'that very disagreeable fathers had very agreeable men for their sons'. Having attended a performance of *Henry IV* (whether Part I or II Hervey does not tell us), and while dressing the next morning, the King told his gentlemen of the bedchamber he had never seen 'so awkward a fellow and so mean a looking scoundrel in his life' as the actor who played the part of the Prince of Wales, a remark everyone pretended to take literally but realized full well was meant as yet one more jibe against his son.

8

Marriage

Why George II thought there should have been any reason for
Frederick to take a leaf out of his own book remains a mystery.
At the age of fifty-two he discovered he had fathered an illegitimate child by his new German mistress.[1] But the King can have
had no cause for complaint when it came to the Prince's conduct
over the arrangements for his marriage. Five members of the Cabinet
Council called upon the Prince to inform him that if he was agreeable
the King would 'demand' the hand of Princess Augusta, and
Frederick 'made answer with great decency, duty and propriety
that whoever His Majesty thought a proper match for his son
would be agreeable to him'. In view of the King's previous unre-
alistic suggestions, we may assume Frederick had received favourable reports on Augusta. The King's newly appointed Treasurer,
Lord De La Warr, was therefore dispatched in March 1736 to
Saxe-Gotha to inform the Duke that his sister was wanted in
England, and in his most acerbic vein Lord Hervey explains why
'Lord Delaware',[2] as Hervey misspelt his name, was chosen 'to
prevent the Prince's having any jealousy of his future bride's affections being purloined on the way by him who was sent to
attend her to England'. He was, thought Hervey, 'the properest
man His Majesty could have pitched upon; for, except his white
staff and red riband, as Knight of the Bath, I know of nothing
belonging to the long, lank, awkward person of Lord Delaware
that could attract her eyes; nor do I believe there could be found
in any of the Goth or Vandal Courts of Germany a more unpolished
ambassador for such an occasion'. A quarter of a century later
Frederick's son, George III, rewarded De La Warr with an earldom.

The Princess's journey to England was expedited because the
King was in a frenzy to return again to Hanover and to the arms
of Madam von Walmoden. But before the seventeen-year-old Augusta
arrived there was, needless to say, a typical family row. She was

to be assigned four ladies-in-waiting, one of whom, the Prince insisted (and this *may* have been indicative of the fact that she was his mistress), should be Lady Archibald Hamilton. But quite overlooking her appointment of Henrietta Howard, her husband's mistress when he was Prince of Wales, the Queen put her foot down, saying that as everyone had believed Lady Archibald to have been Frederick's mistress, such an appointment would be quite improper. In the end they compromised, the Queen agreeing to leave one appointment vacant in case Princess Augusta herself chose to have Lady Archibald as a member of her household. The Prince also asked that the wife of his groom of the bedchamber, William Townshend, son of Lord Townshend and an Opposition MP who had voted against the Excise Bill, be appointed a lady-in-waiting, and then it was the King's turn to be awkward, saying that Townshend was 'the most impertinent puppy in the Prince's whole family', and he was determined not to reward him for being so. The three ladies eventually appointed prior to the arrival of Augusta were the Countess of Effingham, Lady Torrington and Lady Irwin.

In 1733 Anne Irwin's father had tried to procure for her a position in the Queen's household, receiving a polite rebuff. Writing on 11 July that year from Richmond Lodge (or Richemont, as she preferred to spell it), Caroline assured Lord Carlisle, 'C'est avec grande raison que j'estime votre fille', but she regretted, mixing her English with her misspelt French, there was at present 'pas de vaquance dans ma chamber de lit'.[3] On 15 July Carlisle wrote again to the Queen to assure her he 'did not presume to name any time'. If the offer of his daughter's services were agreeable to the Queen, it was left solely to Her Majesty 'to consider in what manner and at what time it might be done with most ease to yourself and most conveniently to your affairs'. If such time should ever come, he assured the Queen, he would look upon it 'as an additional mark of the Royal favour' to his family. He 'sincerely and truly' wished Her Majesty and the King 'a long and prosperous reign' et cetera, et cetera.[4] Now the importuning had paid off. On 15 April 1736 Lady Irwin was writing to her father with a message from the Queen: 'She bid me to tell your Lordship, instead of your thanking her, the thanks was due on her side to you for sending me to Court. . . . Tomorrow I believe the whole thing will be decided. I'm told we are to kiss the King's hand. I

hear nothing of myself or any other persons going to Holland;
therefore I fancy no lady will be sent.'[5]

But Lady Irwin *had* been chosen to travel to The Hague in
order to accompany the Princess on her Channel crossing. As she
had also been the first to receive the Queen's invitation to become
a lady-in-waiting to Augusta, and had been the first to kiss the
Queen's hand, she asked, 'in a respectful manner', if she was not
to be the senior lady-in-waiting. The Queen told her, 'with great
goodness', that as Lady Effingham was a countess she 'must have
the preference in rank, but that was all; that it would be no
detriment to me in any future expectation either as Groom of the
Stole or Mistress of the Robes, which were always chosen by
inclination or interest, and not by eldership'.[6] It is obvious, however,
that in Anne Irwin Caroline had spotted a lady likely to keep an
eye on her future daughter-in-law and to report back, despite
Lady Irwin's lack of experience at court. 'I'm under a good deal
of apprehension of not behaving right,' Lady Irwin told her father,
adding, 'but the Queen I believe will give me her instructions in
every particular, which by observing strictly will secure me from
erring.'[7] Before sailing, Lady Irwin received specific instructions
from the Queen to impart to the Princess 'the conduct that was
proper she should observe', and above all, the Queen desired her
'in the strongest terms to recommend to the Princess to avoid
jealousy, and to be easy in regard to amours, which she said had
been her conduct, and had consequently procured her the happy
state she had enjoyed for so many years'.[8]

Augusta landed at Greenwich on 25 April 1736. Lady Irwin
had previously told her father that the Princess was to be married
the night she arrived, and that she thought 'after a sea voyage,
neither she nor her attendants will be fit for the ceremonies they
are to undergo'.[9] But Augusta remained at Greenwich for two
nights. She was met by no one but Frederick. Not even one of his
sisters troubled to keep the new addition to the family company.
Augusta knew no one in England, spoke not a word of English
and hardly any French. Advised a year before to have her daughter
learn both languages, her mother had said that that was quite
unnecessary, everyone in England spoke German. With considerable
composure Augusta appeared on the palace balcony. Frederick
dined with her, and he entertained her with a trip in his barge as
far as the Tower of London.

Next day Augusta was whisked in one of the King's coaches to Lambeth, then from Lambeth to Whitehall in a barge, and from Whitehall she was carried through St James's Park in the King's sedan-chair. As the wedding was fixed for the evening of her arrival at St James's Palace, 'the whole Court, and almost indeed the whole town' had paraded in their wedding clothes to see her turn up. One absentee was Lady Irwin's father, who had written to Frederick asking to be excused on the grounds of 'his age and infirmities'. Frederick, who had gone on ahead, received Augusta in the garden at the foot of the steps leading to the King's apartments, and led her indoors, where the King and Queen (the King exhibiting his usual impatience) had been waiting more than an hour in the drawing-room. Augusta made an excellent initial impression with sweeping curtsies to the King and Queen, who both embraced her.

The Princess was 'rather tall', Lord Hervey noted, 'and had health and youth enough in her face, joined to a very modest and good-natured face, to make her countenance not disagreeable; but her person, from being very ill-made, a good deal awry, her arms long, and her motions awkward, had, in spite of all the finery of jewels and brocade, an ordinary air, which no trappings could cover or exalt'. One should read this grudging description of a lonely and no doubt rather shy and flustered young girl, uprooted from a provincial dukedom to live in one of the grandest courts in Europe, while bearing in mind that the last thing Hervey would have wished for Frederick was a wife blessed with every gift of self-possession and beauty. The Earl of Egmont found the Princess had 'a peculiar affability of behaviour and a very great sweetness of countenance mixed with innocence, cheerfulness and sense'. Sarah Marlborough, who might have felt cause for pique at Augusta's good fortune, thought 'she always appeared good-natured and civil to everybody', while Sir Edward Southwell found her conversation 'quite easy and unaffected'. He noticed that the Prince 'likes her extremely'. That George II, even though he had hand-picked Augusta, should have approved of Frederick's wife speaks volumes. According to Lord Waldegrave, a talented diplomat highly esteemed by Walpole, Augusta 'had a most decent and prudent behaviour; and the King, not withstanding his aversion to his son, behaves to her not only with politeness but with the appearance of affection'.

As usual, the King and Queen dined alone. The Duke of

Cumberland, who was to give the Princess away, and his sisters dined with the bridal pair, Frederick insisting that William and the girls should sit on stools. So the princesses remained in an antechamber until chairs had been provided for them. The marriage took place at nine o'clock at night. The Bishop of London officiated, Handel obligingly supplied an anthem, and the Queen translated the vows into German for the benefit of Augusta. As on the occasion of the wedding of the Princess Royal, no expense was spared, and as befitted her new rank as Princess of Wales, Augusta wore a crown 'with one bar' set with diamonds. Her four train-bearers wore diamonds 'not less in value than from twenty to thirty thousand pounds each'. The King was in gold brocade, with diamond buttons and stars, while the Queen wore jewels 'of immense value'. According to the *Gentleman's Magazine*, the courtiers' suits cost between £300 and £500 each, a stupendous sum to spend on clothes at that time, while Sarah Marlborough's grandson Charles, who had inherited the dukedom of Marlborough three years previously, outshone everyone in 'white velvet and gold brocade, upon which was an exceedingly rich *point d'Espagne*'.

At the conclusion of the service Frederick and his bride knelt before the King and Queen in the drawing-room to receive their blessing, and at half-past ten everyone sat down to supper, Frederick and Cumberland on the King's right, Augusta and the English princesses on the Queen's left. Frederick made a bit of a fool of himself by consuming several glasses of jelly, winking over his shoulder at the footmen in the sometimes perhaps rather over-familiar way he had, for jelly was believed to be an aphrodisiac. Then came the ceremony of putting the couple to bed. Augusta was formally undressed by her new sisters-in-law, Frederick by his brother, the King doing him 'the honour to put on his shirt'. When 'the Quality' were admitted to see the bride and bridegroom 'sitting up in bed surrounded by all the Royal Family' they were astonished by the sight of the Prince's nightcap, 'which was some inches higher than any grenadier's cap in the whole army'.

The Queen could not resist sending to her oldest daughter, in Holland, a first-hand account of the wedding, both chatty and catty. Griff, 'the half-caste', is Frederick:

Heaven be praised, everything passed off wonderfully well, my dear Anne. The King behaved like an angel. Your sisters will tell you about Griff's silliness and the sweetness of his wife, who, far from being beautiful, has a wretched figure.... She is as anxious as a good child to please.... I felt excessively sorry for her in the chapel, which was beautifully decorated. I told her to take off her gloves and she wanted to give me them to hold. Though I would have taken them willingly I feared the King and her amiable husband for different reasons so I made her hand them to Lord Effingham. I told her to look at me and I would make a sign when she ought to kneel. She clutched my skirt and said 'For Heaven's sake, please don't leave me', but Griff bawled in her ear, making her repeat the marriage sentences.... After the service, she and her husband knelt to ask the King's and my blessing, which the King bestowed most benignly.... Her undress was so miserable that it made me go quite gray [Caroline's spelling].... The bridegroom arrived in a grenadier's bonnet and knelt before the King. She is the best creature in the world, one puts up with her insipidity because of her goodness. As far as one can judge her husband is perfectly pleased with and likes her.... I could scold the old duchess of Gotha for not having given the poor good child a better education.

As one might imagine in any house where Caroline and Hervey lived, gossip next morning was rife. 'The Queen and Lord Hervey agreed that the bride looked extremely tired with the fatigues of the day, and so well refreshed next morning, that they concluded she had slept very sound.' In other words, that the marriage had not been consummated. Whether or not the marriage was consummated on the first night, Augusta was to bear her husband nine children in fourteen years, and the fact also remains that once he had achieved his ambition to be married, Frederick dispensed with mistresses for the rest of his life. By any standards, and particularly by those of royal marriages at a time when the parties involved were almost always total strangers and were brought together purely for political or dynastic reasons, Frederick and Augusta's marriage was a very happy success. It is inexplicable that in his study of eighteenth-century politics Professor Archibald Foord can have dismissed Frederick's marriage as 'forlorn'.[10]

Speeches of congratulation to the Prince and Princess were delivered in Parliament, not all of them entirely to the satisfaction of the King, who was reliably informed that a young whipper-

snapper by the name of William Pitt had had the audacity to
suggest the marriage was no credit to the King, for he had merely
been compelled to give way to popular sentiment. George promptly
deprived the future Lord Chatham of his regimental commission,
an act which merely ensured that Mr Pitt and his like-minded
friends would gather more closely than ever around their focus of
opposition to Walpole the Prince of Wales, who compensated Pitt
for the loss of his commission with a place in his household.

Until now, although Frederick had claimed the right to appoint
members of his own household and had established bachelor
homes, at Kew and in Pall Mall, he could not be said to have set
up any kind of rival court to his father's. His official residence
remained the apartments allotted to him at St James's Palace, and
he had apartments of course at Hampton Court and Kensington
Palace, where the Prince of Wales Court is named after him. Before
leaving for Hanover, the King sent word to the Prince that wherever
the Queen resided, there would always be accommodation provided for him and his wife. While the King pretended this was
meant as a gesture of civility, no one, least of all Frederick, was
in any doubt that it was a veiled instruction on no account to
think of setting up a hive of dissension in the way that George
and Caroline had done at Leicester House. Not only did the King
plan to retain a sharp eye on his son, he intended to keep him on
a tight financial rein, simply increasing his allowance on his marriage from £24,000 a year to £50,000, not to the £100,000 voted
by Parliament. 'The breach between these two parts of the family
grew wider every day,' Lord Hervey wrote in his memoirs, 'and
this circumstance of the £100,000, as it is one of the principal
causes of their disagreements, and indeed the most material point
in dispute between them, it was not likely the breach would ever
be healed, as the one would never cease to think the withholding
half of this income a wrong done to him, and the other would
never be prevailed upon, right or wrong, to give it.'

Once again the King appointed Caroline regent during his absence in Hanover. Frederick, having first of all appeared ready to
accompany his mother to Richmond, where she intended going
into residence until she heard the King had safely disembarked in
Holland, when she would then proceed to Kensington formally to
assume the Regency, announced that his wife was ill and that he
would have to stay in London. According to Hervey, the illness

was first of all described as measles, then as a rash (which might have been the same thing), and eventually a cold. The Queen 'pretended her ill, and with great civility and maternal kindness went with her two eldest daughters [Amelia and Caroline; Anne was in Holland] to see her'. She found Augusta in bed and her bedroom so dark it was impossible to see what condition she was in, so she returned to Richmond none the wiser. Frederick's next snub was to arrive late for the Council at Kensington, but who could blaim him? By rights he should have been appointed regent. He was now twenty-nine, married, and kept by his father in enforced idleness. Naturally, as Hervey asserts, he 'liked better to stay in town and divert himself there'. He had nothing else to do, and he and Augusta took to an itinerant life, constantly travelling, on rotten roads, between The White House at Kew, St James's Palace and Kensington, living the life of gypsies, as the Queen joked, seldom in the same place two days on end.

With the King abroad, commissions in the army remained unfilled and family bickering continued. First of all Princess Augusta was advised by her former governess, sent for from Saxe-Gotha to keep her company, that she ought to attend the Lutheran Chapel in London, but the Act of Settlement was dusted down, the Prince sent the old governess packing, and prevailed on his wife to receive Communion in the royal chapels. The Queen herself privately entertained unorthodox and somewhat radical Protestant beliefs, but she was assiduous in her external allegiance to the Church of England, having prayers read to her every morning and regularly receiving Holy Communion. 'On Christmas Day,' the *London Gazette* had reported on 27 December 1729, 'the King and Queen, the Prince of Wales, the Princess Royal, the Princesses Amelia and Caroline, with several of the nobility and other persons of distinction, received the sacrament in the Chapel Royal at St James's.' On the Feast of the Epiphany the King and the Prince of Wales traditionally made their offering at the altar of gold, frankincense and myrrh. But the King cared nothing for matters ecclesiastical, holding bishops in as much contempt as he did politicians and writers, and throughout her years as Queen Consort, Caroline, in consultation with the Duke of Newcastle, virtually ran the established Church; no senior appointment was made without her consent. It irked the Queen more than somewhat when at one of the royal chapels, in Kensington Palace,

Frederick and Augusta acquired the habit of arriving after the service had begun. This meant a lot of pushing and shoving in front of Her Majesty, who told Augusta that if she was going to arrive late the least she could do was enter by a side door. Frederick told Augusta to take no notice, and the Queen told Lord Hervey 'she believed nobody was ever treated so impertinently as to be told one should not be mistress in one's own house, nor to be able to order what doors should or should not be opened'.

But these were mere skirmishes ahead of the battle yet to be fought. In the meantime the Queen went out of her way to be friendly to Augusta. Having purchased 'a most beautiful hat, curiously made of feathers in imitation of a fine Brussels lace ... the first of the kind ever made in England', the Queen gave it to Augusta. (Even odder, the King gave Frederick a present of £1,000.) The Queen felt certain Augusta lived under her husband's domination, and did only as Frederick told her. Which would not have been very surprising. There was an age difference of a dozen years between the Prince and Princess of Wales (as there was to be between their successors in title in 1981), and Frederick would have felt it natural to supervise the training of a girl of seventeen who had come from such a sheltered background. Just as naturally, the Queen saw things in a different light. 'Poor creature,' she told Lord Hervey, 'if she were to spit in my face I would only pity her for being under such a fool's direction, and wipe it off.' Such was the Prince's influence with Augusta that at any rate he had no difficulty persuading her that Lady Archibald Hamilton had never been his mistress, and with a vacancy still in her household to fill, Augusta wrote to the King in Hanover to ask permission to take Lady Archibald into her service. She ended up mistress of the robes to the Princess, with a salary of £900 a year.

It had been necessary for Augusta to write to Hanover because the King showed no inclination to return to England. Part of the attraction of Hanover was his new mistress; part was simply the fact that he loved bossing his subservient Hanoverian subjects about and detested the thought of having to reign in England over a people he would have preferred to rule. Eventually he prolonged his absence even beyond his birthday, and although no one in England save the Queen loved him, and not one person liked him, it was generally acknowledged that as he was King he ought to be at home. The Hanoverians had not yet attained general acceptance (they still had a serious Jacobite revolt to face), and the King's continual journeys abroad tended only to increase the unpopularity of a parvenu royal house of which Frederick might find himself the head any day. Discontent reached such limits that eventually a poor broken-down old horse was left to wander through the streets with a message attached to it: 'Let nobody stop me. I am the King's Hanoverian Equipage going to fetch His Majesty and his whore to England.'

At the Royal Exchange a notice was pinned up that read: 'It is reported that his Hanoverian Majesty designs to visit his British dominions for three months in the spring.' But the most serious example of popular sentiment appeared on the gates of St James's Palace itself: 'Lost or strayed out of this house, a man who has left a wife and six children on the parish; whoever will have any tidings of him to the churchwardens of St James's Parish, so as he may be got again, shall receive four shillings and sixpence reward. N.B. This reward will not be increased, nobody judging him to deserve a Crown.'

'The citizens of London cry out that their trade is ruined,' Lord Egmont noted in his diary on 28 October 1736. He added: 'Last week one of them in the presence of a friend of mine damned [the King], saying, if he will have a whore, why don't he take an English one and stay at home; there are enough of them to be had cheaper.'

Angered by the employment of cheap Irish labour, weavers in Spitalfields had caused such havoc that the militia were called out and lives were lost. A bomb exploded in Westminster Hall, causing a stampede of judges and barristers. In November the Queen was hissed at the opera. And it was not only the citizens of London who were up in arms during the summer of 1736; in the West Country there were riots against the export of corn. But the most serious disturbance Caroline had to deal with while her husband cavorted in Hanover occurred in Edinburgh, where the execution of a well-known and popular smuggler named Wilson had caused a riot. The mob began to stone the hangman, the commander of the town guard, John Porteous, ordered his men to open fire, and several people were killed. Captain Porteous was then himself tried and condemned to death. Presented with a petition for clemency, Caroline exercised the royal prerogative, but no sooner was it known that Porteous was to be reprieved than the mob took the law into their own hands, broke into the Tolbooth prison where he was being held, released the other prisoners and dragged Porteous out to the Grass Market, where they hanged him from a barber's pole.

As if the Queen had not enough to contend with, in 1736 Walpole decided to try to curb the prodigious consumption of gin, estimated, in London, at two pints a week for every man, woman and child. Gin had become plentiful, cheap and of a lethal quality, and accounted for the almost permanently inebriated condition of thousands of the poor. 'Drunk for a penny, dead drunk for tuppence' was the catch-phrase. Gin was on sale in brothels, prisons, workhouses, factories and barbers' shops. As with the attempt by Walpole to put a curb on smuggling, his efforts to regulate the sale of gin were premature. Indeed, his Gin Act of 1736 was virtually ignored. According to the *Daily Gazetteer*, 29 September, the day the Act was passed, was marked by several people making themselves 'very merry with the death of "Madam Gin", and some of both sexes got soundly drunk at her funeral, of which the mob made a formal procession with torches'. The cry of 'No Excise!' now gave way to 'No Gin, No King!' whenever the Queen ventured forth in her carriage, and all the new act did was to stir up discontent. The debilitating effects of gin on the hungry and homeless who resorted to it for solace continued unabated, with the drunk lying where they fell, in the City slums of St Giles and the precincts of Westminster Abbey. Informers flourished and hawkers took to the streets, offering bottles of Cuckold's Comfort or Colic and Gripe Water. A drop or two of some pink liquid might be added, together with a label that read: 'Take two or three spoonfuls of this four or five times a day, or as often as the fit takes you.'

Frederick seized his chance to show solidarity with the masses, and of course his chance to disconcert Walpole: gin suddenly became his favourite tipple, and he made quite sure he was seen knocking it back in a tavern. By 1743 it was estimated that gin was being sold at one in every eight of the private houses in London, and after seven futile years Walpole's Gin Act was deemed a failure and repealed. When, in the year of Frederick's death, a more serious attempt was made to bring the excessive distribution and consumption of gin under control by means of the 1751 Licensing Act, Londoners finally rose in revolt. By then they had little to lose but their lives, the Bow Street magistrate, Henry Fielding, sternly pronouncing that 'should the drinking of this poison be continued in its present height during the next twenty years there will be by that time few of the common people left to drink it'.

It was now left to the King himself to bring Caroline to the point of distraction. He delayed his departure from Hanover until 7 December, and without even troubling to visit his daughter, the Princess of Orange, who was about to miscarry and very nearly die, he arrived at Helvoetsluys in Holland four days later. By this time of year it could be expected that the weather in the Channel might at least be choppy. In fact, a stupendous storm blew up. Communications between St James's Palace and the Admiralty might as well not have existed at all, for no one had any news of the fate of the King and the royal yacht, and bets were freely laid as to whether or not George was dead. On 17 December, being obliged to hire fifty-four candlesticks and twenty-six dozen knives, forks and spoons at a cost of 5 guineas, Frederick, perhaps unwisely, gave a dinner party at Carlton House for the Lord Mayor of London in gratitude for having been given the Freedom of the City. When told how popular her son had become, the Queen, by now quite frantic with worry, and overlooking her own desire for popularity when she had been Princess of Wales, exclaimed, 'My God, popularity always makes me sick, but Fritz's popularity makes me vomit. I hear that yesterday, on his side of the house, they talked of the King's being cast away with the same *sangfroid* as you would talk of a coach being overturned, and that my good son strutted about as if he had been already king.'

It was not the dinner that had assured popularity for the Prince; it was the popularity he had already earned for which he had been rewarded with the Freedom of the City. In his memoirs, Lord Hervey makes great play of Frederick's supposed glee at the prospect of his father's death, but such conduct would have been contrary to all we know of his character. The worst one can say about the Carlton House dinner was that its timing was tactless.

Walpole was in as big a stew as the Queen, fearing for his own fate if the King really was drowned and Frederick were to ascend the throne. But that we can be expected to believe Lord Hervey's transcriptions of Walpole's remarks to him at this time concerning the character of the Prince is doubtful. They were surely embellished by Hervey for the benefit of posterity. 'What will be the

Prince's case?' Walpole is supposed to have mused to Hervey on
the way to dinner. 'A poor, weak, irresolute, false, lying, dis-
honest, contemptible wretch, that nobody loves, that nobody believes, that nobody will trust, and that will trust everybody by
turns, and that everybody by turns will impose upon, betray, mislead
and plunder. And what then will become of this divided family,
and this divided country, is too melancholy a prospect for one to
admit conjecture to paint it.' These are Hervey's sentiments, not
Walpole's, and they contain just one damning indictment too many
with which to hammer home their repetitious point. One wonders Hervey did not hear Sir Robert Walpole accuse Frederick of
cheating at cards and sleeping with his page, for good measure.

We know what one member of the family was planning to
do, at any rate. Princess Caroline was threatening, the moment
her brother did become king, 'to run out of the house *au grand
galop*'. Surprisingly, Hervey thought the Prince would be likely to
seek the Queen's advice on assuming his duties as sovereign, but
Princess Caroline contradicted him. 'You must know very little of
him if you believe that,' she said, 'for in the first place he hates
Mama, in the next, he has so good an opinion of himself that he
thinks he wants no advice, and of all advice, no woman's.'

The first positive information the Queen received, and it was
hardly the sort to cheer her up, was when Frederick appeared in
her apartments with a letter saying that guns had been heard at
sea as a distress signal, and that part of the fleet escorting the
King's yacht had been dispersed. That night, however, a letter
arrived from the King himself. It transpired that he had never
stirred out of harbour. The wind having died down, it was assumed the King really had set sail at last, but then came news
that a second storm had begun to rage. For ten days there was
no further news of any sort, until the Queen learnt that the royal
yacht had been seen in the midst of the hurricane to tack about –
but whether she had sunk or returned safely to The Hague, no
one had any idea. The general consensus seemed to be that as so
many ships were being found wrecked along the coast the King
of England was almost certainly dead, and Caroline now gave
way to despair. But she pulled herself together sufficiently to attend the Chapel Royal when Sunday came round (it happened to
be what we call Boxing Day), not knowing if she were the Dowager Queen or still Queen Consort, and in answer to her prayers a

second letter from the King was handed to her in her pew. He had indeed set sail, and like the intrepid hero he believed himself to be he had ordered the Admiral of the Squadron, Sir Charles Wager, to sail into the teeth of the gale. Admiral Wager, who knew more about the sea and ships than the King, and in 1739 was appointed First Lord of the Admiralty, decided to disregard the monarch's orders, returned to port and in all probability saved both his and George II's life.

Caroline wasted no time in writing to tell her husband how eager their son had been to wear the crown, and how confoundedly popular he seemed to be, his popularity having soared only to new and dizzy heights when, on learning a great fire had broken out at the Temple (on the night of 4 January 1737),[11] Frederick had dashed out to help extinguish it. 'Crown him! Crown him!' people are supposed to have shouted when subsequently he appeared at the theatre. Hervey's account of the fire (he says the Prince 'pretended to have received two great blows on his head whilst he was assisting the firemen to convey the water') is one of the most sarcastic even he ever penned, and leads to one of the most damning accusations against her son allegedly made by the Queen: '"For you know," said she, "he is the greatest coward in the world."'

A rather different version of this event has come down to us in a letter sent by Lady Irwin to her father:

> There was a dreadful fire last week at the Temple, which has destroyed a vast number of chambers, with manuscripts and writings to a great value. The Prince stayed from 12 at night till 6 in the morning, directing the soldiers and encouraging the firemen to work both by his presence and money, and 'tis said he did a great service. He need not this to make him popular, for the King being obliged to delay his journey, the wind still against him, makes the unreasonable populace so extravagantly angry that 'tis not to be imagined the outrageous things that is every day spoke against the King, and on the other hand how exceedingly the Prince is caressed by all ranks.[12]

But any chance of England's acquiring her first King Frederick were dashed for the time being when on 15 January 1737 George II, looking extremely pleased with himself, arrived safe and sound at St James's Palace. Frederick made haste to accompany his mother as she and the princesses went into the courtyard to receive him, having first of all taken the precaution of professing to Sir Robert Walpole his admiration and esteem. He said he had 'always looked upon him as one of the ablest men in England'. It would be interesting to speculate what appointments, had the King perished at sea, Frederick would have made. Would Bolingbroke have been recalled, with his twin-track records of liberality and Jacobite sympathies? And Lord Chesterfield, that most civilized and able of eighteenth-century politicians? The Earl of Stair, who told Lord Chesterfield in 1739 that he loved the Prince 'for many valuable qualities, especially for his good head; which I think does not dispose him to be overfond of money or power', had told the Queen he had been overlooked by Walpole for appointments he richly deserved. As things turned out, Walpole's prosperous career had only a few more years to run in any case, and it is not inconceivable that Frederick would have retained his services, for despite the outward appearance of over-indulgence and inactivity, Walpole had sagacity and a shrewd pragmatism always valuable in a politician, and a knowledge of public affairs that none could rival. In January 1737 Frederick, in any case, did not possess a soundly established following of his own; by the end of the year things were to be very different indeed.

There is no doubt the King had had a narrow escape, and seemed happy to have found himself still alive. On the journey to London from Lowestoft, where he had been obliged to land, he had had time to reflect on his former conduct, not least towards his wife and elder son. After alighting from his coach he kissed Prince Frederick. 'Everybody,' Lord Hervey reports, 'was astonished at all this unexpected sunshine, but the warmest of all his rays were directed towards the Queen.'

Perhaps the paternal greeting had lulled Frederick into a false sense of optimism or security. In a playful but not very tactful manner he had already drawn attention to his annoyance at having half his parliamentary allowance withheld by the King by writing (or having written for him, versions of the event differ) a fairy-tale called *l'Histoire du Prince Titi*. Frederick was of course the patriotic and misused gallant young Prince Titi. Unfortunately the King and Queen were also clearly identifiable – as his avaricious father, le Roi Guinguet (King Guinea), 'haughty, fierce, partial in his affections', and as his mother, la Reine Tripasse (Queen

Tripe), who managed her husband and hated her son. While Frederick's friends relished the allegory, it was not one of the most brilliant satires of a satirical age and must be counted an obvious cause of his parents' mounting ill-will. It was the sort of prank a naughty schoolboy might be expected to attempt, but not the heir to the throne, whose parents took filial obligations and respect for the monarchy very seriously indeed. But the truth is, Frederick had never as a boy experienced parental control or discipline, and the only people to blame for his retarded development were his parents themselves.

Now he decided to take more positive action, of a very dangerous kind, in order to secure his full civil list grant of £100,000 a year. He would petition Parliament itself. From every point of view, his timing could not have been more unfortunate. The King's eventual safe return had heralded the worst year that Frederick (and in many ways the King himself) was ever to endure. It began with the King taking to his bed, having caught a severe chill while crossing the Channel. And piles, to which he was a martyr, were again causing him agony. But indifferent to the sufferings of others, in particular those of his wife, George II at least had the merit of being an unselfpitying patient, and when one of his lords-in-waiting had the temerity to inquire how he was, the King had him removed from that week's rosta. When the news was broken by Hervey to the Queen that Frederick's Opposition friends were planning to raise the matter of the civil list in Parliament, his and the Queen's first reaction was that quite obviously, bearing in mind the King's present ill-health, Frederick was planning to cause him a seizure.

However, the King took the news quite calmly. This was probably because he was so contemptuous of democracy that he did not fear the consequences of a constitutional crisis should Parliament demand payment of the £50,000 the King continued to withhold, and the King refuse to hand it over; he would simply dissolve Parliament. Afraid that Frederick's support was increasing because people mistakenly believed that the King, having taken to his bed, must be at death's door, George rose to hold his regular levees and was, says Lord Hervey, much more gracious to everybody than he used to be. Nevertheless a majority of anything between ten and forty in Parliament was being predicted for the Prince, and Walpole fully expected to fall if the Prince carried the day.

From the moment he was created Prince of Wales, Frederick had been cheated by his father. Now that he was married, his demands were more just than ever. But neither the Queen nor Princess Caroline 'made much ceremony of wishing a hundred times a day that the Prince might drop down dead of apoplexy', the Queen, so Hervey informs us, 'cursing the hour of his birth, and the Princess Caroline declaring she grudged him every hour he continued to breathe'. Princess Caroline even rebuked Hervey for his weakness in ever having loved the 'nauseous beast'. On the eve of the momentous debate Walpole decided something had to be done, and proposed that the King should offer the Princess of Wales a 'jointure', the sum in question remaining unspecified, and that the £50,000 a year the Prince of Wales was already receiving should be paid automatically, not at the King's pleasure. Ten members of the Cabinet Council – the Lord Chancellor, the Lord President, the Lord Steward, the Lord Chamberlain, three dukes, a couple of earls and a baron – called upon Prince Frederick to inform him of this almost entirely meaningless gesture. Keeping cool, as he always did in a crisis, and assuring his father, through the Council, 'that he had, and should retain, the utmost duty for his royal person', Frederick sent reply that the affair was now out of his hands.

Hervey says the King and Queen were 'both extremely enraged at this reception of the message'. The King turned on Walpole for dreaming it up, and all the Queen could think to do was bicker over whether the Prince had ever previously asked for his allowance as of right. The King said he had not, Frederick said he had, and the Queen went around demanding to know if there were any witnesses. By the following morning Frederick had sunk in her estimation to the 'lowest stinking coward in the world'. She was convinced he was capable of shooting or stabbing her. Hervey was in no doubt the quarrel was farcical, but it seems his supposed influence with the Queen was not as great as he had imagined it to be, for no matter how bluntly he spoke to her she was by now beyond all hope of seeing reason. Even while the Queen and Hervey were chewing over the business in her dressing-room, Frederick was spotted crossing the courtyard. 'Look, there he goes,' exclaimed the Queen. 'That wretch! That villain! I wish the ground would open this moment and sink the monster to the lowest hole in hell.'

So spoke the mother who had abandoned her seven-year-old son, and who was herself, although she did not know it, on the brink of death. Even Lord Hervey seems to have been shocked by this vehement outburst. 'You stare at me,' said the Queen. 'But I can assure you if my wishes and prayers had any effect, and that the maledictions of a mother signified anything, his days would not be very happy nor very many.'

The Prince and his friends had mistakenly counted on Tory Members of Parliament pouncing on any opportunity to vote against the Government. The motion for Frederick's £100,000 was seen as a specifically Hanoverian issue, many Tories still harboured serious Jacobite sympathies, and some forty-five Tories whom the Prince had hoped to muster absented themselves. Thus the debate ended with victory for Walpole and the King, by a majority of thirty in the Commons and by three to one in the House of Lords. The King was particularly pleased, as the outcome had cost him only £900 in bribes. Hervey says the King and Queen were both for turning Frederick out of St James's but that Walpole dissuaded them. They accepted his advice, but made sure they never spoke to their son on any public occasion.

With Hervey as Vice-Chamberlain, Frederick had never stood a chance of establishing even a working relationship with his family, but it was in any case an age when there was no remote conception of training for the monarchy, and it is surprising that kings and queens did not turn out worse than they did. Aware of the Queen's well-educated background, Hervey now decided to amuse his mistress by constructing an essay, *Character of Frederick, Prince of Wales*, comparing the Prince's conduct with that of the Emperor Nero. Many an enjoyable hour was passed with Hervey reading from his manuscript while the Queen and Princess Caroline rocked with laughter. One quotation from this minor masterpiece of invective should be sufficient to suggest its flavour: 'He was lewd without vigour, would laugh without being pleased, and weep without being grieved, for which reason his mistresses were never fond of him, his companions never pleased with him, and those he seemed to commiserate never relieved by him.' It is at least to Hervey's credit that never in his memoirs does he make the least attempt to disguise his prejudiced dislike of the Prince nor the intense pleasure he took in doing him harm.

Once Parliament had risen, the court moved to Richmond, where the King, his infant son by Baroness Walmoden having died, and his ardour for the child's mother having temporarily abated, was easily persuaded not to attempt another trip to Hanover. Instead, he was kept in good humour by a new English mistress, Lady Deloraine – 'that pretty idiot', as Hervey had described her to Stephen Fox in 1731. She was the thirty-five-year-old widow of Lord Deloraine and now governess to the two youngest princesses. She also happened to be married to George Wyndham, sub-governor to the Duke of Cumberland, but she was so vain she continued to use her former title. At court she was universally known as Fly. Walpole thought her 'a lying bitch', and Hervey told him that was no matter, the only person's ear she had was the King's.

9

Expelled from Court

It has always been regarded as the first duty of an heir to the throne to produce an heir of his or her own, and in Frederick's time, if possible several heirs, for infant mortality, even among royal families, was high, and childbirth exceedingly dangerous. Apparently Frederick was forever dropping hints that his wife was pregnant, and frequently told his coachman to take extra care when the Princess was travelling – ironic instructions in view of his own later conduct. But the Queen convinced herself the Princess was not pregnant for the good reason that the marriage had not been consummated, and it had not been consummated because Frederick was impotent. She got round the problem of Anne Vane's son by declaring the father was Lord Hervey. But Hervey assured the Queen that 'little Fitzfrederick', as the Queen referred to her grandson, had indeed been the Prince's child, and that whereas Miss Vane had told him the Prince was 'ignorant to a degree inconceivable' he was certainly not impotent.

The Prince seems to have fretted unnecessarily in the early days of his marriage, imagining his wife would automatically conceive within weeks if not days, while the Queen busied herself trying to get other women with whom she believed the Prince had slept to confide whether he was 'like other men or not'. She and Hervey became so crazed over the subject they even discussed the possibility of Hervey's somehow slipping into the Princess's bed pretending to be Frederick, but the Queen soon went off this idea, saying, 'If I thought you would get a little Hervey by the Princess of Saxe-Gotha to disinherit my dear William, I could not bear it.' Until Frederick produced children, his brother William remained his heir presumptive, and what really worried the Queen was that Frederick might try to plant a warming-pan baby upon the nation if it turned out he was incapable of fathering a child himself. Hence her prurient interest in his sexual activities. The fact that to sleep with the Princess of Wales would have constituted an act of treason must perhaps remove Hervey's and the Queen's musing to the realms of irresponsible fantasy. Frederick's over-anxiety about his wife's condition the Queen attributed to his fear that if she did not produce children people would scorn him. She even expressed her belief that to soothe his vanity Frederick was capable of paying someone to father an impostor by the Princess, a slander to which Princess Caroline eagerly concurred.

But despite the Queen's wild surmises, she and the King were formally notified that Augusta was expecting a child. It was the King's desire that the baby should be born at Hampton Court, so that as many people as possible could be present to see fair play. The Queen told Lord Hervey: 'At her labour I positively will be, let her lie-in where she will; for she cannot be brought to bed as quick as one 'can blow one's nose and I will be sure it is her child. For my part, I do not see she is big; you all say you see it, and therefore I suppose it is so, and that I am blind.'

On 31 July 1737, at Hampton Court, the Prince and Princess of Wales dined in public with the King and Queen. That evening, after she had retired to her own apartments, the Princess suddenly went into labour. At that point the Prince's conduct can only be described as lunatic, and excusable, if at all, by a childish desire to exert independence. He grabbed hold of his wife, and with the aid of an equerry and his dancing master bundled her into a coach, notwithstanding the protests of Lady Archibald Hamilton and the Prince's groom of the bedchamber, William Townshend. Two of the Princess's dressers got in with her. On the top of the coach perched the Prince's *valet de chambre*, who claimed also to be a surgeon and a midwife. At the Prince's urgent command this mad cavalcade (a second coach full of servants and luggage followed) made a headlong dash to London.

By the time the Princess arrived at St James's Palace she was bleeding profusely. No one was expecting her arrival, there were not even any sheets available, and Augusta found herself in a bed made up with table linen. Within forty-five minutes of her arrival at St James's she was, according to Hervey's arresting account of this appalling incident, 'delivered of a little rat of a girl, about the bigness of a good large toothpick case'. At least the Lord President of the Council and the Lord Privy Seal had been found in time to attend, the Lord President being summoned by the Prince from his house in Chiswick. The Lord Chancellor, whom the Prince also tried to contact, was discovered to be in the country, and the Archbishop of Canterbury arrived fifteen minutes too late. Meanwhile, at Hampton Court, totally oblivious that an heir presumptive to the throne had been born, the King continued playing commerce, the Queen quadrille and Lord Hervey cribbage. At eleven o'clock they all went to bed, and were woken at half-past one in the morning by a courier from London. At first the Queen thought the palace must be on fire. Told that the Princess of Wales was in labour she cried out, 'My God, my nightgown! I'll go to her this moment.' She still had no idea that the Princess had been spirited away. It sunk in only when her lady-in-waiting said, 'Your nightgown, Madam, and your coaches too.'

The King's first reaction, as so often when things went wrong, was to turn on the Queen, and to blame her for the nation being about to have a 'false child' foisted on it. Once dressed, the Queen rounded up the two oldest princesses, the Duke of Grafton, Lord Essex, a lord of the bedchamber, a couple of ladies-in-waiting and Lord Hervey, and at half-past two they all went clattering across the cobblestones at Hampton Court in anticipation of catching up with the errant Prince and Princess of Wales before some foundling could be secreted into the Princess's bed. One and a half hours later they were at St James's. Hervey offered to provide hot chocolate for the Queen in his own rooms, whereupon Caroline gave him a wink and said, 'You need not fear my tasting anything in this side of the house.' Upstairs she was greeted by the Prince, in his nightgown, who kissed her hand and her cheek and informed her she was a grandmother. She merely expressed surprise that news of the birth had not been relayed to Hampton Court, but her fears about a pretended birth had been alleviated by news of a girl rather than a boy.

The Queen behaved well in the Princess's bedroom, saying to Augusta, in French as recorded by Hervey, 'Apparemment, Madame, vous avez horriblement souffert.'

Remaining loyal to Frederick, Augusta replied, 'Point du tout, ce n'est rien.'

When Lady Archibald Hamilton produced the baby, the Queen kissed her granddaughter and said, 'Le bon Dieu vous benisse, pauvre petite créature! Vous voilà arrivée dans un désagréable monde.'

Knowing Lady Archibald to be the mother of ten children, the Queen asked her how she could have allowed the Prince and Princess to be so mad, not knowing of course that Lady Archibald had tried to prevent the departure from Hampton Court. Lady Archibald just turned to the Prince and exclaimed, 'You see, Sir!'

His second child by Anne Vane having died within twenty-four hours, Frederick himself was no stranger to the dangers of child-birth, and the Queen was quite right when she told the Prince it was a miracle that the Princess and the child had not both been killed. The circumstances of her birth did not, however, affect the little rat of a girl, who was baptized Augusta in honour of her mother, later married the hereditary prince of Brunswick-Wolfenbüttel, and lived to the age of seventy-six, becoming, in 1768, mother of that unfortunate Princess Caroline who was to make such a disastrous marriage to her cousin, Frederick's grand-son George IV. As for the Princess of Wales, her constitution also seems to have remained unimpaired; within three months she was pregnant again.

To be as fair as one can to Frederick over the affair, when re-porting to Lord Stair 'an extraordinary quarrel at Court' Sarah Marlborough asserted that both the King and Queen knew of long-standing arrangements for Augusta to give birth at St James's, 'where everything was prepared', and that when she went into labour Augusta earnestly begged the Prince to take her to London.

Nine days after the birth of baby Augusta the Queen and the Princesses again drove to London to see the mother and daugh-ter, and if Hervey's account is to be believed, neither Frederick nor the Queen exchanged one word. Frederick disgraced himself by not going to the coach to receive the Queen, but apparently made a great show of seeing her off, kneeling in the street to kiss her hand, but then failed to escort his sisters to their carriage, and did not bother to send a message thanking the Queen for her visit. When all this was recounted by the Queen to the King, Hervey swears blind that George told his wife 'she was well enough served by thrusting her nose where it had been shit upon already'. 'This extraordinary expression of His Majesty's,' Hervey wrote, '(though none of the cleanest) I could not help relating just in the words the Queen reported it to me.'

The christening of Frederick's first child took place on 29 August (this may have been another reason why she was named Augusta),

the King and Queen, oddly enough, agreeing to stand as godparents, albeit by proxy. The Princess's mother was also a sponsor.
Although the prerogative rested entirely with the King, Frederick
announced that the child was to be known as Lady Augusta,
not Princess Augusta, yet she was to be styled Royal Highness.[1]
What lay behind this confused way of thinking it is impossible
to say; what lay behind the Queen's plan to have her son expelled from court but to allow the baby to remain with its mother
was a fear that if anything happened to the child people would
accuse the King and Queen of having murdered it so that their
favourite, the Duke of Cumberland, might yet succeed. The Queen
also had a soft spot for Augusta. Members of the Cabinet Council
argued among themselves about the wisdom of having Frederick
and his family sent packing, but his parents were now determined to disgrace him. At breakfast one morning the Queen
remarked, 'I hope in God I shall never see the monster's face
again', and had the effrontery to add that at one time she would
have given up all her children for him, so fond of him had she
once been, adding (which was rather closer to the truth), 'Now
I wish he had never been born.' Her venom was kept on the boil
by the King, who chimed in with the opinion that Frederick was
'the greatest villain that ever was born'. There were, he explained,
degrees in all things. Bad subjects were very provoking. Bad servants were still more provoking. 'And bad children are the most
provoking of all.'

On 10 September Frederick, his wife and infant were ordered
out of St James's Palace, and out of every other official royal
residence. When informed of this decision, Frederick is said to
have 'changed colour several times', but his behaviour, so Hervey
was informed by the Earl of Pembroke, groom of the stole to the
King and one of three peers deputed to deliver the King's instructions, 'had been very civil, and very decent'. The King had demanded to know whether Frederick had kept the three of them
waiting, and was assured by Lord Pembroke he had not, but
Pembroke told Hervey privately that even if the Prince had done
so they had 'all agreed to lie and say he had not'. The King's
household were distinctly uneasy at their master's conduct, and
the King in turn was scathing about Frederick's 'family'. Lord
Carnarvon he described as 'a hot-headed, passionate, half-witted
coxcomb', William Townshend as a 'silent, proud, surly, wrong-

headed booby', Lord North as a very weak man and Lord Baltimore as a little mad.

Just as George I had done when he threw *his* son and daughter-in-law out of St James's Palace, George II now withdrew the Prince's guards and warned every peer, peeress and Privy Councillor that if they paid court to the Prince they would not be received by the King. Ambassadors were likewise informed that the King would be obliged if they did not call on the Prince of Wales. Never had history so clearly repeated itself. The King even gave instructions that Frederick was not to remove any furniture, and the Duke of Grafton was instructed to make sure he did not. Even Hervey protested that Frederick and Augusta should at least be allowed the use of chests 'as their clothes could not be carried away like dirty linen in a basket'. The King asked, 'Why not? A basket is good enough for them.'

But the Prince and Princess were not exactly homeless. On 12 September a curious and sympathetic crowd watched them depart for The White House at Kew, one of the sentries at St James's Palace, we are told, shedding a tear because he had been forbidden to present arms. However pale Frederick may have turned on being told of his expulsion (and he may have been fearing worse punishment than he received – separation from his daughter, for instance), it is hard to believe that once he and Augusta had considered their position they were unhappy at the prospect of a dramatic exit, enhanced popularity and the chance of unrestricted domestic life. Earlier that summer Lady Irwin had been in waiting at The White House for a fortnight, reporting afterwards to her father: 'The Prince lives there quite in private, without form; passes his time wholly with his [household], whom he treats in so obliging a manner and with such an easy familiarity as makes the attendance very agreeable.'[2]

Back at Kew six weeks after the Prince and Princess had left St James's, Lady Irwin was again writing to Lord Carlisle, to say they would be celebrating the King's birthday 'with fiddles, bonfires, etc.' and that life was extremely agreeable, 'the Prince and Princess wholly conversing with their [household], and so of course we are admitted to share all their diversions, viz: music, play, walking, and whatever amusements can be thought of in the country in a large family of men and women'.[3]

Not content with Carlton House as a London residence, Frederick approached the Duke of Bedford to see if he might rent South-ampton House. When the Duke demurred, Frederick next made overtures to the Duke of Norfolk, to see if Norfolk House in St James's Square might be available. The Duchess of Norfolk took the precaution of seeking an audience with the Queen at Hampton Court to discover if the King and Queen had any objection, and when informed they had not, Norfolk House became one of Frederick's London homes for the next four years, and it was at Norfolk House, on 24 May the following year, that the future George III was born. The Prince paid £1,200 a year in rent, and spent some £2,500 on repairs before he moved in.

There could not have been a greater contrast between the family's reception of Hanover's new princess and the City of London's. The Lord Mayor had the honour to inform the Prince of Wales that he and his aldermen were anxious to express their congratulations, so on 22 September 1737 Frederick received a deputation at Carlton House. It was too good an opportunity for Frederick and his friends to waste, now that in any case the Prince was regarded by his parents as a pariah, not to distribute, as one might at a modern press conference, copies of the King's message expelling Frederick from court. Lord Carteret, who like so many eighteenth-century politicians changed allegiance with bewildering frequency, and in 1743 was to attend the King at Dettingen, declared: 'You see, Gentlemen, how the Prince is threatened if he does not dismiss us. But we are here still, for all that. He is a rock. You may depend upon him, Gentlemen, he is sincere, he is firm.' The Queen retaliated by publishing her own correspondence with the Prince, originally in French but hastily translated by Lord Hervey, and then Frederick threw a final spanner into the royal works by resurrecting a far more damaging exchange of letters between his father and grandfather.

The trouble with The White House, now that Frederick was no longer on speaking terms with his family, was its close proximity to both the Dutch House and Richmond Lodge, but that problem was settled when Frederick alighted on Cliveden (at that time spelt Clifden or sometimes Clieveden, but then, as now, pronounced 'Cliffden'), a seventeenth-century mansion in Buckinghamshire with superb views from 200 feet above the Thames. It had been built in 1666 for George Villiers, 2nd Duke of Buckingham, the son of James I's murdered favourite, but apart from the surviving

south-facing terrace it bore no resemblance to the nineteenth-century
mock Georgian house that stands on the site today and achieved
fame as a centre for social and political intrigue when its owners
were Lord and Lady Astor. Cliveden has twice been burnt down,
and in Frederick's day the house was constructed of red brick.
(Today the extensive grounds are owned by the National Trust,
and the house is run as a luxurious hotel.) Frederick had already
paid at least one visit to the place, and in 1737 he decided to
rent it for £600 a year from the daughter of a previous owner,
the Earl of Orkney, Marlborough's second in command at Blenheim
and England's first field marshal.

George I had dined at 'Clieveden', in great splendour, on 5
September 1724, and on 30 July 1729 Lady Orkney had entertained Queen Caroline, the Prince of Wales, the Duke of Cumberland
and Princess Anne to dinner and supper. 'How they were diverted
I know not,' Peter Wentworth wrote to his brother, 'but I believe
very well, for they did not come home until almost four in the
morning.'[4] Eight years later Frederick found waiting for him grounds
already planted with shrubs 'scarcely to be met with, at that period,
in any other grounds of the same extent', and it was in the garden at Clieveden, during Frederick's tenancy, that in 1740 *Rule
Britannia* was written. As with every new enthusiasm, Frederick
threw himself whole-heartedly into Clieveden – the house and the
gardens. 'The Prince not to be diverted from Clieveden, though
very inconvenient,' one of his political activists, Lord Marchmont,
noted almost straight away.

Clieveden remained Frederick's chief country residence (eventually he took a lease on two other places in addition to Kew and
Clieveden) for the rest of his life. Marlborough's widow noted in
1738 'a good deal of expense at Cliefden in building and furniture' at a time when, again according to the Dowager Duchess,
Frederick and his wife were spending £12,000 a year on clothes
and £25,000 on wages. By this time Frederick had debts of about
£30,000, yet a mere bagatelle compared with the debts of £100,000
run up by his father when he was Prince of Wales.

One of those newly enlisted on the pay-roll was George Lyttleton,
for the past two years MP for Okehampton and a former equerry to the Prince, whom Frederick now appointed as his private secretary. It very much seems to have been a case of out of
court, into opposition, and by November 1737 Lord Chester-

field was writing to Lyttleton to say 'nothing will more hasten [Walpole's] retreat if he is inclined to retire, or his ruin if he is inclined to resist, than the part which the Prince ought and therefore I am sure will act. The Prince at the head of the Opposition and forcing it to act with vigour has everything in his hands'. Lyttleton, two years younger than the Prince, had made his maiden speech during the debate congratulating Frederick upon his marriage. He was given one of Frederick's Cornish seats in 1741, and remained as private secretary until Frederick dismissed him in 1744 when he accepted a government post as a Lord of the Treasury. Four years after Frederick's death Lyttleton struggled as a less than competent Chancellor of the Exchequer, and was got rid of in 1756 by being sent to the House of Lords.

What with The White House at Kew, Carlton House and now Norfolk House and Cliveden to run, Frederick was seriously short of money, and his solution, according to Lord Hervey, was to sack his 'inferior' servants, a move that 'made him many enemies among the lower sort of people, and did not save him much money'. He also 'put off all his horses that were not absolutely necessary'. Frederick was fond of horses. In 1732 he had Lord Malpas, heir to the 2nd Earl of Cholmondeley and his Master of the Horse, searching Scotland for suitable bloodstock. This prompted Lord Carlisle to send the Prince a young gelding and a mare as a present. Carlisle's son, Charles Howard, displayed the horses in Hyde Park and told his father the Prince 'liked them very well'. He liked them so well, in fact, that he gave the servants who had taken care of the animals 20 guineas. But it was late summer before the Prince got round to writing a personal letter of thanks to Carlisle:

My Lord,
   'Tis not out of want of regard to you that I did not thank you sooner for the two fine horses you sent me. I stayed till Cll. Howard's duty would permit him to carry my letter, and shall depend upon him to give you further assurances how agreeable your present is to me. My stables want'd only the Carlisle breed to make them perfect, and I look upon this mark of your affection and regard to me with a great deal a [sic] pleasure.
                Your affectionate, Frederick P.[5]

One reason Lord Malpas had been instructed to search out

horses for the Prince was because in 1732 new royal stables were being built on the north side of what today is Trafalgar Square, and the Palladian construction clearly called for the finest horses money could buy. But Frederick thoroughly disapproved of the style of architecture chosen for this particular project. In September 1732 he and the Queen went to view the site, 'and as soon as he saw the pillars,' Sarah Marlborough reported to her granddaughter Diana, 'he said, "What the devil are these? The beauty of a stable is to see a great many horses, but in this you can only see two or three as you go up between the pillars." I was surprised at his Royal Highness saying what appeared to me so very rational! The Queen sat in the coach and did not go in, so I can't tell you what representation he made to his Mamma, but one that stood by in the stable told me he looked very angry.'

Not even having had Frederick removed from under her roof could modify the almost insane hatred Queen Caroline had come to feel for Frederick since the days when she would accompany him to view some work in progress. 'My dear first-born,' she told Lord Hervey, 'is the greatest ass, and the greatest liar, and the greatest *canaille* [i.e. scum], and the greatest beast in the whole world, and I most heartily wish he was out of it.' But it was Caroline herself, 'still amiable yet over-bearing, good humoured yet tyrannous',[6] whose days were numbered. Terrified of getting into the King's bad books, she had long ago learnt to dissemble where her own indifferent health was concerned. On 10 December 1734 Peter Wentworth had written to his brother:

The Queen has been so ill. I went every day to the backstairs and had the general answer that she was better, but I knew when they told me true and when not, and was often in great pain for my good Queen, but it is not the fashion to show any at Court. The first day that she came out into her drawing-room she told a lady, whom I stood behind, that she had really been very bad and dangerously ill, but it was her own fault, for she had a fever a fortnight before she came from Kensington, but she kept it a secret, for she resolved to appear on the King's birthday. She owned she did wrong, and said she would do so no more, upon which I made her a bow, as much as to say, I hoped she would do as she then said. I believe she understood me for she smiled upon me.[7]

The Queen's most closely guarded secret, known only to the King and a lady-in-waiting, dated back to the birth of Princess Louisa, in 1724, when she suffered a rupture. During the summer of 1737 she had been unwell, and on 9 November, while supervising her new library close by St James's Palace, she was suddenly taken alarmingly ill. The symptoms were acute stomach-ache and vomiting; the remedies applied, needless to say, were bleeding and purging. Eventually her old rupture was disclosed, and while the Queen endured the agony of having her stomach opened and her intestines pushed about by seven unsterilized and incompetent quacks, Princess Caroline, already herself racked with rheumatism, proceeded to suffer from profuse nosebleeds, very probably brought on by nervous tension. The King, meanwhile, found time to fuss about having new ruffles sewn on his shirt.

Lord Hervey's contribution to the prolonged and macabre sufferings of the Queen was to provide her with 'snake-root with Sir Walter Raleigh's cordial'. Letters were sent to The Hague telling Princess Anne to keep away, and when Frederick came up to Carlton House to be as near the Queen as possible in case she would consent to see him, vast quantities of emotional energy were expended by the rest of the family in keeping him away as well. They were convinced he had come only to gloat over his mother's deathbed, and to await impatiently news of her demise.

When an exceedingly anxious Robert Walpole came waddling out of the Queen's bedroom he said to Hervey, 'My Lord, she is as much dead as if she was in her coffin. If ever I heard a corpse speak, it was just now in that room.' Never having taken care of his wife's health, always forcing her to attend the opera, a ball or a Drawing Room when she was unwell, even the King now became thoroughly alarmed, and began to realize the Queen was undoubtedly dying. She returned to him a ruby ring he had given her at their coronation, and expressed concern that her country property, Richmond Lodge, might pass to Frederick, who by this time had received written instructions not to visit his mother. The Queen commended the two youngest princesses to Caroline.

As for you William [the Queen told the Duke of Cumberland], you know I have always loved you tenderly, and placed my chief hope in you. Show your gratitude to me in your behaviour to the King. Be a support to your father, and double your attention to make up for the disappointment and vexation he must receive from your profligate and worthless brother. It is in you only I hope for keeping up the credit of our family when your father shall be no more. Attempt nothing ever against your brother, and endeavour to mortify him in no way but by showing superior merit.

Much debate ensued as to whether the Archbishop of Canterbury, Dr John Potter, should be summoned. As Bishop of Oxford he had preached the coronation sermon on the accession of George II, and he had been translated to Canterbury on the advice of the Queen only nine months previously. The Queen had expressed no desire for spiritual comfort, and many thought this bad form, so the Archbishop arrived to pray for her. Then it was noticed she had not received Communion, and rumours spread that the Archbishop had denied her the sacrament unless she consented to be reconciled to Frederick. But this is most unlikely. Potter, although the son of a draper (the 103rd Archbishop of Canterbury, George Carey, is far from being the first working-class holder of that office), was a sound scholar, and although of a High Church persuasion he would have been most unlikely to have tried to coerce a free spirit like Caroline. But never had the court been so prone to gossip, and at one time the room adjoining the Queen's became so thronged with courtiers that they had to be told to clear out. Having paraded his mistresses in front of Caroline all his life, disregarded her health, derided her intellectual pursuits and snapped her head off whenever he felt like it, the King now spent hours at a stretch extolling her virtues: no man had ever had a better wife, no family a more loving mother, no nation a more devoted queen. As soon as he entered her bedroom, however, he reverted to his normal peevish ways. 'How the devil should you sleep, when you will never lie still a moment?' he demanded of the woman who had undergone surgery without an anaesthetic.

When not rehearsing the merits of his wife, the King bored everyone to death by rehearsing his own. One evening, alone with Princess Amelia and Lord Hervey, the King was ranting on about his bravery in the storm the previous year, and noticed that the Princess's eyes were closed. 'Poor good child,' he said, imagining the Princess to have fallen asleep, 'her duty, affection and attendance on her mother have quite exhausted her spirits.' As soon as his back was turned, 'Princess Emily started up and said: "Is he gone? Jesus, how tiresome he is!"' But these domestic harpings, in part brought on by the strain of waiting for the Queen to die, were to last only two more days. About ten o'clock on the evening of 20 November 'the Queen began to rattle in the throat'. The King and Princess Amelia were asleep in the Queen's room and were woken up by the Queen's dresser. Princess Caroline and Lord Hervey were sent for, the Queen asked for prayers, but hardly had Princess Amelia begun to pray, and before Caroline and Hervey were able to reach the room, the Queen was dead. She was fifty-five.

For several nights afterwards the King had a page keep him company when he went to bed. Otherwise he behaved much as before, bragging and boasting and relating to Lord Hervey and his daughters every minute detail of his military and amorous conquests, while Walpole and the other ministers plotted as to who was to receive the ear of the King as his mistress, Lady Deloraine or Baroness von Walmoden. Walpole was in favour of the German lady, who was sent for the following spring and installed by Lord Hervey in lodgings at St James's Palace. She proved to be discreet, but soon got the hang of selling peerages. One of her satisfied customers was the grandson of a footman; another the son of a Barbados pedlar.

The main prop and purpose of his life – the Queen – having been removed, Hervey now fell into a paranoid depression, and on 1 December he wrote to Walpole to say it was obvious he was considered fit only to carry candles and to set chairs. He wanted advancement, and if none was forthcoming he was prepared to quit public life. Walpole hastened to assure Hervey he thought the world of him and persuaded him to remain at his post, promoting him to the Cabinet as Lord Privy Seal in 1740.[8] In closing his memoirs, Hervey tells us that Walpole's enemies were anxious for Hervey to make trouble with the King and bring about his downfall, but Hervey was to remain a reluctant Walpole supporter for another five years. He went into opposition on Walpole's resignation in 1742, and died on 8 August the following year, an embittered and prematurely aged invalid of forty-six. His last inexcusable act of spite was to cut his loyal and long-suffering wife out of his will.

Having been denied any opportunity of a last-minute reconciliation with a mother whose love had always been denied him but for whose maternal affection he must always have craved, Frederick was now excluded from her funeral. Even the King felt unable to attend, and the chief mourner was Princess Amelia. For a month the Queen's body lay in its coffin in her bedroom. The walls were hung with purple and black, tapers burned around the bier, and gentlemen pensioners with their axes reversed stood guard at the door. On the evening of 16 December the Archbishop of Canterbury conducted a service in the room, attended by the King, the Duke of Cumberland and the four princesses, and by torchlight the body was conveyed to the Prince's Chamber in the Palace of Westminster, where it lay in state until the following evening, when a funeral procession of some splendour made its way to the Henry VII Chapel in Westminster Abbey. The choir of the Chapels Royal sang yet another specially composed anthem by Handel, and the Queen was laid to rest in a sarcophagus in the vault, there to await her husband's arrival by her side twenty-three years later. On her deathbed she had implored him to marry again, but this he declined to do, and life at court became duller than ever. The saddest part of Caroline's relatively early death was that she never knew about George's and Cumberland's heroic deeds at Dettingen, in which she would have revelled.

With the birth at Norfolk House on 24 May 1738 of her second child, the Princess of Wales again provided a fright. The baby was a boy, hence heir apparent to the throne after his father, but he was born two months prematurely and no one expected him to live.[9] So he was baptized that evening, and given the names George William Frederick. But he survived, thanks apparently to his wet-nurse, Mary Smith, to whose 'great attention', George III wrote on her death in 1773, 'my having been reared is greatly owing'. When he came to the throne he rewarded her by appointing her his laundress, a position later filled by her daughter. Obviously as tough as his sister Augusta, George overcame his unpromising start to live until the age of eighty-one, and succeeding to the throne at the age of twenty-two he was to reign for fifty-nine years, beating the previous record holder, Henry III, by three years, an achievement so far exceeded only by his granddaughter Queen Victoria, who occupied the throne for sixty-three years. But unfortunately, from unstable genes somewhere in his Guelph ancestory, Prince George was to develop the most pronounced symptoms of porphyria ever to torture a member of his family, ending his days as a white-haired wraith in the north wing of Windsor Castle while his oldest son had to act as regent.

But for all his unfortunate failings, and particularly his political ineptitude, George III was to possess an acute intellectual curiosity and love of art, dismantling and reassembling complicated clocks, producing architectural drawings faultless in execution, enlarging the Royal Collection of Old Master drawings by purchasing two important Italian collections, including no fewer than forty-six etchings by Canaletto, eagerly quizzing Fanny Burney on the trials and tribulations of being an author, and with great humility stealing up on Samuel Johnson in the library at Windsor for the pleasure of complimenting him on his own work and discussing, among much else, Lord Lyttleton's *History of the Life of Henry the Second* and the universities of Oxford and Cambridge. For the inspiration for many of George III's civilized and endearing qualities it is reasonable to take into account the childhood influence of his father, who organized amateur theatricals for his children and their friends, and encouraged their education.

Only a year passed after the birth of Prince George before a second son, Edward, later created Duke of York and Albany, appeared on the scene. He was to live only to the age of twenty-eight. Being so close in age, naturally George and Edward were educated together, and it was George Lyttleton's brother-in-law, the Reverend Francis Ayscough, whom Frederick and Augusta chose as the boys' first tutor. But Mr Ayscough does not seem to have ensured that when separated from their parents the young princes were always dutiful letter-writers. 'I think you might have spared a quarter of an hour of your employments to please me in hearing of you,' a plaintive Prince Frederick once had occasion to write to George and Edward. 'Therefore for the future let one of you two always do it. Your sister has not forgot you, but has writ to you both. See how much more attentions she has than either of you, and those attentions (I have often told you) please and keep up mutual friendships.' Frederick, who went out of his way all his life to please people, chided George for 'not caring enough to please', a fault the future king never entirely remedied.

It is a sad and mysterious fact that although Frederick would not have raised a hand to his children, George III did not hesitate to have his own sons thrashed by tutors, and proved in every way to be a hopelessly incompetent father. Indeed, Frederick never failed to express his love for his children, nor to encourage them to treat him as a friend as well as a father. To Edward he wrote on one occasion: 'I rejoice to find you have been so good, both, pray God it may continue. Nothing gives a father, who loves his children as much as I do, so much satisfaction as to hear they improve or are likely to make a figure in the world.' George was admonished never to forget his duty but always to be a blessing to his family and country; this was the prayer of his 'friend and father', a father who had adopted a comparatively civilized if unorthodox method of curing George of infantile bed-wetting. While escorting her daughter Princess Caroline on her journey to England in 1795 to marry the future George IV, Augusta of Brunswick-Wolfenbüttel, Caroline's mother and George's sister, told Lord Malmesbury (according to Malmesbury's diary) how she had disliked sharing a bed as a child with George because he wet it, explaining in somewhat ambiguous terms that Frederick 'cured him of his fault by making him wear the blue ribbon [of the Order of the Garter] with a piece of china attached to it which was *not* the George'.

Against his better judgement, George II was persuaded by his ministers, who feared criticism from the Opposition, to invest Prince George with the Garter when the boy was eleven. The ceremony was performed in private, on 22 June 1749, and Frederick does not appear to have been invited. But he, or the boy's tutor, was careful to dictate a very proper letter of thanks: 'Sir, I hope you will forgive me the liberty I take to thank Your Majesty for the honour you did me yesterday. It is my utmost wish and shall always be my study to deserve your paternal goodness and protection. I am with the greatest respect and submission, Sir, Your Majesty's most humble and most dutyfull subject, grandson and servant, George.'

Why, when Frederick was already tenant of a substantial country property, Cliveden, he should have decided, probably in 1738, to purchase Park Place, near Henley, and hence, like Cliveden, again by the Thames, is a mystery. The estate belonged to the Hamiltons, with whom Frederick and Augusta were as close as ever; in 1738 Lady Archibald Hamilton was appointed governor to the newly born Prince George, and Lord Archibald had become Surveyor-General to the Prince's Duchy of Cornwall. They had owned Park Place since 1719 and had built a second house, into which they now moved. John Wootton painted Park Place somewhere around 1742, depicting one of Frederick's barges being hauled upstream, and Frederick himself wearing the Garter and surrounded by grooms and huntsmen. The estate was particularly beautiful, with wooded hills, and Frederick retained Park Place until his death, when Augusta sold it to a cousin of one of Frederick's detractors, Horace Walpole.

There can be no doubt what attracted Frederick to the idea of paying £300 a year in rent for a decade to his lord of the bed-chamber, Lord North, for yet another country house, Durdens at Epsom. When Henry VIII's magical palace of Nonsuch, near Ewell in Surrey, was demolished, some of the building materials were carried off, in 1682, by the Earl of Berkeley to be incorporated in Durdens. An intrepid traveller, Celia Fiennes, who made a journey from Land's End to Newcastle, alighted on Durdens in 1711, and left an account which describes the house very much as Frederick would have found it when he took possession in 1737:

You enterd a noble lofty hall, plaine but neate painted white; on the right is a little parlour the lesser hall hung with armes, a butlers office with bedchambers and closets, thence goes the kitchen, schullery, bakeing-room, laundry into a court of all the offices and the stable yard; out of the little parlour goes into a pretty Chappel which has a balcony closet looking into it for the Lord and Lady.

The left hand of the hall led into a great parlour which runnes to the end of the house and makes the front, and short again into another great parlour or dineing-roome which makes the end front of the house; this also opens into the staircase, it leads on to a drawing-roome closet bed chamber two dressing roomes, which with the great staircase makes up the front backward and the other end front, which lookes into the stable yard and a garden railed in with a large pond or cannall.

The house had extensive gardens and a park, but alas can no longer be viewed. The Durdens Frederick knew was demolished shortly after he relinquished the lease in 1747, and the present house, once the home of Lord Rosebery, dates from 1764.[10]

In addition to Durdens, Lord North[11] owned Wroxton Abbey

near Banbury. And in 1739 Frederick and Augusta honoured the
Norths with a visit, stopping off at Blenheim Palace on the way.
Lady North was thrown into the sort of confusion that attends
most recipients of royal visits, being torn between intense pride
and a terror that things might go wrong. 'Their Royal Highnesses
have notified to us their design of coming to us at the Race,' she
wrote to her mother, 'so we are busy preparing for this great
honour and trouble.' She might have added, great expense. The
Prince and Princess with all their entourage had invited themselves
for four nights, which meant that Lady North had to get in an
extra cook from London, 'for there must be two dinners and two
suppers every day, because she must not dine with gentlemen. It
is odd to turn the master of the house to the second table, but
such is royal ceremony, but they reckon they shall give no manner
of trouble'.

Provisions seem to have been a headache. 'We have four bucks
already sent us,' Lady North informed her mother, 'and expect
more, but fruit we are sadly distressed about; there is none in this
country, one pineapple Lady Baltimore has sent us from Epsom.'
In all, Lady North 'settled fourteen bills of fare', arranging 'that
chicken broth shall always be supplied at the Royal table'. Perhaps
aware that catering for royalty presented difficulties, Frederick
obligingly arrived with a gift of '12 partridges and some pheasants',
and having, on his arrival at Banbury, been presented by the Mayor
with an enormous cake, he no doubt also handed this over to his
hostess. Frederick and Augusta had been up since five o'clock on
the day of their arrival at Wroxton Abbey, and having been delayed
poking around Blenheim they did not arrive until late evening,
and asked for supper straight away. The Princess, so Lady North
reported, did not look 'a bit tired or haggered' but the journey
had nearly done for her two ladies-in-waiting, both a good deal
older than she, who retired to bed at once, being 'almost dead'.

In the event the visit to Banbury was a great success, the Prince
and Princess insisting on having the Norths' children with them
all the time, and insisting too on the children's nanny attending
both the races and a ball. 'They was most excessively obliging
and seemed pleased with everything,' Lady North was able to tell
her mother when the visit was over. She thought Augusta had
'the easiest, sweetest manner and temper I ever saw, and no sort
of ceremony or pride'. Having supplied her guests with a 'cold

loaf' and wine for their homeward journey, Lady North was gratified to discover the Prince had distributed money to the poor of
Banbury and Astrop (a village just south-east of Banbury), as well
as Wroxton, and had left 60 guineas as tips for her servants.

But were the cold loaf (some sort of meat loaf presumably) and
the wine intended to sustain the Prince and Princess on a return
journey to Cliveden? It is inconceivable that Frederick and Augusta
did not honour other friends by staying with them. They were
unusually sociable and gregarious for royalty at that time, and
curious to inspect new and imposing houses. Just such a one was
Easton Neston, a convenient distance away from Banbury, at
Towcester. Easton Neston was the only country house entirely
designed and built by Wren's pupil Nicholas Hawksmoor. By 1739
it had been standing thirty-seven years. Its proud owners were
the Earl and Countess of Pomfret. In 1727 Lord Pomfret had
been appointed Master of the Horse to Queen Caroline; Lady
Pomfret had been a lady-in-waiting to the Queen. Frederick would
have known them well. Did he also know that for the past four
years twin portraits of himself and his brother, by Amigoni, had
hung in the house? It has been said that these portraits were
commissioned by the 1st Duke of Dorset, which might make sense;
his son, Lord Middlesex, was at one time Master of the Horse to
Frederick. But why should they have passed from the Sackville
family to the Fermors? There is no record among the Duke's
accounts, bills or abstracts of bills for payments to Amigoni.[12]
Although Easton Neston is bereft of archives, the most likely explanation for the existence of these portraits of Frederick and
Cumberland in the house is that they were commissioned by the
Queen (in 1735), were a gift from the Queen to Lady Pomfret,
and have always hung there. There is alas no hard evidence that
Frederick ever paid a visit to Easton Neston, but the chances that
he did – and probably on leaving Banbury – must remain high.

Whether Frederick would have ventured as far north as York
remains more problematical, but not far off from the city stood
Vanbrugh's Castle Howard, begun in 1700 (and not finished until
after Frederick's death), now the home of Lady Irwin's brother.
The 5th Earl of Carlisle made a tantalizing note on paper water-
marked 1812 about the Gold Bedchamber at Castle Howard, referring to 'a state Bed of red figured velvet, made to receive Geo.
P. of Wales, the Kings Father the whole richly covered with broad

gold lace'. The King in 1812 was of course George III, and it seems quite obvious the Earl absent-mindedly alluded to 'George' when he meant 'Frederick'. But a number of country houses contain beds prepared for royalty who never turned up (Knole, home of the Sackvilles, has a bed prepared for James I, but he never slept there), and there is no conclusive proof that Frederick ever visited Castle Howard, although his grandson George IV undoubtedly did so, as Prince of Wales, in August 1789.

No doubt having received favourable reports from Princess Amelia following her visit to Bath in 1728, a decade later, in the autumn of 1738, Frederick and Augusta decided to sample the spa waters and to view the newly emerging town for themselves.[13] (When Amelia was there it had barely been more than a village.) They were received by the Master of Ceremonies, Beau Nash, at one time a penniless adventurer, who had been drawn to Bath in 1708 because of his addiction to gambling. Bath had been a health resort since Queen Anne paid a much-needed visit in 1703, in search of a cure for her dropsy, but Nash had found the place ill-run, rowdy, dirty and expensive. It was he who took the town in hand and established its reputation for elegance. Frederick presented him with a gold snuff-box, and Nash in return erected an obelisk in Queen's Square, 'In memory of honours conferr'd and in gratitude for benefits bestow'd in this city by His Royal Highness Frederick Prince of Wales and his Royal Consort.' When Nash died in 1761, aged eighty-seven and once again penniless, he was buried in Bath Abbey. One of the honours that had been bestowed on the city was a silver-gilt cup, costing £104. 9s. 6d., 'richly embellished with arms of his Royal Highness on one side and the arms of the City on the other, and his Highness's crest on the cover, all finely ornamented and interspersed with the fruit of the vine and its leaves: the handle composed of two snakes, whose tails are beautifully interwoven and twisted amidst the grapes and leaves . . . the whole of an entire new taste and much admired'.

A distinct benefit for some was conferred when Frederick gave instructions that all the town's debtors should be released from prison. Britain was still far from universally happy with the Hanoverian succession, and this was one reason Frederick never missed an opportunity to pull off an act that would make not only himself more popular but the monarchy too. He had the common touch in any case, and saw no reason not to put it to good use. 'The amiable Frederick, Prince of Wales' was seen by a contemporary observer visiting Bartholomew Fair by torchlight. We are told, too, 'he walked the streets unattended to the great delight of the people ... would enter the cottages of the poor, listen with patience to their thrice told tales and partake with relish of their humble fare'. It was because there was no competition, from his father, his brother or his sisters, all of whom were permanently buttoned up and bedecked by the trappings of protocol, that Frederick so easily acquired his reputation for largess and liberality. And never once, from the day he arrived in England, did he ever consider returning to Hanover, a realm to which he was as much the heir as he was to the kingdom of Great Britain.

Frederick let it be known that when he succeeded to the throne he would be perfectly happy for the Duke of Cumberland to become Elector of Hanover. It had always been his grandfather's desire for Hanover in some way to be separated from England, and the prospect of such a move remained an attractive one to those who regarded Hanover as nothing but a drain on England's resources of men and money.[14]

It is indicative of the uncertain place the House of Hanover held in the fickle affections of the nation that when Queen Caroline was warned by Lord Hervey that the Prince might be going to suggest to Parliament that he renounce his rights to Hanover in exchange for the £50,000 a year still being withheld from his portion of the civil list, she had scoffed at the idea on the grounds that she believed Frederick would prefer to retain Hanover as a possible safe haven in the event of the Stuarts being invited to return.

10

The Patriot Prince

In 1738 the semi-exiled Jacobite sympathizer Lord Bolingbroke was back in England to pay a short visit to Alexander Pope, and Frederick again went out of his way to meet him. Bolingbroke, like Pulteney, had been a contributor to the Opposition newspaper *The Craftsman*, and it was now that he put on paper the most famous formulation of those liberal political ideals he had long carried in his head. The result, *The Idea of a Patriot King*, remained in manuscript until, about five years later, Pope, to whom the manuscript had been entrusted, published an unauthorized edition. When Bolingbroke revised the work and had it officially published in 1749 it carried a dedication to Frederick, who by that time saw himself as a patriot prince. Lord Chesterfield, who had himself not only written for *The Craftsman* but for two other Opposition publications, *Fog's Weekly Journal* and *Common Sense*, declared that until he read *The Idea of a Patriot King* he did not know 'the extent and power of the English language'. The Introduction comprises an essay on the Spirit of Patriotism, addressed to George Lyttleton; and there is an appendix on 'The State of Parties at the Accession of George I'. Bolingbroke believed – and so did Frederick – that the heir to the throne should participate in a 'legal course of opposition to the excesses of regal or ministerial power'. All true patriots were to be employed by the Crown; away with narrow factions; the royal family was to be established on a 'broader and more solid foundation'. Until the dawning of this happy day, opposition by the Prince of Wales would at least 'blast many a wicked project, keep virtue in countenance, and vice, to some degree at least, in awe'.

Bolingbroke's desire was to have the heir apparent trained for the duties of sovereign by suffering in the cause of the people. 'He would be formed in that school out of which the greatest and best of monarchs have come, the school of affliction.' And on inheriting the throne he would be thoroughly versed in the 'ways of thinking and acting to so glorious a purpose as the re-establishment of a free constitution'. Frederick was left in no doubt that upon succeeding his father his duty would be to 'purge his Court' and eliminate the party element in his choice of ministers, admitting only high-minded patriots to his administration. So high-minded would the King then appear to be that no troublesome Opposition would in future be able to prevail against his will. But *The Idea of a Patriot King* was also intended as a rallying-cry to the present Opposition, whose clear duty was to overthrow the existing 'establishment' so as to form a new (high-minded) 'establishment', an establishment whose rule would be so beneficent that opposition would never be called for again. What Bolingbroke's manifesto was really proposing was the creation of a benevolent dictatorship; he had no concept of the role of an Opposition as a corrective parliamentary device in a democracy. He scarcely comprehended the concept of a constitutional monarchy, towards which, albeit unwillingly, George II had been inching throughout his reign; after he came to the throne he never attended the Cabinet, and already he had learnt the futility of appointing as his first minister a man who could not command the support of the House of Commons.

Bolingbroke's Utopia was not an entirely original concept; it was very similar to Lord Oxford's in the reign of Queen Anne. He too had advocated the abolition of parties, the sole criteria for office being altruistic 'patriotism', the desire to serve the commonwealth for the benefit of all. But George II remained an ardent Whig all his life, and it was not until the death of Queen Victoria that an English monarch deemed it advisable to keep quiet about his political allegiance. Edward VII strongly disapproved of democracy *per se*; George V and George VI were both Conservatives, but behaved with perfect constitutional propriety towards their Labour ministers; it is reasonable to assume that in private life Queen Elizabeth II would vote Tory, the present Prince of Wales probably Liberal Democrat. Whether, had he succeeded to the throne, Frederick would have hastened the day of the officially neutral monarch we shall never know, but there was not much inducement while he remained Prince of Wales for him to show equal favour to all, however attractive he may have found Bolingbroke's ideas in principle. He always needed supporters whose good offices he could secure by promises of patronage upon his eventual succession, and it remained in the interests of Opposition politicians to cultivate Frederick as a focus for discontent. Had he adopted a totally non-partisan approach in 1760 (the year of his father's death), he might have found he had no loyal servants at his command at all. But he undoubtedly found the general concept of Bolingbroke's *Idea of a Patriot King* congenial.

By the closing weeks of 1739 events were occurring which would lead within three years to the downfall of Bolingbroke's and Frederick's sworn enemy, Robert Walpole. A war with Spain, with its roots in the Caribbean slave-trade, had been brewing for some time, and for once Prince Frederick and his father found themselves united – in a desire for war. The country had become bored with a quarter of a century of peace – one of Walpole's great achievements – and both the King and the Opposition found themselves in tune with public sentiment. Only the King's ministers, well aware that taxation would have to be raised if a war was fought, counselled conciliation. But as every schoolboy knows, in 1738, in order to hurry things along, the Opposition produced a sea captain by the name of Robert Jenkins, who claimed that his ear, which he produced for inspection on every conceivable occasion, had been cut off by a Spanish coastguard eight years before. There were those who said the unwholesome exhibit was not an ear at all; others that even if it was the captain's ear, he had lost it in a tavern brawl, not in the patriotic pursuit of merchandise. But the seizure of foreign ships by the Spanish on the pretext of searching for smuggled goods was the issue at stake. 'The right of search,' Frederick's secretary pronounced, 'is the root of all our grievances', and when the first British squadron sailed off 'to annoy and distress the Spaniards', Frederick himself publicly drank a toast at Temple Bar to the success of the enterprise.

Walpole had been pressured into a war – the War of Jenkins's Ear – which he always believed the nation would live to regret. But all was jingoism and jubilation when in November 1739 Admiral Edward Vernon, with only half a dozen ships at his disposal, captured a major Spanish base, Porto Bello. The British navy had always been, and was to remain, well manned, well disciplined and well equipped, with ships commanded by professional officers whose seagoing apprenticeship often began when they were incredibly young. (Nelson's flagship *Victory* numbered among its crew six boys of thirteen, four who were twelve, and a lad of ten.) But in peacetime no one approved of a standing army, which in any case was led by gentlemen entitled to purchase a regiment while still in nappies. Hence no military back-up had been supplied for Vernon, and when an expeditionary force of ten thousand men was eventually recruited, and dispatched in 1741 to reinforce Vernon's victory by capturing Cartagena, it was too late to capitalize on the naval success. Yellow fever decimated the military forces, and they were withdrawn the following year. Admiral Vernon, who seems to have done quite well out of the war, spending £291. 13s. 5d. on silverware while on leave in February 1743, told the King that soldiers had never been necessary anyway, and could never preserve him; the security of his realm depended solely on the navy. The King disagreed, and history has proved him right. The slow-witted Duke of Newcastle never comprehended the importance of co-ordination between sea and land forces. 'This war is yours,' Walpole told the Duke. 'You have the conduct of it. I wish you joy of it.'

Before he learnt how badly things had gone in the Caribbean, George II spent six months in Hanover. By the time he returned in the autumn of 1740 the country was about to become embroiled in a second conflict, this time on land: the War of the Austrian Succession. The Holy Roman Emperor, Charles VI, had no legitimate son and had persuaded Britain, Hanover, France, Spain and Prussia to guarantee that on his death his formidable daughter, Maria Theresa, would peacefully inherit his lands. Charles died in October 1740, just as George's nephew, Frederick the Great, inherited his wealth and beloved army. Frederick promptly invaded Silesia, and then suggested that Maria Theresa should cede the property to him in return for his protection. She declined this impertinent offer, and Spain and France valiantly rushed to her aid, hopeful of acquiring new territory in the process. Saxony and Bavaria, however, declared their support for Frederick of Prussia. The scene was set for the dismemberment of the Empire.

Greatly to the distress of Walpole, Maria Theresa reminded him of Britain's treaty obligations, and asked for help. The King knew how ambitious his impetuous nephew was likely to become, and believed there was great danger in a Franco-Prussian alliance. Hence he chivvied Walpole into action, and Maria Theresa was sent £300,000 and a mercenary force of twelve thousand. By June 1741, however, a Franco-Prussian alliance had been forged, and war seemed inevitable. Walpole's gifts, so unsuited to war, were now to be put to the test in a major military conflict, one he never desired, and one for which, if things went wrong, he would surely become the scapegoat. If he were to lose the support of the House of Commons, not even the King would be able to save him. Meanwhile it began to look as if it was Hanover that was in need of rescue, with a French army poised to invade. At this stage, neither Britain nor Hanover were at war with France. George managed to secure a French promise to respect Hanover's neutrality, and to wrest from Maria Theresa the twelve-thousand-strong army Walpole had sent her in order to have it now protect his Electorate in case the French reneged. All this he achieved without consulting his English ministers, who were disgruntled to find the heroine of the hour left high and dry. In a last desperate attempt to avert war, Walpole then managed to persuade Maria Theresa to appease Frederick of Prussia by ceding Silesia after all.

Things could not have been going better for Frederick of Wales and his friends. They had a whale of a time fighting a general election in April 1741. 'The Prince bid me tell you that he has had uncommon success in the Elections in Cornwall,' Lady Irwin reported to her brother from Kew on 4 June. 'Out of 44 he has carried 27.'[1] The election want so badly for Walpole that having in the past been able to rely on the support of some 150 Members of Parliament, he was left with a probable working majority of only a dozen, which left little room for desertions in the event of things going badly overseas. Between them, Frederick and the Duke of Argyll brought twenty-two new anti-court members into Parliament, and in 1743 Frederick's personal followers in the House of Commons numbered forty. So now it was Prince Frederick's turn to be bought off – if only he would consent to be.

In January 1742, in return for the votes in Parliament of his obstreperous friends, Frederick was offered by Walpole the additional £50,000 a year he had always craved, the payment of his debts, which now amounted to an embarrassing £200,000, and a return for himself and his followers to court. There was a small stipulation attached to this handsome bribe: knowing the King's character as he did, Walpole told his messenger, the Bishop of Oxford, to tell Frederick that as a quid pro quo it would be necessary for him to write a contrite letter to his father. But had the Bishop been sent by his father or by Walpole? 'The Prince,' Lord Egmont recorded, 'who has a quick and lively imagination and is remarkably ready, at once asked the Bishop whether His Majesty had sent him.'[2] The answer of course was much as Frederick had suspected, and presumably he reasoned thus: his father was now nearly sixty; surely he could not live much longer. Then all this lovely money – and a great deal more – would be his by right, and his friends would be in office anyway. Why save Walpole now? He blamed, or pretended to blame, Walpole for the rift between himself and the King, and told the Bishop of Oxford: 'I have all the duty imaginable for my father . . . but I cannot approach him while Sir Robert Walpole continues about him, nor never will.'[3]

Walpole's ploy had failed. Between 1741 and 1742 he suffered seven defeats in the House of Commons, and eventually he was driven to having sick and ailing supporters carried into the House to vote for the Government. It was ironic that a year before, in February 1741, Walpole had survived a motion of censure initiated by Lord Carteret, calling upon the King 'to dismiss Sir Robert Walpole from his presence and councils for ever', for now his end came about over 'the trumpery issue of the Chippenham election'.[4] The last days of Walpole's administration are amusingly – if with some of his accustomed exaggeration – revealed by Horace Walpole (he was at this time MP for Callington in Cornwall) in a letter to Horace Mann: 'It was a most shocking sight to see the sick and dead brought in on both sides! Men on crutches, and Sir William Gordon from his bed, with a blister on his head, and flannel hanging out from under his wig.' Horace Walpole said there was a plan to persuade his father to 'retire with honour. All that evening there was a report about the town, that he and my uncle were to be sent to the Tower, and people hired windows in the City to see them pass by'.[5]

By declining his bribe, Frederick had denied Walpole a reliable working majority, Robert Walpole had lost the support of the House of Commons once too often, and on 1 February 1742 he was received in audience by the King and offered his resignation. Such was George II's comprehension of the evolving British constitution that he realized he had no alternative to accepting it. After twenty-one years, Walpole was out of office, if not out of royal favour. As noted in Chapter 5, the King conferred upon him the earldom of Orford (a title defunct since the death in 1727 of Edward Russell, created Earl of Orford by Queen Anne), granted

his illegitimate daughter the style and dignity of the daughter of
an earl, promised Walpole a pension of £4,000 a year, not knowing, perhaps, that his former First Lord was about to walk off
with £7,000 from the Secret Service fund, and 'fell on Sir Robert's
neck, wept and kissed him and begged to see him frequently'.

On 2 November 1741 Horace Walpole had penned a telling
reflection on the running battle between Frederick and his father,
again in a letter to his correspondent Horace Mann, at one time
envoy at Florence: 'I forgot to tell you that the Prince was at the
Opera; I believe it has been settled that he should go thither on
Tuesdays, and Majesty on Saturdays, that they may not meet.' It
had been during the summer of 1741, the year that saw the birth
of his fourth and perhaps cleverest child, Elizabeth[6] (physically
crippled in some way and always ailing, she lived only to the age
of eighteen), that Frederick realized he would have to vacate Norfolk
House. In the same letter to her brother, in which she had reported
success among the Prince's Cornish constituences, Lady Irwin explained: 'The Prince has met with a great disappointment in regard
to Norfolk House; upon making some repairs the workmen found
the house in a dangerous condition; upon this it was examined
by two or three head builders, who report the front to the square
to be in a falling condition – several cracks and failures in the
wall. Upon this the Prince has left it, and proposes being in the
country all winter.' The house was demolished seven years later.

The oddest sequel to Walpole's downfall, so largely engineered
by Frederick, was that on 17 February 1742 'the Prince, attended
by two of his lords, two grooms of the bedchamber, and Lord
Scarborough, his treasurer, went to the King's levee. The King
said, "How does the Princess do? I hope she is well." The Prince
kissed his hand, and this was all! He returned to Carlton House,
whither crowds went to him.' This account of the frosty reconciliation between the King and Frederick we owe to a letter from
Horace Walpole to Horace Mann dated 18 February 1742, in
which Walpole adds that the King 'had sworn that he would not
speak to the Prince at their meeting, but was prevailed on'. So
fluid were party politics at this time that Lord Carteret, who spoke
fluent Swedish and Spanish as well as French and German, and
whose great abilities the King fully recognized despite Carteret's
previous support for Frederick, accepted the seals of office in
Walpole's stead.[7] Previously ostracized Tories attended court, the

Prince's guards were restored to him, and he and Augusta travelled to the City to receive the congratulations of the Lord Mayor. On the evening of Frederick's reception by the King, the Duchess of Norfolk gave a masked ball, attended, according to Horace Walpole, by five hundred guests 'in the greatest variety of handsome and rich dresses I ever saw, and all the jewels of London – and London has some!' He observed Augusta 'covered with diamonds' – £40,000 worth, but she had been obliged to borrow them. Even the King put in an appearance, and Augusta was so overcome with emotion that when she attended court a few days later 'she fell at the King's feet and struggled to kiss his hand, and burst into tears'.[8]

Peter Quennell's pen portrait of Robert Walpole cannot be bettered, and explains among other things why he was unlikely ever to have survived as a successful prime minister in the thick of a European war:

His bulk overshadows an entire epoch. Nor is he impressive merely as a gifted and unscrupulous statesman who was to retain office longer than any previous chief minister since the days of Lord Burleigh. He is also a figure-head of the age he lived in – an age that he represented both in his merits and in his shortcomings, in his intellectual ability and his physical grossness. Bodily and spiritually his build was opulent. He had an abundance of good and inferior qualities; and these qualities were jumbled together like the personages of one of Hogarth's swarming street scenes, without propriety but, equally, without self-consciousness. . . . He was extraordinarily industrious, but seldom hurried. He had, indeed, that aptitude, peculiar to Englishmen of the governing caste, for seeming to transact business as an afterthought and never allowing the claims of business to disturb his leisure. The business would get done – and it did get done. But, before he opened the dispatches on his table, he would read a letter from his gamekeeper in Norfolk describing the state of his Houghton coverts. The continental statesman who was a slave to his duty – some plotting cardinal secluded in the depths of his cabinet – would have aroused the good-natured contempt of the Norfolk squire.[9]

The year that saw Walpole's downfall witnessed also, on 24

May, the opening, at a cost of £16,000, of a new pleasure venue, Ranelagh Gardens in Chelsea. Frederick and Augusta, accompanied by the Duke of Cumberland, attended, together with 'much nobility, and much mob besides'. Horace Walpole was there the following night, 'did not find the joy of it', and told Horace Mann he thought Vauxhall 'a little better; for the garden is pleasanter, and one goes by water'.[10] Vauxhall had been so conspicuously patronized by Frederick that in 1740 the proprietor, Jonathan Tyers, had had himself painted by Francis Hayman taking tea with his wife and family, and over the fireplace in the painting hangs a medallion portrait of the Prince. This picture can be seen at the National Portrait Gallery.

By midsummer 1742 the King was thinking of making another trip to Hanover, 'If he can avoid leaving the Prince in his place,' as Horace Walpole told Horace Mann. By the autumn Walpole was reporting that the expense of the King's journey had been 'computed at two thousand pounds a day!' and that 'the Regency has been settled and unsettled twenty times: it is now said that the weight of it is *not* to be settled on the Prince'.[11]

The Prince was in for indignities even greater than being for-ever denied the Regency when the King went abroad. In April 1743 George set sail for the Continent, to take charge in person of an array of British, Hanoverian, Austrian and Dutch troops posed to challenge the might of France – and by his side was Frederick's younger brother, the twenty-two-year-old, 20-stone Duke of Cumberland. At home, a Council of Regency consisting of fourteen members had been commissioned. Frederick was not among them. He was, however, the new occupant of Leicester House, the very house his father had occupied as Prince of Wales when he was expelled from court by George I.[12] When George II came to the throne he had sold Leicester House to Sir George Savile for £4,200, but in 1728 the Earl of Leicester moved in, and lived there until his death in 1737. His brother, the 7th and last earl (the current earldom of Leicester dates from 1837), paid rates on the house from 1737 until 1742, when he agreed to rent the property to Frederick for £580 a year. Frederick took out a fourteen-year lease on 16 August 1743, but not before he had settled £4,000 of a £5,000 bill for repairs begun in June. The first essential seems to have been the knocking down of a shop (the owner was duly compensated) in front of the house, to enable sedan-chairs to be carried more easily into the courtyard. Another small problem were the vermin, with which the house was periodically overrun. Despite the sums of money spent on it, Leicester House remained relatively small and inconvenient by the standards of an eighteenth-century royal residence. Water was supplied from the two wells for '14 close-stools', twelve of them made of oak, two, for the princesses, of mahogany. There appear to have been four reception-rooms at the front of the house and only six bedrooms, so that the Princess of Wales's maids of honour had to be lodged in Duke Street, St Albans Street, Leicester Square and Lisle Street, the pages in Gerrard Street.

Nevertheless Frederick did his best to ape royal splendour, furnishing a State Room with two state chairs and a canopy of crimson damask. Benjamin Goodison was called in to embellish several rooms with carvings and gilded picture frames for Frederick's ever-expanding art collection.

Augusta was to retain the use of Leicester House for fifteen years after Frederick's death (it was demolished in 1792), and clearly the couple regarded Leicester House as far more of a home than Carlton House, to which Augusta finally retreated in 1766. For a year after Frederick's death the entire house was draped in black, and in the year of his death his two oldest sons, George and Edward, took up residence at Savile House next door, while William and Frederick moved into Nos 28 and 29 Leicester Square. For a brief time after his mother moved out, Prince Henry lived at Leicester House. As early as 12 May 1743 Horace Walpole was recounting to Horace Mann 'a comical circumstance at Leicester House: one of the Prince's coachmen, who used to drive the Maids of Honour, was so sick of them, that he has left his son three hundred pounds, upon condition that he never *marries* a Maid of Honour!'

The army over which George II now took control, in June 1743, was encamped on the right bank of the Main, at Aschaffenburg. The baggage train with which he had equipped himself was on a scale so pretentious as to suggest the King had no concept how an army was expected to deploy or march; his luggage, which included nine hundred napkins, was carted about in a convoy of eighty-nine wagons. As though on a state visit, he had ordered thirteen berlin carriages. His personal stable of horses numbered a staggering 662; perhaps he imagined one steed would be shot from beneath him every minute. While the troops, seriously short

of food, committed 'great disorders' in search of supplies, the
King rode about inspecting fortified positions, but he seems to
have had no overall plan of campaign to impart to his officers.
Meanwhile the French commander was organizing what looked
like a very promising encirclement of George's forces, with 28,000
men positioned near the village of Dettingen.

It was not long before the French were openly aiming their
cannon at the person of the King himself, who was excitedly rushing
about, anxious to be seen in action by all and sundry, sending
one officer after another to summon up his own artillery, stationed
far too far in the rear. It had not been since the glorious battle at
Oudenarde that George had had an opportunity to display his
valour. (He was not to know that Dettingen would prove the last
occasion on which a British sovereign was to take the field. William
IV fought at the Battle of Cape St Vincent and George VI at
Jutland, but neither was even heir apparent at the time.) Fortunately
for the Allied army, the French second in command left his strong
position near the village too soon, enabling an open battle to
commence. Now on horseback, now on foot, the King ordered a
combined force of British and Hanoverian infantry to clear a wood
through which the French were working their way. Then he had
a six-gun battery brought up and personally directed their fire.
Frederick of Prussia saw his uncle 'putting himself in the posture
of a fencing master and flourishing his sword'. It was all the King
knew to do; the actual tactics of warfare were quite beyond his
comprehension, and so he simply exposed himself in a reckless
manner, encouraging his troops by force of personality and a fearless
exposure to danger.

At one point the King's horse decided it had seen enough of
the action and bolted. Having reined it in, the King dismounted,
saying he could at least trust his own legs not to run away. With
the enemy only sixty paces away, the King shouted, 'Now boys!
Now for the honour of England! Fire, and behave bravely, and
the French will run!' Before long the French did indeed flee in
disorder, taking shelter behind their horse. Then ensued a fierce
cavalry action, which saw the virtual elimination of the Third
Dragoons. Dettingen, like Waterloo, was a close-run thing, but
British volleys eventually decided the issue, leaving piles of dead
gendarmes. Lord Stair was all for following up the costly victory
with a pursuit; the King advised caution, and thought in any case

a more romantic end to his exciting day would be to wander the battlefield knighting his fellow-heroes. He started with Lord Stair, and ended with a trooper from what was left of the Dragoons.

Cumberland too had acquitted himself well, receiving a wound – according to Horace Walpole, 'in the calf of the leg, but slightly'.[13] Despite a general voicing of dissatisfaction over the King's military tactics, in particular his failure to follow up the victory at Dettingen with a rout, or to seem to know how to pursue the war in general, George returned to England in November to a triumphal reception. 'We were in great fears of his coming through the city after the treason that has been published in these two months,' Horace Walpole wrote to Horace Mann on 17 November 1743, 'but it is incredible how well his reception was beyond what it had ever been before. . . . They almost carried him into the palace on their shoulders; and at night the whole town was illuminated and bonfired. He looks much better than he has for these five years, and is in great spirits. The Duke limps a little.' Frederick, with Caroline and Amelia and a group of Privy Councillors, received the King 'on the stairs', but even flushed with military glory George could not bring himself to speak. 'Pas un mot,' Walpole recorded. And this in spite of the fact that his grandson Prince George was ill with smallpox, and the day before Augusta had yet again given birth, to a boy christened William and later created Duke of Gloucester. Perhaps the King was not best pleased to discover that Frederick and Augusta were disporting themselves at Leicester House, where on 15 December, and again the following day, Augusta received congratulations on the birth of her new baby.

There was a constitutional aspect to the rapidly expanding nursery at Leicester House. By 1743 Cumberland, who had been allowed to go to war when Frederick's request had been refused, and, if his father had his way, would inherit the throne, had dropped to seventh in line of succession. Even were Frederick to die now, Cumberland's chances of inheriting the Crown – thanks to Frederick's contented and fruitful marriage – had virtually vanished for ever. There were compensations for the Duke, however. Although, before Dettingen, Cumberland had never been in action, and although in 1745 he was still only twenty-four and inexperienced, he was appointed Commander-in-Chief of what was called the Pragmatic Army, and while the heir to the throne remained in England, his brother was about to take to the field of battle again. In the

spring of 1745 the King inspected his army, then left Cumberland
in charge and paid a visit to Hanover. On 11 May Cumberland,
good at administration but indecisive in the field, led 44,000 assorted
troops against a firmly entrenched French force of 76,000, under
the command of a master of the art of war, Maréchal Saxe. The
British infantry were first brought to a halt, and then, ominously,
beaten back by a charge of the Jacobite Irish Brigade.

Saxe followed up this victory at Fontenoy by capturing the British
base at Ostend. Now the twenty-five-year-old Prince Charles Edward,
known to history as the Young Pretender, stood poised to reclaim
the British throne for his father. And it is quite conceivable that
it was the bloody nose Cumberland received at Fontenoy that
dictated the evil revenge by which he obtained his soubriquet after
Culloden.

The danger of a second Jacobite attempt on the throne had been
evident for some time. Yet in a letter to Horace Mann from the
House of Commons on 16 February 1744, Horace Walpole wrote:

> There has been some difficulty to persuade people of the immi-
> nence of our danger; but yesterday the King sent a message to
> both Houses to acquaint us that he has certain information of
> the young Pretender being in France, and of the designed invasion
> from thence, in concert with the disaffected here. Immediately
> the Duke of Marlborough, who most handsomely and seasonably
> was come to town on purpose, moved for an Address to assure
> the King of standing by him with lives and fortunes.

A week later: 'There is no doubt of the invasion: the young Pretender is at Calais, and the Count de Saxe is to command the
embarkation.' Three hundred arms had been seized in a French
merchant's house in Plymouth and attempts made to raise the
clans in Scotland, 'but unsuccessfully'. This letter concluded: 'All
is at stake; we have great hopes, but they are but hopes!'

Frederick had been in the House of Lords to hear his father's
message delivered, and to hear also Robert Walpole rise to speak
in the Upper House for the first and last time, shocked by the
apathy of his fellow-peers and indignant that initially it was proposed only that 'the papers should lie on the table'. Frederick
was delighted by Lord Orford's urgent plea than an Address should
be conveyed to the King assuring him of their loyalty. Lord Egmont

confided in his diary that the Ministry was greatly alarmed 'though they do not show it publicly for fear of sinking the public credit'. Eventually it was a storm that saved England from invasion, but not before the old Dowager Duchess of Marlborough, with only seven months to live, had expressed her certain belief that before long the country would be overrun by Frenchmen.

On 25 February an expedition of 15,000 men was ready to sail from Dunkirk. A dozen transport ships were destroyed and the rest put back into harbour. Charles had always depended upon French support, but the French had bigger fish to fry on the Continent, and left him stranded on the beach. It was not until July the following year that he made his pathetic landing in Scotland, with only seven men in attendance. Nevertheless he raised his standard at Glen Finnan, and because the local Hanoverian commanders were hopelessly unprepared he managed to attract sufficient followers to occupy Edinburgh and to carry off a victory at Prestonpans. For four heady weeks Charles Edward preened himself in the capital as if he were the lawful sovereign, and with a combination of good luck and sheer audacity crossed the border and got as far south as Derby. London now decided it was time to panic. Alas for Charles, however, his Scottish followers began to drift home, and a mere three hundred Englishmen could be induced to replace them. He had no alternative but to retire to Scotland, and by December he was encamped at Stirling. There he and his brave, foolhardy warriors awaited their fate.

Meanwhile the eventual vanquisher of Charles, the Duke of Cumberland, was not doing too well on the Continent. In May 1745 he had lost another battle to the French, at Tournay. 'I pity the Duke,' Walpole wrote to Mann on 11 May, ignoring Fontenoy, 'for it is almost the first battle of consequence that we ever lost. . . . However coolly the Duke may have behaved, and coldly his father, at least his brother has outdone both. He not only went to the play the night the news came, but in two days made a ballad. It is in imitation of the Regent's style [the French regent, Philippe II, Duc de Chartres and d'Orléans], and has miscarried in nothing but the language, the thoughts, and the poetry'. Thirteen days later Walpole was reporting: 'All the letters are full of the Duke's humanity and bravery: he will be as popular with the lower classes of men as he has been for three or four years with the low women.'

Frederick's timing, as with his Carlton House dinner when the

King was missing, may have been tactless, but he was probably both bored and not too upset at the news of his brother's discomfiture. Even Walpole had to admit, writing to George Montagu on 13 July 1745: 'If it were not for the life that is put into the town now and then by very bad news from abroad, one should be quite stupefied.' It was certainly odd, what passed for intelligent conversation. Apparently Lord Baltimore 'said to the Prince, t'other day, "Sir, your Royal Highness's marriage will be an *area* in English history"'.[14] Perhaps he was anticipating the birth (on 27 October) of yet another son to Augusta, Prince Henry, who lived a dissolute life and in 1766, a year after his bachelor uncle William, Duke of Cumberland, died, was created by his brother, George III, Duke of Cumberland and Strathearn.

On 16 April 1746, just as George II had been the last British sovereign to lead his army in battle, so his younger son was to take the field in the last battle ever fought on British soil.[15] It lasted less than an hour and took place at Culloden Moor, five miles east of Inverness. The battle was lost before it began, for Prince Charles chose to fight on flat, open land, a site ideally suited to Cumberland's cavalry and artillery, and fatal for the only tactics known to Charles's unsophisticated Highlanders – undisciplined charge, followed by hand-to-hand combat armed with broadsword and dirk. Charles had by now mustered a respectable five thousand men, but Cumberland had nine thousand. To coincide with an overture from the English artillery, sleet and snow blew into the faces of the rebels. Communications in the Scottish ranks were chaotic, Charles's order to charge was never delivered, and all Cumberland had to do was mow down the clansmen as they stumbled forward. While just fifty Hanoverian troops were killed, 1,200 Jacobites perished, most of them murdered after Prince Charles had been led away. Cumberland followed up the carnage by burning castles and hanging captors. Then he returned to London in triumph and was proclaimed a national hero. Handel set to work on a new oratorio, *Judas Maccabaeus*, and asked Frederick to recommend a librettist. The Prince came up with the name of Dr Thomas Morell, quite unaware at the time that the work was 'Designed as a compliment to the Duke of Cumberland upon his returning victorious from Scotland.' *Judas Maccabaeus*, composed in July and August 1746, was first performed on 1 April 1747, and became Handel's most popular oratorio in his lifetime.

Frederick would have known Morell because he was churchwarden at St Anne's on Kew Green, where in later years George III and his family became regular worshippers.

Horace Walpole believed the Duke of Cumberland to have had a lion's courage (which may have been true), vast vigilance and activity, 'and, I am told, great military genius'. On that last point Walpole was misinformed. Cumberland never won a serious battle; Culloden was a walkover. Nevertheless London was illuminated, fireworks were lit, and the Duke voted £25,000 a year. Walpole enjoyed himself immensely at the London trial of the traitors, but told Horace Mann, on 1 August 1746: 'The King is much inclined to mercy; but the Duke, who has not so much of Caesar after a victory, as in gaining it, is for the utmost severity. It was lately proposed in the city to present him with the freedom of some company; one of the aldermen said aloud, "Then let it be the *Butchers!*"'[16] And with good reason. Walpole, who had an even more enjoyable time watching the traitors being executed, was shocked by Cumberland's conduct. On 20 July 1749 he was writing to George Montagu to say that the Duke's 'savage temper increases every day'. A soldier who had gone absent without leave to see some friends had been sentenced to two hundred lashes, but Cumberland, 'who loves blood like a leech, insisted it was not enough'.

There was a humane postscript to the bloody butchery at Culloden, to the public beheadings in London and the final collapse of all Jacobite threats to the Hanoverian succession. Frederick interceded, successfully, for the life of Lord Cromartie, whose wife was pregnant. And when the legendary twenty-five-year-old Flora Macdonald, who had so bravely befriended Prince Charles during his flight to Skye and eventual escape to exile in France, was captured and brought to London, Frederick went to see her. But Frederick's kindness towards Flora and his good impression of her very much angered Princess Augusta. Frederick told her he hoped that, had he been in the condition in which Charles found himself, Augusta would have behaved as Flora had done. The Patriot Prince was no mere political pawn but a man of genuine compassion and liberality, virtues he passed on in certain important respects even to his self-centred grandson: when in 1788 the future George IV heard that Flora Macdonald, by then sixty-six, was still alive and living in poverty, he arranged for her to receive a pension of £50 a year.[17]

11

'An Unwearied Friend to Merit'

The eighteenth-century antiquarian and engraver George Vertue said of Frederick, Prince of Wales: ' . . . no prince since King Charles I took so much pleasure nor observations on works of art or artists'. This was undoubtedly true at the time, and save perhaps for the example of George IV, surely remains so. Frederick's chief enthusiasm was reserved for seventeenth-century Flemish master-pieces, but his taste was catholic, his eye discerning. All that his father ever patronized was music. Frederick encouraged silver-smiths, wood-carvers, sculptors, boat-builders, frame-makers, in-terior decorators, cabinet-makers, landscape gardeners, and as well as purchasing paintings already executed he commissioned a great many himself. While the whereabouts of some sixty pictures col-lected by Frederick are now unknown, no fewer than eighty have come to rest in the present Royal Collection, and hence are held in trust for the nation. Denied the throne, and thus any oppor-tunity to test his ultimate destiny, Prince Frederick's permanent claim to fame must rest upon his success as a patron of the arts. His son King George III enhanced the Royal Collection, as did Prince Albert, but on a more limited scale. His grandsons George IV and William IV commissioned fabulous porcelain, as did his great-granddaughter Queen Victoria. But in the comprehensiveness, not to mention financial astuteness, of Frederick's activities as a collector there remains no member of the British royal family with whom to compare him before or since King Charles I, who amassed a staggering 1,500 pictures. (Queen Mary, the consort of George V, possessed the magpie's instinct, but many of the *objets d'art* with which she embellished her private collection were gifts from cowered acquaintances.)

One day the Prince escorted Vertue round his Leicester House collection, telling him (as Vertue later recorded): 'I have something of every kind as I love Arts and Curiositys.' Frederick discussed

with Vertue the possibility of establishing an academy, a plan
thwarted only by the Prince's death, and eventually put into effect
by George III. 'We hear,' the *London Advertiser* reported on 26
March 1751, 'His Royal Highness the Prince of Wales, two days
before he was taken ill, offered £500 a year for the Encouragement
of an Academy of Painting and Sculpture, which was going to be
established here: and that Exeter Exchange was intended to be
taken until a house could be built for that purpose.' It may have
been from his father that George III inherited his remarkable gifts
as a draughtsman; while still in Hanover Frederick drew a ground
plan of Herrenhaüsen, now at Windsor. But Frederick also had
Prince George taught drawing by the French artist Joseph Goupy.
On a visit to Carlton House, George Vertue found Frederick and
Augusta just finishing dinner, 'both setting still at their Table,
waiting their Fruit and desert being brought in, and their stood
near them waiting their two Eldest young princes their sons, prince
George and prince Edward, having each a little knapkin on their
armes. They staid for some time and his royal highness was so
kind as to mention to them who I was, and that he would show
them some of my curious works.'

Throughout his life Frederick sat for fashionable portrait painters
– for so many that no distinctive group of portraits such as Van
Dyck produced of Charles I emerged. As a boy in Hanover he was
frequently painted at the behest of his relatives, and as befitted a
prince in direct succession to a throne he was often shown in armour,
and decked in an ermine-trimmed cloak. It was in Hanover that
he first sat for Philippe Mercier, but for Mercier, and later for
Antoine Pesne, he dispensed with martial attire. These were paintings
intended for exhibition in England, where no one had set eyes on
Frederick, and they showed him as his future subjects would wish
him to be, handsome and possessed of royal refinement. Examples
of both types of portrait can be seen, when the rooms are open
to the public, in the suite at Hampton Court occupied by the Duke
of Cumberland when he was a young man. Both are by unknown
artists. In the same room as these two youthful portraits, one in
armour, one in civilian clothes, painted when Frederick was perhaps
fourteen, is a strange semi-allegorical image of Frederick by Martin
Maingaud, and charming portraits by Maingaud of his sisters Anne
and Amelia, aged about twelve and eleven, and, again by Maingaud,
a more sophisticated painting of Anne, Amelia and Caroline.

Although painted on horseback while still in Hanover, for the equestrian image of monarchy remained very potent, once Frederick had arrived in England, and was in a position to begin commissioning his own portraits, he soon dispensed with State portraiture in favour of informal settings. This reflected his enjoyment of outdoor life and convivial company, but portrayed him too as a man of taste and discernment, as a rival even of the great arbiter of Palladianism, Lord Burlington. As backgrounds to these informal portraits Frederick would choose his newly laid-out gardens at Kew and Carlton House. He enjoyed forming dining and drinking societies. One was called the Henry V Club, Frederick having identified himself with the gallent young king whose supposed exploits as Prince of Wales, in the company of convivial if probably mythical friends like Falstaff, had so inspired Shakespeare. In 1730 Bolingbroke wrote an essay hailing the virtues of Henry V, and Frederick had a meeting of his Henry V Club recorded for posterity, with a bust of Henry V shown above the fireplace of the room in which they met. This work is attributed to Charles Philips, a painter of conversation pieces who died in 1747 at the age of thirty-nine. In 1732 Philips produced two small full-length portraits of Frederick, standing in a baroque hall decorated with painted trophies. Already he had begun distributing portraits of himself as presents for friends, and one of these two portraits, in which Frederick is wearing the Star and Ribbon of the Garter, landed up at Chatsworth, where despite its clear signature it was for some time attributed to Dorothy, Countess of Burlington, and even labelled 'George III', although it had been painted six years before George III was even born.[1] There is also an early family group portrait at Chatsworth by William Aikman, who died in 1731, wrongly attributed to Philippe Mercier. This depicts Frederick with Cumberland, Anne, Amelia, Caroline, Mary and Louisa. Other country houses in receipt of portraits of Frederick include Wilton, Warwick Castle and Goodwood, which is not surprising as the Duke of Richmond ('I couldn't have lost anybody more affectionate, and a more sincere friend,' George II said of him when he died) had been Master of the Horse to the King.

Another of Frederick's societies was called the Round Table, for the example of King Arthur in seating his knights in a circle so that no one could claim superiority appealed to his own democratic ideals. And it was in 1732 that he commissioned from

Charles Philips a painting of nineteen members of the Round Table, at 4 guineas a figure, all of them dressed in Frederick's hunting livery. Philips also charged expenses of £21 'in going and whilst attending at Hampton Court' and a further 8 guineas for a 'Gold Frame finely carv'd'. Much talking and imbibing is taking place, and like many of Frederick's early commissions, it reflects the romantic yearnings of a young man, still tied to his parents financially, for independence, approval and attention.

Someone to whom Frederick presented a portrait as a present – it was a parting gift – was his mistress Anne Vane. It was executed by a Venetian, Jacopo Amigoni, who had arrived in England in 1730 and for whom Frederick sat three times, and appropriately enough it has come to rest in the dining-room of Lord Barnard's home, Raby Castle. Anne bequeathed it to her brother Henry, later created Earl of Darlington. Another of Amigoni's portraits, showing Frederick seated in a highly decorative manner (Amigoni was much addicted to embellishing his paintings with cupids), was given to Dodington and now hangs at St James's Palace. It was painted in 1735, the same year that Queen Caroline sat for Amigoni. (Also in the Royal Collection at St James's Palace is an important portrait of Frederick by Joseph Highmore.) An earlier family collaboration occurred in 1729 when the *Daily Courant* reported that Mercier was 'painting the picture of His Royal Highness the Prince of Wales, at full Length, for the Princess Royal'. This is believed to be a portrait of Frederick presented by Caroline to the Earl of Grantham.

After his marriage the portraits of himself that Frederick commissioned became more formal, although his desire to behave informally was as strong as ever. Hoping to watch the Lord Mayor's procession in 1736 incognito, Frederick managed to get jostled by the crowd, and was rescued when several members of the Saddlers' Company hauled him into their private stand. In gratitude he agreed to become their Perpetual Master, and sat for a dignified portrait, in an embroidered suit and wearing a sword and the Garter collar and star, to be hung in their hall. It became a victim of the Blitz in 1940. Freemasonry also benefited from the Prince's more orthodox activities. On 26 February 1742 the *Daily Post* was able to report: 'We hear that at a full Lodge of the Free-Masons at the Cardigan's Head on Wednesday Night Last, Mons Andue being in the Chair, it was proposed by Dr Beaumont to have his Royal Highness the Prince of Wales's Picture painted by

Mr Thomas Frye, to be hung up in the Lodge, which motion was immediately agreed Nemine Contradicente.'

Since there were then no photographs with which to illustrate newspaper reports of the Prince and his activities, portraits of him were widely distributed. Hence in 1741, to commemorate his earlier visit to Bath, Frederick had 'two Capital Pictures' of himself and his wife, attributed to Jeremiah Davison, a Scot who had produced a State portrait of Frederick in 1730, delivered in London to Beau Nash, who duly presented them to the Corporation of Bath. After they had been hung in the Town Hall (now the Guildhall) 'the Mayor his Brethren of the Corporation and several Gentlemen of Distinction assembled in the Evening and drank the Health of his Majesty, the Royal Donors, and the rest of the Royal Family; the Night concluded with ringing of Bells and other publick Demonstrations of Joy'. In some ways, Frederick's distribution of portraits, especially to friends he wished to reward or thank for loans of money or personal services rendered, was not unlike the use made in later times of the honours system. Lord and Lady Archibald Hamilton, whose loyalty to Frederick never wavered when other courtiers threw in their lot with the King, received portraits, as did William Pulteney, in 1742, the year of his elevation to the peerage as Earl of Bath.

Pulteney's gifts, presented in gratitude for political support over many years, were fine examples of the work of the Frenchman Jean-Baptiste Van Loo, who arrived in England in December 1737. Within three months Frederick and Augusta 'did him the honour to sit by him and see him paint two Heads, and afterwards ordered him to prepare the Clothes for the Painting their Royal Highness's and Princess Augusta's Pictures'. 'Their Royal Highness's' referred to several of Frederick's children. Van Loo's portraits of Frederick and Augusta have been described as 'perhaps the most accomplished and impressive known images of the royal pair'. They are attired in court dress and have no inhibitions about displaying their expensive dress and jewels.

One of the most extraordinary images of the royal couple was commissioned by Augusta after the Prince's death. Painted by George Knapton, *The Family of Frederick, Prince of Wales* was intended partly as a keepsake, and partly as a reminder to posterity of the Prince's achievements as progenitor of the royal line. Frederick makes his own appearance as a misty-grey ethereal figure in a portrait in the top left-hand corner, indicating down below the wife and children he loved. Augusta nurses the posthumous baby princess; her eldest daughter, tall and graceful, stands beside her. In various postures, on the floor, romp the other children, accompanied by their pet dogs and their toys. The future George III and his brother Edward examine a map. William and Henry play with a boat. Louisa strums her mandolin. This enormous, brilliantly executed, altogether remarkable work hangs on public view in the room at Hampton Court in which George II was accustomed to dine in public.

Frederick had alighted on Van Loo's studio with unerring instinct. With equal discernment he was to patronize John Wootton, England's leading sporting painter at the time. Hunting was one of Frederick's passions (his ability to ride fearlessly in the hunting field was to some extent a compensation for his permanent exclusion from the battlefield), and Wootton's pastoral woods and fields, in which Frederick and his companions delighted, was another way for Frederick to advertise his association with the way of life so precious to his future subjects. In 1740 Wootton depicted a shooting party, for example, with Frederick, the 3rd Duke of Queensberry and John Spencer, father of the 1st Earl Spencer. *The Death of the Stag* and *The Return from the Chase* are set in Windsor Great Park. They were painted in 1737 and hung in the gallery at The White House in Kew. One of Frederick's most quixotic commissions from Wootton was a portrait of the Duke of Cumberland with the Battle of Dettingen in the background, although the Duke's head was contributed by Thomas Hudson; Wootton never claimed to be much good at portraiture. This picture, together with two other enormous battle scenes, was displayed at Leicester House.

In addition to Van Loo, another artist commissioned by Frederick to paint his family was Thomas Gibson, who was summoned to Cliveden in November 1742. George Vertue tells us: 'Mr Thomas Gibson lately recommended to Draw the children of the Prince of Wales – being four on a large Cloth – which was so well approved on that Her Royal Highness the princess of Wales also sat for her picture, a half length in which he succeeded very well her picture being very like.' The children were again painted, in 1747, by an artist from Switzerland, Barthélemy du Pan. Six children appear, in the garden at Carlton House, and it is noticeable how much more sumptuously dressed Frederick's daughters are than his sisters were at their age. Prince George is in the uniform of the Royal Company of Archers; Edward, busy loading a flintlock, is in military uniform. A bill for £52. 10s. presented in 1749 by George Knapton was for 'A large Picture in crayons containing 3 figures Viz: their Royal High. Lady Elizabeth, Prince William, & Prince Henry, representing the Spring, Summer, & Winter, drawn according to his Royal Highness the Prince of Wales his directions & commands.' William, draped in grapes and vine leaves, was actually doing his best to look like autumn.

Frederick sat for at least seventy portraits. A few have gone abroad, and the present whereabouts of some are not known. Two dozen are in the Royal Collection, one of them, a full-length portrait in Garter robes, possibly by Charles Philips, having been purchased by Queen Mary as recently as 1931. Two years previously, Queen Mary acquired another portrait of Frederick in Garter robes, possibly painted on the occasion of his marriage. There are portraits at the National Portrait Gallery of Scotland, in the Victoria and Albert Museum, and at the National Portrait Gallery in London, where in addition to its version of *The Music Party* can be seen a not very flattering equestrian painting of Frederick by Bartholomew Dandridge, with a poorly executed background, painted about 1732 and purchased by the gallery in 1898. Full-length portraits by Charles Philips of both Frederick (in Garter robes) and Augusta in the Royal Collection can be seen in the King's Presence Chamber at Kensington Palace, and when the State Apartments at Windsor Castle are open an amusing early equestrian portrait of Frederick, with a large grin on his face, painted in Hanover by Joachim Kayser and Johan Anton Klyher, can be viewed above the fire-place in the Queen's Guard Room. In the private apartments at Windsor are two paintings attributed to David Morier.

Frederick was well aware of the example set by his great-great-great-uncle Charles I, and shared his admiration for Van Dyck. As a result, one of his most moving purchases, in 1748, was Van Dyck's *Thomas Killigrew and (?) William, Lord Crofts*, painted in 1638 and depicting the youthful playwright Thomas Killigrew in mourning for his wife, and probably in the company of his bereaved brother-in-law. Frederick displayed it in Leicester House, and it remains in the Royal Collection, as do six of the other seven Van Dycks purchased by Frederick. An important purchase he made in about 1740, *St Martin Dividing His Cloak*, was believed at the time to be by Rubens, but has since been identified as the work of Van Dyck. This too was hung in Leicester House, and is now normally on display at Windsor Castle. From the studio of Van Dyck Frederick rescued a portrait of King Charles's wife, Henrietta Maria. The Royal Collection is strangely lacking in landscapes (it does not contain a single example of the work of Turner or Constable) and in his day Frederick made amends by purchasing landscapes by Rubens, Jan Brueghel and Claude. It may have been Frederick's leasing of Cliveden that encouraged him in 1747 to buy *Winter* and *Summer* by Rubens, both now at Windsor Castle (and normally on view to the public), for they had originally belonged to the 1st Duke of Buckingham, the father of Cliveden's first owner.

As well as collecting Old Masters, Frederick commissioned new work from contemporary artists. *Boys Playing with a Goat* was probably painted for Frederick around 1735 by Jacopo Amigoni, and was recorded at Kensington Palace in 1818. A companion piece, *Boys Playing with a Lamb*, seems to have become separated; it was recorded a year later at St James's Palace. In 1736 Amigoni was paid £63 for a picture of a child with cupids, but this has gone missing. For a sixteenth-century work by Jacopo Bassano, *Diana and Actaeon*, Frederick paid £73. 10s. in 1742. This too has disappeared.

Some of Frederick's purchases were made on his behalf at sales, some came from wealthy connoisseurs, others from friends. *Jacob Peeling the Rods*, painted in the mid-seventeenth century by Cagnacci, had belonged to Frederick's Master of the Horse. Even judging by the value of money at the time, some of Frederick's purchases were amazing bargains. For a miniature of the 'Dutchess of Richemont' he paid 3 guineas, and for one of 'the late Earl of Pembroke when young' 6 guineas. Another miniature cost 4 guineas. A painting by the seventeenth-century artist Abraham Diepenbeeck cost Frederick only 12 guineas.

Among names to conjure with, Frederick acquired work by David Teniers, a painting of St Jerome by Dürer, a very fine oil on panel of the 3rd Duke of Norfolk by Hans Holbein the Younger and a self-portrait by Peter Lely. In 1742 he paid £47. 5s. for a work that may have been by Poussin. It has vanished. *An Old Man's Head* by Rubens, which Frederick had cleaned in 1747 and was observed hanging in Leicester House two years later, has likewise vanished. So has a Tintoretto, and no fewer than five Titians, one of them, *Diana and Actaeon*, a favourite classical subject, having cost Frederick £173. 5s. A Velázquez, for which Benjamin Goodison made a frame in 1748, has suffered a similar fate. But an album of drawings by Poussin remains in the library at Windsor.

Prince Frederick was collecting in competition with the nobility, most of them far richer than he, but he managed to acquire works of art that can be compared, in quantity and quality, to almost any other collection in eighteenth-century England, and this at a time when large new country houses were being built, all in need of paintings and statues, mostly imported from the Continent. In 1735 Frederick was buying pictures from France for Carlton House, but his bill included £25. 4s. for Dresden porcelain. Later that year 'several rich Paintings [were] lately arrived from Italy, for his Royal Highness the Prince of Wales, in order to be put up in his house in Pall-Mall'. Frederick employed his own artistic spies, sending Joseph Goupy, a cabinet-painter by profession, to hunt around in France in 1748, and again in 1750; but he returned from this second visit, after a month, empty-handed.

With never less than four homes at any one time to furnish, Frederick spent a very considerable portion of his income on works of art, furniture, silver and china. In 1749 he retrieved from Rotterdam twenty-two tapestries sold from the collection of Charles I exactly a century before. Furniture had to be mended, pictures reframed, and with eight children rushing around, broken china had to be replaced. The barges needed regilding, stage designs for his family entertainments needed painting. The children were trained by a professional actor, and in 1749 George, Edward, Augusta and Elizabeth took part in Joseph Addison's *Cato*; the next year, at Leicester House, it was *Jane Grey*. Frederick collected maps and other military documents. Plants and statues for the gardens added to a ceaseless if pleasurable expense, and in 1739 Frederick enjoyed the satisfaction of having the fourth volume of a work containing plans and views of country estates, *Vitruvius Britannicus*, dedicated to him.

Frederick had the sense to take advice from the best sources available. One person he consulted was General John Guise, who himself owned works by Claude and Poussin. When he died in

1765 Guise bequeathed 1,734 Old Master drawings to Christ Church, Oxford, where a selection is always on display in the picture gallery situated on the right of Canterbury Quad. By examining this collection Frederick would have been influenced in his own choice of purchases, and he even bought a Claude from the General. Sir Luke Schaub, whose diplomatic career took him to France, Spain and Italy, also amassed a large collection of paintings, and he too placed his expert knowledge at the Prince's disposal. Many of Frederick's Flemish paintings were brought from Spain to England by an Irish merchant, Sir Daniel Arthur.

Although in theory the apartments provided for Frederick at court, at St James's Palace, Kensington Palace and at Hampton Court, were furnished for him, he was ordering additional furniture soon after his arrival in England. For £50 he acquired a 'large pier glass in a tabernacle frame gilt'. Once he had taken over The White House and Carlton House he was in need of quantities of furniture, much of it walnut or mahogany, but very little has survived. His Palladian taste in architecture was apparently much in evidence in the style of furniture he commissioned. Two 'Large Mohogany Piller & Claw Tables' cost him the very reasonable sum of 4 guineas, a 'Rich Carved & gilt Table frame to match another and a fine Purple Slab', £24. A 'Wallnut tree Table with a Drawer to stand under' came to £2. 15s.

Far and away the most expensive items commissioned by Frederick were his silverware, much of it truly magnificent. An early gilt tea service survives in the Royal Collection, made about 1733. This was the year that Frederick appointed George Wickes his silversmith. Soon Wickes had delivered a 'fine cup and cover' and a 'fine bread basket'. The cup cost £80, the basket £50. By the year of his marriage Frederick was ordering dishes, sauce-boats, plates, castors, salvers, soup ladels, candlesticks ... and ran up a bill for £3,244. 6s. 8d., paid with borrowed money. Before long Wickes was employed providing items for the baby Prince George and his sister Augusta. The nursery porringers, spoons, forks, mugs and cups were all made of silver. Prince George's kettledrums came to £49. 5s. 6d. The drumsticks were 2 shillings extra.

George Wickes was born at Bury St Edmunds on 7 July 1698, the eighth child of a reasonably prosperous family of ten. His father James was an 'upholder' or upholsterer. For seven years Wickes was apprenticed to a goldsmith in London, at a cost of

£30, and became a member of the Worshipful Company of Gold-
smiths, although he worked most frequently in silver. By 1722,
when he was only twenty-four, he had a business in Threadneedle
Street, and in the year he was appointed goldsmith to Prince
Frederick, probably on the recommendation of Lord North, for
whom he had made a magnificent pair of candelabra to commemorate North's appointment to Frederick's household, Wickes
moved to Panton Street. Hence when Frederick moved into Leicester
House he had his goldsmith almost next door. The company that
Wickes founded was to become in the nineteenth-century Garrard
& Co., currently Warrant Holders to the Queen.

In 1743 Frederick ordered a pair of silver tureens, engraved
with his coat of arms, and gave one of them to his doctor, Matthew
Lee, which Dr Lee's widow eventually gave to Christ Church,
Oxford. Two other silver-gilt tureens made for Frederick by Wickes
cost £456. 14s. 1d. Wickes was doing well. In 1748 he landed an
order for £1,000 worth of gilt plate. The most stupendous piece
of silverware commissioned by Frederick, in 1741, was a 27-inch-
high centrepiece, punched not by Wickes but by Paul Crespin and
probably fashioned by Nicholas Sprimont. Now in the Royal
Collection, it has been described as 'the purest rococo creation in
English silver'.

The eighteenth century was a great period for clock-making,
and Frederick paid £61. 2s. for a clock with a French case, the
face 'Enamel'd White & Blue with the Days & Months & Signs
of the Zodiack', and £31 for an eight-day clock 'that strikes the
Quarters on Six Bells, as it goes, and when pull'd'. A clock on
view in the King's Drawing Room at Kensington Palace belonged
to Augusta, and originally played music by Handel and Corelli.
Compared with silverware, clocks and jewellery seem to have been
inexpensive. A gold snuff-box with diamonds and rubies cost
Frederick only £46 (four years' pay for a kitchen-boy, nevertheless),
a pair of diamond knee buckles £47. But in 1738 he splashed out
on new Garter regalia, spending £1,033. 10s. (Today Garter regalia
is supplied by the sovereign and returned on the death of the
recipient.) In June 1741 Frederick spent £4,000 on jewellery from
Peter Dutens. Dutens received another order for jewellery worth
£4,000 in September 1742, and was paid £3,000 in January 1745.
Another jeweller by the name of Isaac Lacam supplied Augusta.

In the field of literature Frederick played a minor role, befriending rather than patronizing, and lending his friendship only to writers who were amusing company, men like John Gay and Alexander Pope, whose home at Twickenham he visited. In 1736 Lord Egmont was noting in his diary how pleased he was 'to find the Prince had read so much and had so good a memory', but the less said about Frederick's own literary efforts perhaps the better. They were of a standard well below that attained by even an average amateur man of letters of the eighteenth century, but he was always struggling to express himself in a third language, being fluent in German and nearly so in French. His English was never entirely literate, even allowing for a relaxed attitude towards spelling and grammar that still prevailed in polite society. Yet in the breadth of his interests he was very much in the mould of the Renaissance prince, exercising an enlightened curiosity in a whole range of subjects. He sought the friendship, for example, of Stephen Hales, a cleric and inventor, a founder of the Society of Arts, the author of *Vegatable Staticks* and the discoverer of the phenomenon of arterial pressure. Frederick was fascinated by English history, and by the time he met Hales the kindly old man had lived under seven monarchs; born in the reign of Charles II, he was to see Frederick's son ascend the throne.

Probably only two other members of the royal family, Prince Albert and Queen Mary, have shown as much personal interest as Frederick did in the Royal Collection. A year before his death Frederick commissioned a catalogue not only of his own possessions but of the pictures at Windsor Castle, Hampton Court, Kensington Palace and St James's, starting off the catalogue himself. According to George Vertue, at The White House one afternoon Frederick 'called for paper and pens and began to write down the names of his most Capital pictures at Leicester House', going on to catalogue his paintings at Carlton House, The White House and Cliveden as well as his father's at Windsor, 'writeing down each particular picture, name of Master, and the storys or portraits represented. He was surely above an hour and a half or near 2 hours writeing swiftly, all this by memory which when done he gave those sheets to me for my use'. Vertue then proceeded to catalogue both the Royal Collection and Frederick's own, for which, 'Considering my Labour time & study' Frederick 'genrosly appointed to be paid to me thirty guineas, which I recevd and his promises of the continuance of his friendship'.

Frederick took as much pains over the framing of his pictures as he did over choosing them originally, and gained the approbation of contemporary experts. Vertue wrote of Frederick's collection that there were 'no bad pictures many very excellent, and well chosen'. Horace Walpole, with seldom a kind word for Frederick during his lifetime or after his death, had to admit that his pictures were very fine. One is entitled to dismiss as utterly ludicrous the patronizing judgement made by an otherwise impeccable modern historian, Professor Basil Williams: 'He . . . took, or at least affected to take, a far greater interest in the arts, painting and literature than George I and II even pretended to do.'[2] Smollett was rather nearer the mark when he wrote of 'this excellent Prince . . . a munificent patron of the arts, an unwearied friend to merit'.

12

'Thy Will Be Done'

One need look no further than to the fact that Robert Walpole
had driven into opposition Pulteney, Carteret, Townshend and
Chesterfield to explain Prince Frederick's determination to aid the
Opposition himself; and they were only the four most able men
kept out of office by Walpole. Now that Walpole had gone, and
the King had been obliged to take into his new administration
men with whom he had previously scarcely deigned to pass the
time of day, the need for virulent opposition, and consequently
Frederick's influence over friends who now accepted government
office, began to wane. His overriding objective, the fall of Walpole,
having been achieved, Frederick spent the next four years or so
prepared to support the Government, and in 1746, when his at-
torney-general failed to fall in line behind the Duke of Newcastle
and his brother Henry Pelham, into whose hands the reins of
power had fallen, the Prince dismissed him. But following Pulteney's
farcical attempt to form an administration in 1746 (he lasted forty-
eight hours as Prime Minister) Frederick had a change of heart,
and once again ordered his followers to vote against the court.
And he continued to oppose the Pelhams for the rest of his life,
for he realized that even though it would almost certainly be
impossible to dislodge them during his father's lifetime, it would
be necessary to have opposed them if he were to get rid of them
on his accession. Another reason Frederick returned to opposition
was because he still feared an attempt by the court to alter the
succession in favour of the Duke of Cumberland.

In 1747 Frederick was forty years of age, regarded as well into
middle age in those days. By forty most men in public life had
already attained high office, whereas Frederick had spent the past
twenty years with no defined tasks. Without four homes to furnish
and gardens to tend, and without an agreeable wife for company,
a large circle of admiring friends and children to educate and

play with, he would have become very bored indeed. His official involvement in the life of the country extended merely to his member-ship of the House of Lords and the Privy Council; from the actual councils of the King and his ministers, however, he was totally excluded. That his father was to live to be seventy-seven and to reign for thirty-three years could scarcely have entered into his calculations. By the time Frederick was forty and George sixty-four it was only to be expected that the Prince would be sustained by reasonable hopes of succeeding to the throne within the not very distant future. He can be forgiven for occasionally whiling away the time by jotting down the names of men he would include in his first ministry when eventually his father did die.

But driven perhaps by an innately active metabolism now stoked by a measure of frustration, he went even further. Late at night on 4 June 1747, at Carlton House, Frederick drew up 'The Carlton House Paper'. Concerned about party strife and 'a general depravity of morals diffused throughout this country', Frederick's instructions to Lord Talbot and Sir Francis Dashwood were to assure the Opposition of his 'upright intentions'. His proposals for the fu-ture included the abolition of political parties, exclusion from the House of Commons of army officers under the rank of colonel (which would have barred from Parliament the young ensign Pitt) and naval officers below the rank of rear-admiral. There were to be inquiries into abuses in office, by which presumably Frederick meant the widespread distribution of sinecures (Walpole had died in 1745, narrowly avoiding prosecution), and he added an assurance that when he did come to the throne he would not accept a civil list in excess of £800,000. The ironic result of 'The Carlton House Paper' was to ensure that the very Opposition party Frederick would abolish when king was once again in the headlines, and it was no coincidence that his rallying-cry to all good men and true was made just as Bolingbroke's *Patriot King* was being officially published.

While promising to save the nation £100,000 a year 'when we shall have the misfortune to lose his Majesty', His Majesty being at this time in poor health, plagued not only with intermittent attacks of piles but by 'agues', for which he was prescribed 'Jesuits' bark', Frederick distributed large pay rises among his household. In 1742 salaries had amounted to £21,195 a year; by 1749, by which time the household had doubled, to provide profitable employment for as many of his adherents as possible, salaries had risen to £38,892. The most conspicuous government deserters now included the Earl of Middlesex, heir to the Duke of Dorset, the fair-weather and faintly ludicrous George Dodington, the Lord Chief Justice and most importantly Lord Egmont's bright young son, who succeeded to his father's earldom in 1748. The new Lord Egmont became leader of the Leicester House rebels, and was sarcastically referred to as 'Prime Minister Egmont', clearly in the expectation that on George II's death, Egmont would be called upon to form an administration.

But at no time did Frederick's newly formed Opposition pose any serious threat to Newcastle's government; its main purpose was to provide a springboard for the new reign. In 1746 Frederick's Opposition was numbered at 122, and although a general election was not due to be held for another two years Newcastle was sufficiently worried about the Prince increasing his lead at the polls that he sprang a general election on an unprepared Opposition in 1747. It proved one of the most docile ever, and left Newcastle with a reliable majority of around forty-three, sufficient by which to survive, particularly as there was no guarantee that Tory Members of Parliament would always vote with Frederick's supporters.

The Prince's hopes of succession to the throne were very nearly realized in 1748 when his father, on a visit to Hanover, was thrown from his carriage. But George II was born a lucky man, and walked away from a potentially lethal accident unscathed. A year later, academic disappointment was to follow. Frederick allowed his name to be put forward for the chancellorship of Cambridge, a perfectly proper and harmless ambition. But George could not resist any opportunity to snub and insult his heir. The university was sent a message to say the application was without the King's 'consent or privity', and that 'tho' his Majesty does, by no means, intend to interfere in their election, yt he is persuaded, from the regard & affection which he has always show'd for the University, & from their duty to him, that they will not chuse any one of his family without his approbation'. Frederick would have made an admirable chancellor, but the university took the King's heavy hint of reprisals and the post was filled by the Duke of Newcastle, who 'invited, summoned, pressed the entire body of nobility and gentry from all parts of England' to a series of installation dinners.

Frederick contented himself by composing an ode. Although entitled 'The Charms of Sylvia' it was addressed to his wife, who in 1749 gave birth to their seventh child, a fragile baby hastily baptized, as Prince George had been in 1738, *in extremis*. She was given the name Louisa, and although she did survive infancy, like her sister Elizabeth she was never strong and died when she was nineteen. Several of Frederick's children appear to have been weak by disposition. His namesake, born in 1750, died when he was only fifteen, and the daughter born after the Prince's death, Caroline, was released by death at the age of twenty-four from marriage to a madman, her cousin King Christian VII of Denmark.

Frederick cared deeply about his family, keeping in touch with the children by letter when they were separated. He often failed to date his letters, but it was almost certainly in 1749, after the performance of *Cato*, that he sent the following round robin.

My Dr Children,
You have giv'n me too much Joy to-day, that I should omitt answering yr letters. There are different Reasons for liking Letters, some are agreeable for the Stile, others for the Turns, but those I prefer to all these are when they are full of good Sentiments. Yrs are so, in particular Lady Augusta's; I have allways wished you would come to like reading, it is only by that one forms ones-Self, and one mak's proper Remarks of Caracters; these you make of yr Play are exceeding Just, and if you keep yr prudent Resolution you'll be happy, and make the proudest Father so too, who has the Kindest Intention for yr future happiness. Yr Mama sends you her blessing, and wee send kisses to the 3 little on's, which you 3 Eldest will distribute in our Nam's. Yr hand, my Dr George, grows much better, and I'm obliged for yr compliment, to my boy Edward. Pray God you may grow in every Respect above me.
Good night my Dr Children. Do'nt expect us before near 11 a clock at night, therefore go to bed; my Compliments to Mrs Herbert, and Schrader, and order Hoggnell and the 2 Grooms to be at the Relays at Colebroke at 9 a'clock.

To his eldest son, who had been ill, he wrote:

My dear Boy,
thank God, Mrs Herbert tells me yr better and that Edward and Augusta are so too. Make them my compliments, and write

to me to morrow, how they all do. You can't imagine how happy you have made me yesterday. Any mark of a sincere or a sensible feeling heart giv's me much more Joy than any signs of Wit, or of Improvement in yr learning; which I daresay will come also in time. You have a Father who lov's you all tenderly, and (who tho' peevish against yr faults, be-cause he wants you Should Shine), allways by the Father again when he sees you mend. Good night to you all.

Your Mama sends her blessing to you all. If you are not well, let Augusta write.

Frederick P.

As well as expressing concern for their welfare, Frederick was full of encouragement. His letters, too, are delightfully geared towards the age of their recipients. 'Yr German letter was a very good one,' he assured Prince George on one occasion, 'and I hope you'll know soon to write the letters too. [He meant the German script.] I am very well, so is Mama, Cosi and Billy. I did not care to shew my self at the Drawing room, therefore I staid here, my face is a little like Edward's usual face, which in these times is not a good Drawing room Face. Ev'ry body sends compliments to you all and the little on's. I send mine in particular to Edward, who I hope, as well as you, learns his lessons well. Good night Dr Boy, Frederick P.'

It was in September 1749, when George was eleven, that Frederick appointed Lord North, at a salary of £1,000 a year, governor to the two oldest princes. He did this without referring the matter to the King, who was in Hanover at the time. North's duties were to 'go about with Prince George and appear with him in public'. The boys' actual lessons were entrusted to a new tutor, George Scott, a devotee of Lord Bolingbroke, and the less than efficient Francis Ayscough was told merely to concentrate on religious instruction. Perhaps to emphasize the security of this tenure, Ayscough commissioned a portrait from Richard Wilson, now in the National Portrait Gallery, of himself with his two pupils; the boys are side by side on a settee while the pedant stands beside a table heaped with improving literature. Frederick took such a close personal interest in the boys' life that he drew up a daily timetable himself. They were to get up at seven o'clock, and to read from eight until nine. Instruction of one sort or another was to take place until half-past twelve, when the boys were free to play until three o'clock, when they were to have their dinner. Three afternoons a week they were to receive dancing lessons. Supper was at eight o'clock, and between nine and ten they were to be in bed. It was a long and strenuous day for boys of their age, judged by modern ideas, but nothing out of the ordinary for an eighteenth-century lad destined for Westminster or Rugby.

'On Sundays,' Frederick instructed George Scott, 'Prayers exactly at half an hour past 9 above stairs. Then the two Eldest Princes, and the two Eldest Princesses, are to go to Prince George's apartment, to be instructed by Dr Ayscough in the Principals of Religion till 11 o'clock.' In addition to dancing, the boys received instruction in fencing. They were encouraged to enjoy music, and Frederick made sure they were taught history as well as Latin and mathematics. Desperate for reassurance about their educational progress, he wrote one day from 'Clifden':

> Dr George,
> Thank God you are all well. We are so too. How do you advance in the English History and in what Reign are you, and why do'nt you write me what you have learnt with Ayscough and Funge? As you and Edward are both in Town I think one might speak of ev'ry bodys health, and th'other acquaint me with the Progresses you make with yr Masters, but Edward has forgot me, and has giv'n me no signs of life this fortnight, which hurts me. For the Future I beg both may take it by Turns, to tell me in writing once a Week what you have read, it will imprint it better on yr mind, and convince me that you both aply, which will make me happy, as nothing can do that more, than a Prospect, to say my Children turn out an Honour to me, and a Blessing to my Country.

Annoyed by George's dilatory habits where letter-writing was concerned, Frederick reminded him of his ultimate destiny and the responsibilities it entailed. 'You of all people should take more trouble,' he told the boy, 'as God has giv'n you so high a Mark to govern one day so many Nations, and if you do not please them, they wo'nt please you in return. Read this carefully and keep it, as it comes from a Father who (what is not usuall) is

your best friend.' He added a peevish postscript: 'Mama, tho'
you neglect Her both, sends both of you her blessing.'[1]

One's first reaction to Frederick's choice of tutor for the princes
was that anyone recommended by Lord Bolingbroke would be
likely to instil Jacobite sympathies as well as the mildly radical
sentiments of the author of the *Patriot King*. But Frederick's decision
to employ George Scott was one of his major acts of enlightenment,
a serious service to the future welfare of the monarchy – or intended as such, at any rate. Scott was a considerable scholar. He
was destined to become the friend of Samuel Johnson and the
great historian Edward Gibbon. And because his father was a
diplomat, Scott had actually been born in Hanover, and from the
first had been firmly attached to the Hanoverian cause. Indeed,
his credentials were beyond reproach, for Prince George's great-
great-grandmother Sophia had been his godmother.

Frederick's genuine love of children and appreciation of the
joys and sorrows of parenthood can be judged from a letter he
wrote in 1744 from Durdens to the father of Lady Archibald
Hamilton, one of whose younger brothers had died:

> My Dr Lord,
>
> I won't tell you how much the loss you have had has struck
> us all here; Lady Archibald is vastly concerned as you may
> imagine, but bears it with that Christian patience you know
> she has. I hope you make use of the reason you have. I own in
> losing so promising a Boy you want it. Pray tell Miss Hamilton
> her Mama is well, and I hope she takes care of you, and her-
> Self. I hope you have sent for Freddy, and William home, and
> keep 'em some days with you, which will be some comfort to
> 'em. I know the trouble you have in writing, therefore desire
> not to answer me.
>
> Ldy Archibald will come home to-morrow night. Believe me
> Allways your good Friend,
>
> Frederick P.

The Hamiltons' son William was to become Sir William Hamilton, British envoy in Naples, whose second wife, Emma, was
the lover of Horatio Nelson – Nelson being the great-grandson of
Robert Walpole's sister Mary.

It is only in very recent times that the fantasy has been created that children born to reign need to be sheltered from the knowledge, and are themselves unaware of their destiny until some sudden and dramatic event brings it home to them. In Frederick's day royalty were well aware of their station in life from the youngest possible age; indeed, it was deemed their duty to know who they were and to behave accordingly. So Frederick's reminders to Prince George of his destiny came quite naturally. On 13 January 1749, at the age of only forty-one, and when his heir was still only ten, Frederick produced 'Instructions for my son George, drawn by myself, for his good, that of my family, and for that of his people, according to the ideas of my grandfather, and best friend, George I.' This testifies to the dependence Frederick had had upon visits to Hanover from his grandfather while abandoned there as a boy. It also indicates that Frederick may for some reason have harboured a premonition that, young as he still was, he might not come to the throne, for he wrote: 'I shall have no regret never to have worn the Crown, if you do but fill it worthily.' The ideas of his grandfather which he so warmly commended to his son relate to the separation of Hanover from Britain. 'This has always been my design,' he wrote, 'and the latter years have still more convinced me of the wisdom of this project.' But during the reign of George III the King's dual sovereignty ceased to be a political issue.

Frederick passed on to his son some general moral guidance, to the effect that 'When mankind will once be persuaded that you are just, humane, generous, and brave, you will be beloved by your people and respected by foreign powers', and in a somewhat idealistic frame of mind he told the boy 'that a good deal of the national debt must be paid off before England enters into a war'. Unfortunately, as George III's biographer has sagely observed, the enemies of England might not be prepared to wait.[2] Frederick also urged his son to live economically, advice he took to heart only in part; George III allowed his equerries barley water and spent £10,000 a year on candles. But the chapel at Windsor was kept so cold in George III's day that one of his equerries told Fanny Burney: 'Not a soul goes to chapel but the King, the parson and myself; and there we three freeze it out together.' He was so frightened of getting fat that he sometimes ate nothing but mutton and stewed pears, but he indulged himself on Sundays with a plate of roast beef. His was to prove a contradictory character. Like his father he spoke to his servants with easy familiarity, and would engage complete strangers in conversation while walking alone in Windsor Great Park, but he failed to follow his father's example with regard to protocol indoors, where it remained so rigid that even his daughters waited for their father to address them before they spoke. The King once made William Pitt stand for two hours during an audience although like so many of his contemporaries he was almost incapacitated by gout. These human defects, and particularly his inability to cope with his adolescent sons, can be attributed to the tragic fact that George was denied his father's benevolent influence throughout the formative years of his own adolescence, when it cannot be doubted that, had he lived, Frederick would have given his son a thoroughly liberal training.

By the end of 1749 Frederick seems to have put aside thoughts of not inheriting the throne, for Lord Egmont and George Dodington found themselves summoned by the Prince, on 12 November, to consider 'the immediate steps to be taken upon the demise of the King, more particularly with relation to the Civil List'. The most extraordinary conversation seems to have ensued, with Frederick weighing up the pros and cons of letting the existing ministers settle the civil list, 'and then part with them and the Parliament'; of dismissing 'four or five of the principals, but to vote the Civil List before the Parliament was dissolved'; or thirdly 'to dismiss the Parliament immediately, to turn all those out whom he did not design to continue, and to throw himself upon the country for a new Parliament and a provision for himself and family'. There was general agreement that the third suggestion would be best, whereupon 'His Royal Highness came heartily into it, gave us his hand, and made us take hands with each other to stand by, and support it.' These were the rather childish antics of a clique bored with opposition and hungry for power, and as far as Frederick's own conduct was concerned, it displayed that unseemly side to his nature driven in part because he was so sure that things were being conducted badly at present, and that as king he would be a great improvement on his father.

According to Horace Walpole, March 1750 found Frederick canvassing 'in a green frock (and I won't swear, but in a Scotch plaid waistcoat) sat under the Park-wall in his chair, [hallooing] the voters on to Brentford'.[3] On 19 May Walpole was complaining that Augusta was 'lowering the price of princes, as the earthquake had raised old china; she has produced a fifth boy'. This was a reference to the birth of Frederick, her eighth child in thirteen years, and to the fact that in March there had been an earthquake 'that lasted', Walpole had reported to Horace Mann on 11 March, 'near half a minute, with a violent vibration and a great roaring'. On 23 June George Montagu was informed by Walpole that 'Lord Granby's temper had been a little ruffled the night before: the Prince had invited him and Dick Lyttleton to Kew, where he won eleven hundred pounds of the latter, and eight of the former, then cut, and told them he would play with them no longer, for he saw they played so idly, that they were capable of *losing more than they would like*.'

It was at this time that Frederick renewed his interest in the garden at Kew, getting Dodington to lend a hand in February. By 12 October 1750 George Vertue was able to record Frederick's 'directing the plantations of Trees exotics with the workmen – adviseing & assisting. where wee were receivd gratiously and freely walking and attend the Prince from place to place – for 2 or three hours. seeing his plantations and his Gardens. water works. canal – & great numbers of people labouring there his new Chinesia Simmer hous. painted in their stile & ornaments the Story of Confucius & his doctrines &c'. It is not known where Frederick's House of Confucius, for work on which a carpenter was paid £207. 18s. 11d., a plumber 25s., originally stood. It was removed to a position in the north-east corner of the garden after Frederick's death and taken down in the nineteenth century.

July 1750 found Frederick and Augusta, with William, now seven, five-year-old Henry and their oldest child, Augusta, back in Bath, at the start of a progress through the West Country. There were picnics and meals on barges, an excursion to the Isle of Wight, and a visit to Southampton. When they reached Portsmouth 'his Highness landed at the Sally port . . . and walked round the fortifications attended by one of the engineers with a plan of them'. Words could not express 'the joy and pleasure all ranks and degrees of people expressed at this presence amongst us'. And from Portsmouth Prince George was kept informed of events by his father: 'I wo'nt go to bed without telling you that we are all here after our Passage of 3 hours, we are well, and mightyly pleas'd with the Ship's and the rest of the curiositys. Both yr brothers are with us vastly well, and grown. My Compliments to Edwd and the rest. Good bless you all.'

Frederick himself was not to remain well for much longer, and his thoughts seem again to have been turning towards things eternal. On 9 September, while at Cliveden, he penned, in German (presumably so that his thoughts would not be at the mercy of his shaky command of English): 'Fear God and honour his name so shalt thou live happily in the Land of thy Fathers and the blessing of the Highest shall be with thee.' In March 1751 he attended the House of Lords, where the King was 'passing some bills'. He returned to Carlton House, 'very hot, where he unrobed, put on a light unaired frock and waistcoat, went to Kew, walked in a bitter day, came home tired, and lay down for three hours, upon a couch in a very cold room at Carlton House, that opens into the garden. Lord Egmont told him how dangerous it was, but the Prince did not mind him'.[4] Dodington's laconic diary entry merely relates: 'Went to Leicester House where the Prince told me he had catched cold the day before at Kew.' It may be that the cold developed into pleurisy. Three doctors were called to Leicester House, and despite their usual best endeavours to kill their patient (they bled the Prince, thus reducing his resistance to infection), Frederick seems to have begun to recover. The first thing George II said, on being told of his son's death, was, 'Why, they told me he was better!' But according to Horace Walpole's information: 'The cough continued; the Prince laid his hand upon his stomach, and said, "Je sens la mort!" The page who held him up felt him shiver, and cried out, "The Prince is going!" The Princess was at the feet of the bed; she catched up a candle and ran to him, but before she got to the head of the bed, he was dead.'[5]

When Ayscough broke the news to Prince George, now, on the death of his father, Duke of Edinburgh, the boy turned pale, laid his hand on his heart, and said, 'I feel something here, just as I did when I saw two workmen fall from the scaffold at Kew.' Sent to tell the King that the heir to his throne was dead, Lord North found George II playing cards with Princess Amelia, the Duke of Grafton and the Duchess of Dorset. The King immediately sent his condolences, and the morning after Frederick's death he called at Leicester House, burst into tears, and told the boys they were to be brave, 'obedient to their mother, and deserve the fortune to which they were born'. On 20 April Prince George was created Prince of Wales and Earl of Chester and given his own household.

Frederick's dukedom of Cornwall, in remainder only to the oldest
son of the sovereign, reverted to the Crown, and George II proceeded to enjoy its revenues.

'Unhappy day,' George Vertue wrote in his Note Book on 20
March. 'O God, thy will be done.' Although left distraught, and
with her ninth child on the way, Augusta that evening had the
sagacity to destroy Frederick's copy of his plans for his accession,
not knowing, perhaps, that another copy had been retained by
Lord Egmont. Next day she wrote to her father-in-law: 'Sire, The
grief which overwhelms me makes me not the less sensible of
Your Majesty's kindness. The only thing, Sire, which could console
me is the gracious assurance which Your Majesty has conveyed
to me. I throw myself, with my children, at your feet. We commend
ourselves, Sire, to your fatherly love and royal protection, and I
am with the utmost submission, Sire, etc., Augusta.'

Frederick was buried on 13 April in the Henry VII Chapel at
Westminster Abbey, and not one member of his family followed
the coffin. Eight boy choristers were paid half a crown each for
their services. The epitaph on Lord Clarendon – 'Here lies Tom
Hyde, It's a pity that he died' – was instantly polished up for
Frederick: 'Here lies Fred, Who was alive and is dead; Had it been
his father, I had much rather; Had it been his brother, Still better
than another; Had it been his sister, No one would have missed
her. . . .' 'This has been a fatal year to my family,' the King noted
at the end of 1751. 'I have lost my eldest son, but I was glad of it.'

Less delighted were Frederick's friends in opposition. The day
after Frederick's death they met at the house of their leader, Lord
Egmont, but failed to concoct any coherent plan of campaign. All
their immediate hopes of office had been dashed. In case the King
should die before Prince George's eighteenth birthday it was necessary to make provision for a regency. The King's natural inclination was for Cumberland to be named, but even George had to
accept there might be some truth in rumours that, given half a
chance, his son would try to usurp the throne, and that his
unpopularity in the country (grossly unjustified in the King's opinion)
was a factor that had to be taken into account. Hence he yielded
to those who advised that the Dowager Princess of Wales should
be appointed, doing so on condition that if the necessity for a
regency should arise, Augusta should be assisted by a council of
twelve, with Cumberland as president.

In the event, George III, twelve when he became heir to the throne, was twenty-two when he succeeded, and no regency was necessary. Lord North was now dismissed as governor to Prince George, and replaced by a reliable Whig, Lord Harcourt, a man of little imagination who had discharged his duty conscientiously, Horace Walpole considered, 'if on no account he neglected to make the Prince turn out his toes'. In later life George III was to dismiss Harcourt as 'well intentioned, but wholly unfit for the situation in which he was placed'. Of his new preceptor, Thomas Hayter, Bishop of Norwich, George recalled *him* as being 'an intriguing, unworthy man, more fitted to be a Jesuit than an English bishop'. But as a consequence of the death of Frederick the man who really took charge of George's education was the Earl of Bute, to whom George became slavishly devoted. We can be pretty sure that Frederick would have wanted to reign rather than rule, and it was the tragedy of the reign of George III that he wanted too desperately to rule. The man who instilled this concept of monarchy into his head was Bute. George's love for and dependence upon Lord Bute seriously retarded his emotional development as well as damaging his political judgement. Bute encouraged the Prince to develop an unseemly contempt for his grandfather, and even worse, for Pitt, arguably the greatest statesman of his age.

It is also reasonable to suppose, knowing what we do of Prince Frederick's character, that had he lived anything like a normal lifespan and reigned for even ten years, perhaps twenty (he would have been fifty-three on coming to the throne), some of the barbarity that marred public life for so long would have been mitigated. Between 1770 and 1830, for instance, perhaps seven thousand people were strangled to death on the gallows, often in batches as large as twenty at a time.[6] For what we can say with absolute certainty is that Frederick was a decent, cultivated, enlightened, kind and generous man, who transcended the traumas of his family background with humour. His most reckless action, absconding from Hampton Court with his pregnant wife, was folly on the grand scale, but would never have occurred had his parents behaved towards him with a shred of common decency. Together he and Augusta made a very considerable success of their marriage at a time when few royal or aristocratic couples remained faithful any longer than necessary.

Frederick's patronage of the arts speaks for itself. His political philanderings were no more dangerous or damaging than those of professional politicians who flitted from side to side in search of honours and financial profit whenever it suited their purpose. For an heir apparent who does not succeed to the throne it is never easy to leave a firm or lasting impression, for his entire life will have been spent waiting in the wings. But at least one contemporary, who had ample opportunity to gather impressions as an eye-witness, Tobias Smollett, had no doubt about the worth of Frederick, Prince of Wales. In his *History of England* he wrote that Frederick's death afflicted 'all who wished well of their country'. He was 'possessed of every amiable quality which could engage the affection of the people – a tender and obliging husband, a fond parent, a kind master, liberal, generous, candid and humane . . . well disposed to assert the rights of mankind in general and warmly attached to the interest of Great Britain'.

It can be rash to judge how a man might have turned out who has not been fully tested, and many people of Frederick's mercurial temperament mature only when given the opportunity to exercise responsibility. But whatever view we take of the imponderables, we cannot say that Frederick's life was wasted; simply that he was never allowed to attain a potential that would surely have confounded his most purblind critics, and enhanced immeasurably, long before it achieved popularity, the all too often tarnished reputation of the House of Hanover.

Notes

1 Hanover's Good Fortune

1. There has been considerable confusion and conflict of opinion over the date of Prince Frederick's birth. There seems, for example, not to be a scrap of evidence for 6 January, the date given in the *Dictionary of National Biography* and followed by a modern American researcher into Frederick's achievements as a patron of the arts, Kimerly Rorschach (*Princely Patriotism and Political Propaganda*, Yale, 1985). Nor for 20 January (Elaine Barr, *George Wickes: Royal Goldsmith*, Studio Vista, 1980). Nor yet for 31 January, the date favoured by R.L. Arkell in *Caroline of Ansbach* (OUP, 1939).

In his biography of Frederick's mother, *Caroline the Illustrious* (1904), W.H. Wilkins dates a dispatch from the British envoy to Hanover, reporting the birth of Frederick, 5 February. The same date is given by Sir George Young in *Poor Fred: The People's Prince* (1937). But although the envoy wrote that 'last night ... the Princess was delivered of a son', Wilkins also dates the birth of that son 5 February, whereas, if the envoy dated his dispatch the day after the birth, it must have occurred on 4 February. 5 February for Frederick's birth is the date adhered to by Peter Quennell in *his* biography of Frederick's mother, *Caroline of England* (1939), but he too seems to have failed to realize the date of the dispatch and the date of the birth cannot be the same.

There were two calendars operating at the time of Frederick's birth, the Gregorian calendar in use in all countries on the Continent except for Russia and Turkey, and, in England, the Julian calendar, eleven days behind the Gregorian calendar, and abolished on 31 December 1751. It is reasonable to assume that for the first twenty-one years of his life, while he lived on the Continent, Frederick would have celebrated his birthday according to the Gregorian calendar, and equally reasonable to assume that after taking up residence in England, in December 1728, he would have adjusted his birthday to the Julian calendar, as everyone else did. Had he done so, and had he been

221

born on 4 February, his birthday in England would have fallen on
24 January. However, in the archives at Castle Howard there appears
to be almost conclusive proof that the Prince was born on 23 January
by the Julian calendar, and therefore on 3 February by the Gregorian.
Writing in 1733 to her father, the 3rd Earl of Carlisle, Lady Irwin,
a lady-in-waiting to Frederick's wife, the Princess of Wales, remarks:
'The entertainment my Lord Tankerville gave upon the Prince's birthday
was one of the finest things that has been known upon that occasion.' This letter is dated 23 January. One of two things therefore
appears to have happened. Either Lord Tankerville's entertainment
was so fine that writing perhaps on 24 February Lady Irwin misdat-
ed her letter, which would make the date of Frederick's birth by the
Gregorian calendar 4 February, or the envoy began his dispatch on
4 February, the day after the birth, and dated it 5 February on com-
pletion. This seems the most plausible explanation, for if Lady Irwin's
letter is correctly dated, and there is no serious reason to think it is
not, Frederick was undoubtedly born on 3 February.

2. Georg August was created Duke of Cambridge in 1706, three
months before the birth of Prince Frederick, and not, therefore, as
some commentators have asserted, as a reward for securing the
succession.

· 3. Not the 'Act of Succession 1700', as in Wilkins, op. cit.

4. Frederick and Charles both died in 1690 (Charles in battle),
Christian in 1703 and Sophie Charlotte, the wife of Frederick I of
Prussia and mentor to Prince Frederick's mother, in 1705.

5. Alternatively spelt Guelf.

6. '. . . all of the Electress Sophia's elder brothers and sisters were
either dead in 1701, or they and their descendants were Roman
Catholics'. Letter from Dr Edward Gregg, Associate Professor of History
at the University of South Carolina and author of *Queen Anne* (1980),
to the author, 14 November 1991. In *Pretenders* by Jeremy Potter
(Constable, 1986) it has been estimated there were fifty-seven Stuart
descendants with a better claim than Sophia, but all were Catholics.

7. Mary Beatrice of Modena, who died in 1718, was fifteen when
she married the Duke of York in 1673 following the death of the
Duke's first wife, Anne Hyde. The marriage was so unpopular at the
time that Charles II was obliged to prorogue Parliament to prevent
addresses against its consummation.

8. On the death of William III in 1702 there was talk among the
Tories of Prince George of Denmark being made king, as William
had been, with the right to reign alone in the event of Anne's death.

Nothing came of this, and Prince George predeceased his wife by six years.

9. In the spring of 1706 Queen Anne had nominated sixty-two Commissioners from Scotland and England, and in the early summer a treaty was agreed, one of the provisions of which was to apply the Hanoverian succession to Scotland as well as to England.

10. *George II* (1973).

11. King George VI refused to countenance a suggestion that he should create his heiress presumptive, Princess Elizabeth, Princess of Wales on the grounds that the title was exclusively for the use of the wife of the heir apparent.

12. Prince Georg August was also granted the courtesy titles of Marquess of Cambridge, Earl of Milford Haven, Viscount Northallerton and Baron Tewkesbury.

13. Chenevix-Trench, op. cit.

14. For a discussion of Queen Anne's apparent agreement, albeit short-lived, to fall in with Tory plans to invite the Electoral Prince to reside in England in 1703, see Gregg, op. cit., pp. 183–5.

2 A Murder in the Family

1. Normally the Tour did not take in England; it was more often from England that young lads set out to discover the architecture and paintings on the Continent. The term Grand Tour did not come into use in print until 1760, but continental tours had become commonplace by the middle of the seventeenth century. See Christopher Hibbert, *The Grand Tour* (Thames Methuen, 1987).

2. While living in London, Philipp von Königsmarck got in some juvenile experience of living dangerously when he was almost certainly implicated, along with his elder brother, in the murder of Thomas Thynne of Longleat.

3. *The Four Georges* (1860).

4. It was because Sophia Dorothea was divorced from Georg Ludwig before Georg succeeded as Elector of Hanover and was therefore never Electress, and because Georg never remarried, that when she was widowed her mother-in-law the Electress Sophia was not known as the Dowager Electress.

5. Not in January 1706, as given in Young, *Poor Fred.*

3   *Abandoned*

1. In *Poor Fred*, George Young mistakenly identifies Princess Amelia as the Princess Royal.

2. Maids of honour at the English court, however, would be unmarried on appointment, although they might be promoted women of the bedchamber on marriage. Queen Victoria had eight maids of honour in addition to her women and ladies. On being appointed a maid of honour in 1887, Marie Adeane was asked whether she could speak, read and write German and French; play the piano; 'read easily at sight in order to play duets with Princess Beatrice'; ride; and whether she was likely to become engaged. No maids of honour have been appointed since the death of George V.

3. At that time the bishopric of Rochester and the deanery of Westminster were always held by the same person.

4. Not at Hampton Court, as stated by Averyl Edwards in *Frederick Louis: Prince of Wales* (1947).

5. The *Weekly Journal* of 22 September 1714, which would indicate that in *The First Four Georges* (1956) J.H. Plumb is in error in dating the landing of the King as 29 September. Even odder, in *George III* (1972) John Brooke says that George I landed on 30 September. Both the King's entry in the *Dictionary of National Biography* and Wilkins in *Caroline the Illustrious* give the date as 18 September, and this is undoubtedly correct.

6. On 12 February 1715 the Prince of Wales took the oath as Duke of Rothesay and his seat in the House of Lords on 17 March that year.

7. Marlborough House had been built by Sarah, Duchess of Marlborough in the first decade of the century with money purloined from the Privy Purse. As the Duke could scarcely afford the upkeep of Blenheim Palace, his real motive in offering to part with Marlborough House was probably a desire to relieve himself of financial burden.

8. *A Foreign View of England in the Reigns of George I and George II* (John Murray, 1902).

9. This anecdote, told by William IV to Viscount Duncannon, was repeated by Duncannon to Charles Greville. *Greville Memoirs*, 13 December 1843.

10. Saussure, op. cit.

11. Lady Cowper's Diary.

12. Chenevix-Trench, *George II*.

4 'They Are All Mad'

1. For a more detailed discussion of George I's constitutionally important decision to absent himself from the Cabinet, see Plumb, *The First Four Georges*.

2. The Order of the Garter is restricted to twenty-four members excluding the sovereign, Royal Knights and Extra Knights Companion.

3. In his essay on George I in *The Four Georges*, Thackeray applies Lady Mary Wortley Montagu's description of the young Prince Frederick to his father, George II. Thackeray was frequently contemptuous of historical accuracy, alleging, for example, that Bath was patronized by George II and Queen Caroline, neither of whom ever visited the city, and stating that in 1729 George II paid a two-year visit to Hanover when he was there only six months.

4. Young, in *Poor Fred*, is mysteriously mistaken in suggesting that Hervey succeeded his father.

5. Walpole must have meant His Electoral Highness, for in England the Prince of Wales was always addressed by this time as His Royal Highness.

6. Geraldine Norman, *The Independent*, 13 February 1992.

7. In 1801 Houghton was inherited by the 1st Marquess of Cholmondeley, who preferred his home in Cheshire, and for most of the nineteenth century Houghton was closed. This at least had the beneficial result that the original upholstery and textiles have survived unfaded. In 1994 just two pairs of Walpole's gilt side chairs from Houghton fetced £729,000 at auction.

8. George II's entry in the *National Dictionary of Biography* is incorrect in asserting that Prince George William was born at Leicester House.

9. *Survey of London*, Vol. XXXIV. Wilkins, in *Caroline the Illustrious*, places Lord Grantham's house in Albemarle Street, but he may have been mistaken.

10. In *The Life and Times of George I* (Weidenfeld & Nicolson, 1973) Joyce Marlow states that the separation of the Prince and Princess of Wales from their children had a long-term effect on the relationship between the future George II and his sons. Neither son was affected. Frederick was being brought up in Hanover and the Duke of Cumberland was not yet born.

11. *Memoirs of Louis XIV and the Regency* (London, 1888).

12. To the Raugravine Louise, 6 March 1718.

13. The suggestion has been made in Marlow, op. cit.

14. Lady Cowper's Diary.

5 'Von Big Lie'

1. Robert Walpole was knighted in 1725 when George I revived the Order of the Bath, and received the Garter a year later, the only commoner so honoured at that time. The first new knight admitted to the Most Honourable Order of the Bath was Frederick's four-year-old younger brother, Prince William Augustus, later Duke of Cumberland.

2. As clear and concise an account of the South Sea Bubble as any, and the way in which it led to the rise to supreme power of Walpole, can be found in Basil Williams, *The Whig Supremacy: 1714–1760* (OUP, 1939; rev. ed. 1962).

3. In 1740 Mary married Frederick of Hesse Cassel; she died in 1772. In 1743 Louisa married the King of Denmark; she died in 1751, the same year as Frederick.

4. Lord Chancellor King's Diary, 24 June 1725.

5. Ibid.

6. *The Memoirs of Wilhelmina, Margravine of Bayreuth*. In 1886 these memoirs were translated into English by Queen Victoria's daughter Helena, Princess Christian of Schleswig-Holstein.

7. The 'blue riband', which would have been worn across the King's left shoulder, was of course the dark-blue broad ribbon of the Order of the Garter, and on his left breast the King would have been wearing the Star of the Order.

8. Twillet, according to George I's entry in the *National Dictionary of Biography*; Twittel, according to Wilkins, *Caroline the Illustrious*.

9. *Lord Hervey's Memoirs, et seq.* Quotations throughout are taken from the 1952 Batsford edition, edited by Romney Sedgwick.

10. Saussure, *A Foreign View of England*.

11. *A Prime Minister on Prime Ministers* (Michael Joseph, 1977).

12. A friendship between Swift and Prince Frederick has been claimed, but they could not even have met in England.

6 Homes and Gardens

1. An admirable biography of Prince Frederick's godson is Brian Fothergill's *The Mitred Earl: An Eighteenth-Century Eccentric* (Faber & Faber, 1974). In 1734 the Prince also stood as a godparent to Lord Jersey's son.

2. Not 1727, as in *The Macmillan Dictionary of Biography*; nor 1728, as in Regnhild Hatton, *George I* (1979).

3. *Manuscripts of the Earl of Egmont* (1920).

4. Not in 1729, as in Young, *Poor Fred*.

5. Egmont MSS.

6. Sometimes his name is spelt Doddington, but the *Dictionary of National Biography* has settled for Dodington. He was eventually raised to the peerage, in 1761, as Lord Melcombe. (Not 'Lord Melbury', as in Young, op. cit.)

7. *Caroline of England*.

8. In *Frederick Louis, Prince of Wales* Averyl Edwards refers to Prince Frederick and his three older sisters playing in a quartet. Only three of the sitters are engaged on instruments, and whatever it was Frederick, Anne and Caroline were supposed to be playing, it was not a quartet. Nor, as has sometimes been asserted, is Caroline playing a medieval instrument called a mandore.

9. *The Tudor, Stuart and Early Georgian Pictures in the Collection of Her Majesty the Queen* (1963). In *Lord Hervey's Memoirs* the version of *The Music Party* in the Royal Collection has been attributed, presumably incorrectly, to Joseph Nollekens.

10. Kimerly Rorschach, *Apollo*, October 1991.

11. Not now at the Victoria and Albert Museum (as in Edwards, op. cit.), where it was on temporary loan until after the Second World War. It was restored on arrival at Greenwich, and again refurbished to coincide with the opening of the National Maritime Museum's new Barge House in 1977.

12. *Read's Weekly Journal*, 15 July 1732.

13. Letter from Horace Walpole to the Hon. H.S. Conway, 27 June 1748.

14. *The Remembrancer*, 20 April 1748. It would have been Prince George's tenth birthday treat. He had been born on 24 May 1738, according to the Julian calendar, but after 1751 he celebrated his birthday on 4 June.

15. By Patrick Montague-Smith and Hugh Montgomery-Massingberd, 1981.

16. *The Wentworth Papers*, 1705–39.

17. Ibid.

18. Ibid.

19. Wilkins, *Caroline the Illustrious*.

7 'No Excise!'

1. The year of birth of Frederick's illegitimate son is incorrectly given as 1733 in Edwards, *Frederick Louis, Prince of Wales*.

2. Egmont MSS.
3. Ibid.
4. Ibid.
5. Sometimes spelt de Roussie. She and her brother were the children of the 1st Earl of Lifford, a former French count ennobled in the Irish peerage by William III.
6. *The Marriage, Baptismal and Burial Registers of the Collegiate Church or Abbey of St Peter, Westminster* (London, 1876), from which also are taken details of the boy's baptism and his sister's birth and death. Young, in *Poor Fred*, is incorrect in his assertion that Frederick's son was christened Fitz-Frederick Vane.

8 Marriage

1. A son was certainly born to Baroness von Walmoden, later created Countess of Yarmouth, but there has been some dispute as to whether he was the King's child. Obviously it was greatly to the benefit of the Baroness to claim that he was. His length of life is also in some doubt.
2. The 7th Baron De La Warr.
3. Carlisle MSS at Castle Howard.
4. Ibid.
5. Ibid.
6. Ibid.
7. Ibid.
8. Ibid.
9. Ibid.
10. *His Majesty's Opposition: 1714–1830* (1964).
11. Not Christmas Day 1736, as in Young, *Poor Fred*.
12. Carlisle MSS.

9 Expelled from Court

1. Both Mary II and Queen Anne had been known as Lady Mary and Lady Anne in childhood.
2. Carlisle MSS.
3. Ibid.
4. *Wentworth Papers*.
5. Carlisle MSS.
6. Quennell, *Caroline of England*.
7. *Wentworth Papers*.

8. Not in 1739, as in Quennell, op. cit.

9. Prince George was not born at Carlton House, as stated by Sir Charles Grant Robertson in *England under the Hanoverians* (1911).

10. Celia Fiennes's *Through England on a Side Saddle in the Time of William and Mary* was not published until 1888. The manuscript is preserved at Broughton Castle in the private possession of Lord Saye and Sele. Much fascinating information about Nonsuch, and the use to which building materials from the palace were put at Durdens, can be obtained from John Dent, *The Quest for Nonsuch* (Hutchinson, 1962).

11. Lord North also held the barony of Guilford, frequently misspelt 'Guildford'. In 1752 he was created Earl of Guilford, and was the father of George III's prime minister, Lord North.

12. Letter from the Senior Research Archivist at the Centre for Kentish Studies in Maidstone to the author, 25 November 1994.

13. Princess Caroline and Princess Mary followed Prince Frederick in 1740.

14. Hanover eventually became a kingdom, the King of England retaining the Crown of Hanover until the death of William IV, when the Hanoverian throne was devolved upon William's brother, Prince Ernest Augustus, Duke of Cumberland, fifth son of George III. He died in 1851 and was succeeded as King of Hanover by his son, Prince George. In 1866 Hanover took part in the Austro-Prussian War, but unfortunately on the wrong side, and as a result of the peace treaty the former electorate was absorbed into the ever-expanding sovereign state of Prussia, to which new links were attached when Queen Victoria's oldest daughter married the heir to the Prussian throne. The last King of Hanover, Frederick's great-grandson, having lost his throne, died in 1878.

10 The Patriot Prince

1. Carlisle MSS.

2. Egmont MSS.

3. Ibid.

4. Chenevix-Trench, *George II*.

5. 22 January 1742. His uncle was also called Horace Walpole.

6. Her birth has been omitted from Frederick's entry in the *Dictionary of National Biography*, as also has the birth of Princess Louisa, in 1749.

7. Students of constitutional history will find an interesting and

detailed account of the parts played by the King and Prince Frederick in the formation of a new administration following the resignation of Walpole in Foord, *His Majesty's Opposition*, chap. 6.

8. Letters from Horace Walpole to Horace Mann, 18 and 25 February 1742.

9. Quennell, *Caroline of England*.

10. 26 May 1742.

11. 25 September 1742.

12. In Derek Jarrett, *Britain: 1688–1815* (1965), the date of Prince Frederick's removal to Leicester House is incorrectly given as 1728 – fifteen years before the event.

13. Letter to Horace Mann, 24 June 1743.

14. Horace Walpole to George Montagu, 13 July 1745.

15. The Battle of Britain was of course fought in the air.

16. George II's inclination to show mercy deserted him entirely eleven years later when he declined to reprieve the unfortunate Rear-Admiral John Byng, executed on the quarter-deck of HMS *Monarque* on 14 March 1757 *pour encourager les autres*.

17. Readers interested in detailed accounts of both Jacobite uprisings should consult James Lees-Milne, *The Last Stuarts* (1983).

11   *'An Unwearied Friend to Merit'*

1. Memorandum from Peter Day, Keeper of Collections at Chatsworth, to the Duchess of Devonshire, 6 October 1994.

2. *The Whig Supremacy* (1939).

12   *'Thy Will Be Done'*

1. Frederick's idiosyncratic spelling, grammar and punctuation are at times so bizarre that they have been tidied up in a few minor instances in order, while retaining the flavour of his letters, to render them at least instantly intelligible.

2. Brooke, *King George III*.

3. Horace Walpole to Horace Mann, 11 March 1750.

4. Horace Walpole to Horace Mann, 21 March 1751.

5. Ibid.

6. John Adamson, reviewing *The Hanging Tree: Execution and the English People 1770–1868* by V.A.C. Gatrell (Oxford, 1994) in the *Sunday Telegraph*, 30 October 1994.

Select Bibliography

Place of publication is London, unless otherwise stated.

Ashley, Maurice, *The Glorious Revolution of 1688* (Hodder & Stoughton, 1966).

Brooke, John, *King George III* (Constable, 1972).

Chapman, Hester W., *Queen Anne's Son* (André Deutsch, 1954).

Chenevix-Trench, Charles, *George II* (Allen Lane, 1973).

Edwards, Averyl, *Frederick Louis, Prince of Wales* (Staples Press, 1947).

Foord, Archibald S., *His Majesty's Opposition: 1714–1830* (Oxford: Oxford University Press, 1964).

Grant Roberton, Charles, *England under the Hanoverians* (Methuen, 1911).

Gregg, Edward, *Queen Anne* (Routledge & Kegan Paul, 1980).

Halsband, Robert, *Lord Hervey* (Oxford: Oxford University Press, 1973).

Harris, R.W., *England in the Eighteenth Century* (Blandford Press, 1963).

Hatton, Regnhild, *George I* (Thames & Hudson, 1979).

Hill, B.W., *The Growth of Parliamentary Parties: 1689–1742* (Allen & Unwin, 1976).

_____, *Sir Robert Walpole: First and Sole Prime Minister* (Hamish Hamilton, 1989).

Jarrett, Derek, *Britain: 1688–1815* (Longmans, 1965).

Jordan, Ruth, *Sophie Dorothea* (Constable, 1971). (Her name is more usually spelt Sophia.)

Lees-Milne, James, *The Last Stuarts* (Chatto & Windus, 1983).

Mason, Alfred Bishop (ed.), *Horace Walpole's England* (Constable, 1930).

Plumb, J.H., *The First Four Georges* (Batsford, 1956).

_____, *Sir Robert Walpole* (The Cresset Press, 1956).

_____, *Men and Places* (The Cresset Press, 1963).

Quennell, Peter, *Caroline of England* (Collins, 1939).

Thackeray, William Makepeace, *The Four Georges: Sketches of Manners, Morals, Court, and Town Life* (1860).

Ward, Adolphus William, *The Electress Sophia and the Hanoverian Succession* (Goupil & Co., 1903).

Wilkins, W.H., *Caroline the Illustrious* (Longmans Green, 1904).

Williams, Basil, *The Whig Supremacy: 1714–1760* (Oxford: Oxford University Press, 1939).

Young, George, *Poor Fred: The People's Prince* (Oxford: Oxford University Press, 1937).

Index

Adam, Robert 85
Addison, Joseph 202
Aikman, William 196
Aislabie, John 82–3
Albert, Prince Consort 111, 194, 205
Alfred the Great 19
Algarotti, Francesco 102
Amelia (Emily, second sister of FL) 46, 53, 59, 84, 86, 88, 107, 114–15, 145, 169–70, 176, 189, 195–6, 217
Amelia (illegitimate daughter of FL) 121
Amigoni, Jacopo 175, 197, 201
Anne, Princess Royal and Princess of Orange (oldest sister of FL) 45–6, 53, 59, 80, 85, 89, 107–8, 122–5, 127–8, 130, 132, 142, 145, 149, 164, 167, 195–7
Anne, Queen 17–27, 29–33, 42, 45–6, 48–9, 59, 65, 68, 76, 128, 176, 179, 183
Argyll, 2nd Duke of 60–1, 66, 67, 182
Arthur, King 196
Arthur, Sir Daniel 203
Astor, 2nd Viscount 164
Astor, Viscountess 164
Atterbury, Bishop Francis 48–9, 84
Augusta of Brunswick-Wolfenbüttle (oldest daughter of FL) 158–61, 170, 172, 202–3, 216
Augusta of Saxe-Gotha, Princess of Wales (wife of FL) 109–10, 133, 138–42, 145–6, 157–62, 171–6, 184–7, 192–3, 195, 198–200, 204, 215–18

Ayscough, Revd Francis 171, 211–12, 217

Bacon, Roger 64
Baltimore, Lady 174
Baltimore, Lord 121, 134–5, 162, 192
Barnard, 2nd Lord 120
Barnard, 11th Lord 197
Bassano, Jacopo 201
Bedford, 3rd Duke of 120
Bellenden, Hon. Mary 65, 74
Berkeley, 2nd Earl of 90, 128, 173
Bernstorff, Baron Andreas Gottlieb von 52, 66
Bolingbroke, Viscount 48–9, 52, 59–60, 88, 97, 104, 152, 178–9, 196, 208, 211, 213
Bolton, Duchess of 55
Bolton, 3rd Duke of 130
Bothmar, Baron Hans Caspar von 52, 65–6
Bristol, Countess of 67–8
Bristol, 1st Earl of 68–9
Bristol, 3rd Earl of 117
Bristol, 4th Earl of and Bishop of Derry 100
Bristol, 1st Marquess of 102
Brown, Launcelot ('Capability' Brown) 85
Brueghel, Jan 201
Brunswick-Wolfenbüttel, Duke of 160
Buckingham, Duchess of 77
Buckingham, 1st Duke of 210
Buckingham, 2nd Duke of 163
Burlington, 3rd Earl of 112, 130, 196

Burnet, Bishop Gilbert 26
Burney, Fanny 110, 171, 214
Bute, 3rd Earl of 219

Cadogan, General Charles 66
Cagnacci, Guido 201
Canaletto (Giovanni Canal) 18
Carey, Archbishop George 168
Carlisle, 3rd Earl of 105, 113,
    139, 162
Carlisle, 4th Earl of 175, 182
Carlisle, 5th Earl of 175–6
Carlton, Lord 112
Carnarvon, 1st Earl of 161
Caroline, consort of Christian VII
    of Denmark (youngest daughter
    of FL) 210
Caroline (third sister of FL) 46,
    59, 80, 84, 107, 115, 125, 132,
    136, 145, 150, 154, 158, 167,
    169, 189, 195–6
Caroline of Brandenburg-Ansbach,
    Electoral Princess, Princess of
    Wales and consort of George II
    (mother of FL) 31 *et seq.*
Caroline of Brunswick-
    Wolfenbüttel, consort of George
    IV 160, 172
Carteret, 2nd Lord 79, 163,
    183–4, 207
Cathcart, Lord 58
Catherine the Great 71
Celle, Duke of 25, 91
Chambers, Sir William 110
Charlemagne, King of the
    Franks 17
Charles I 19–22, 194–5, 200, 202
Charles II 18–20, 32, 47, 51, 54,
    62, 95, 114
Charles VI, Holy Roman
    Emperor 181
Charles, Archduke 40–2
Charles, Duke of Cambridge
    (half-brother to Queen Anne) 27
Charles Edward (The Young
    Pretender) 84, 190–3
Charles, Prince of Wales 179
Charlotte (daughter of George IV)
    114

Charlotte, consort of George
    III 108, 110
Charlotte of Denmark 131
Chenevix-Trench, Charles 24
Chesterfield, 4th Earl of 37, 78–9,
    91, 112, 117–19, 122, 130, 152,
    164, 178, 207
Cholmondeley, 2nd Earl of 165
Christian VII of Denmark 210
Churchill, Lady Anne (Countess of
    Sunderland) 119
Clarendon, 1st Earl of 32, 218
Claude 201–3
Clerk, Sir John 23
Clinton, Lord 130
Cobham, Viscount 110, 116
Compton, Sir Spencer (Earl of
    Wilmington) 90, 93, 97
Constable, John 201
Corelli, Arcangelo 204
Cornwall Fitz-Frederick
    (illegitimate son of FL) 121,
    136
Cowper, Countess 54–5, 58–9, 62,
    65, 67, 69, 71, 79, 80
Coxe, Archdeacon William 104
Crespin, Paul 204
Cromartie, Lord 193
Cumberland, Duke of ('Butcher'
    Cumberland), *see* William
    Augustus

Dandridge, Bartholomew 200
Darlington, Countess of, *see*
    Kielmannsegge, Baroness Sophia
    von
Dashwood, Sir Francis, Bt. 208
Davison, Jeremiah 198
Defoe, Daniel 48
d'Eke, Countess 44
De La Warr, 1st Earl 138
Deloraine, Countess (Mrs George
    Wyndham) 122, 156, 169
de Robethon, Jean 52, 65, 67
de Roucy, Lady Charlotte 126
Derwentwater, 3rd Earl of 62
de Saussure, César 56, 58
de Twillet, Count 89
Diepenbeeck, Abraham 201

Dixie, Sir Wolstan, Bt. 37
Dodington, George Bubb 106,
112, 116, 121, 125, 128–9, 197,
209, 215–17
Dorchester, Countess of 51, 77
Dorset, Duchess of 128, 217
Dorset, 7th Earl and 1st Duke
of 52, 128, 175, 209
Duncannon, Viscount (4th Earl of
Bessborough) 56–7
du Pan, Barthélemy 199
Dürer, Albrecht 201
Dutens, Peter 204

Edward VII 37, 179
Edward VIII 37
Edward, Duke of York and Albany
(second son of FL) 171–2, 187,
195, 199, 202
Effingham, Countess of 139,
140
Effingham, 1st Earl of 143
Egmont, 1st Earl of 104–5, 121,
123, 141, 147, 182, 190, 205,
209
Egmont, 2nd Earl of 104, 209,
215, 217–18
Eleanor of Saxe-Eisenach
(grandmother of FL) 38
Elizabeth I 27, 76
Elizabeth II 37, 179, 204
Elizabeth (second daughter of FL)
184, 200, 202, 210
Elizabeth Christina of Brunswick-
Wolfenbüttel 86
Elizabeth, Queen of Bohemia 20
Elizabeth-Charlotte, Duchesse
d'Orléans 23, 29, 60, 76
Eltz, Baron von 41–2
Ernst August (great-grandfather
of FL) 17, 36, 41
Ernst August, hereditary Bishop of
Osnabrück and Duke of York
and Albany (great-uncle of
FL) 50–1, 67, 72, 89, 91–2,
98–9
Essex, 3rd Earl of 159
Eugène, Prince of Savoy 27
Evelyn, John 108

Falaiseau, Pierre de 26
Fielding, Henry 148–9
Fiennes, Celia 173
Fitzherbert, Maria 47
Foord, Professor Archibald 143
Fortrey, Samuel 107
Fox, Henry (1st Lord
Holland) 100
Fox, Stephen (Lord Ilchester)
100–102, 122, 156
Frederick I of Prussia 38, 40–1
Frederick V of Bohemia 20
Frederick (youngest son of FL)
187, 210, 216
Frederick, Duke of Saxe-
Gotha 133
Frederick the Great 40, 85–6,
181–2, 188
FREDERICK LOUIS, PRINCE OF
WALES birth 17, 44; relations
with parents 36, 50, 68, 84–5,
91, 114, 124, 126, 133, 152,
154–5, 161, 166–7, 184;
antecedents 37; nicknames 45;
homes 46, 106–7, 109–13,
163–4, 172–3, 186, 216; made
KG 67; character and
appearance 67–8, 80, 100,
105–6, 162, 177; created Duke
of Gloucester and Duke of
Edinburgh 68; relations with
Hervey 68–9, 100–103, 117,
121–2; marriage plans 86, 88,
92, 119, 122; disinherited 91;
finances 93, 113, 126; arrives
England 97; created Prince of
Wales 103; meets Bolingbroke,
and influence of 104, 178;
robbed 105; appoints Dodington
106; plays cello 107–8; State
Barge 110–11; appoints Kent
112; denied regency 113, 186;
takes mistress, discards, birth
and death of two illegitimate
children and death of mistress
120–1, 134, 136; patronizes
Italian opera 127 and Handel
128; against Excise 129–30;
relations with Walpole 129–30,

150, 152, 182–3, 190; relations
with Lady Archibald Hamilton
133–4, 139; pastimes 136;
Freedom of City 136, 149;
marries 142; appoints Pitt 144;
opposes Gin Act 148; fights
Temple fire 151; writes satire
152; petitions Parliament 153;
birth of children 158, 170–1,
184, 189, 192, 210, 216 and
influence on 171, 211–12, 214
and letters to 171, 211–12 and
love for 172; expelled from
court 161; publishes family
correspondence 163; appoints
Lyttleton 164–5; visits Bath 176;
supports War of Jenkins's Ear
180; success in elections 182;
provides librettist for *Judas
Maccabaeus* 192; visits Flora
Macdonald 193; patronage of
the arts 194–206; appoints
Wickes 203; catalogues royal
collection 205; supports
government and returns to
opposition 207; Carlton House
Paper 208; appoints Lord North
governor 211; visits West
Country 216; catches cold and
death 217; funeral 218
Frederick William I of Prussia 40–1
Frye, Thomas 198

Gainsborough, Thomas 117
Gay, John 97, 127, 205
Georg Wilhelm (great-great-uncle
of FL) 17
George I, Elector of Hanover
(grandfather of FL) 17 *et seq.*
George II, Electoral Prince, Duke
of Cambridge and Prince of
Wales (father of FL) 17 *et seq.*
George III (oldest son of FL) 20,
37, 57, 108, 110–11, 117, 138,
163, 170–2, 176, 187, 189,
192–5, 199, 200, 202–3,
210–12, 214–19
George IV (grandson of FL) 47,
108, 112, 114, 160, 172, 176,
193–4

George V 37, 179, 194
George VI 37, 93, 179, 188
George of Denmark, consort of
Queen Anne 19, 21, 33, 76,
114
George William (infant brother of
FL) 73, 75
Germain, Lady Betty 128
Germain, Sir George 128
Gibbon, Edward 213
Gibbons, Grinling 110
Gibbs, James 85
Gibson, Thomas 199
Godolphin, Sidney (1st Earl) 25
Goodison, Benjamin 98, 107, 187,
202
Goupy, Joseph 195, 202
Gower, 1st Earl 77
Grafton, 2nd Duke of 114–15,
159, 162, 217
Granby, Lord 216
Grantham, 1st Earl of 57, 74, 77,
197
Guise, General John 202–3
Guy, Thomas 83

Hales, Revd Stephen 205
Halifax, 1st Earl of 26
Hamilton, 3rd Duke of 133
Hamilton, Lady 213
Hamilton, Lady Archibald 133–4,
139, 146, 158–60, 198, 213
Hamilton, Lord Archibald 172,
198
Hamilton, Sir William 213
Handel, George Frideric 24, 39,
64, 92, 127–8, 142, 170, 192,
204
Hans Holbein the Younger 201
Harcourt, 1st Earl of 219
Harcourt, 1st Viscount 29
Harrington, 1st Earl of 120
Haversham, 1st Lord 26
Hawksmoor, Nicholas 175
Haydn, Joseph 108
Hayman, Francis 186
Hayter, Bishop Thomas 219
Hedges, Revd Charles 104
Henrietta Maria, consort of
Charles I 201

Henry III 170
Henry V 196
Henry VIII 120, 173
Henry, Duke of Cumberland and
   Strathearn (fourth son of FL)
   187, 192, 199, 200, 216
Hervey, Lord (Lord Hervey of
   Ickworth) 46, 68–9, 72, 78, 90,
   93, 97–8, 100–103, 105–6,
   108–9, 112, 115–18, 120–8,
   130–8, 141, 143–6, 149–50,
   152–63, 165, 167–9, 177
Highmore, Joseph 197
Holland, Henry 112
Howard, Hon. Charles 165
Howard, Henrietta 46–7, 55, 73,
   75, 83, 139
Howard, Hon. Henry 46, 55, 75
Howe, Emmanuel Scrope 44–5
Howe, Hon. Sophia 55
Hudson, Thomas 199
Hyde, Anne (Duchess of York) 32,
   120

Irwin, Lady 105, 125, 139–40,
   151, 162, 175, 182, 184

James I 19, 20, 51, 176
James II (Duke of York) 18–21,
   23, 27, 32, 51, 55, 77, 120
James Francis Edward (The Old
   Pretender) 20, 22, 28–30, 48,
   60–2, 84
Jenkins, Robert 180
John Frederick, Margrave of
   Brandenburg-Ansbach
   (grandfather of FL) 38
Johnson, Samuel 37, 78, 171, 213
Jones, Inigo 19
Jones, John 109

Kayser, Joachim 200
Kendal, Duchess of, see
   Schulenburg, Melusine von der
Kenmuir, 6th Viscount 62
Kent, William 51, 62, 71, 85,
   108–10, 112–13
Kielmannsegge, Baroness Sophia
   von (Countess of Darlington)
   49, 86

Killigrew, Thomas 200
King, Lord 84–5
Kingston, 1st Duke of 67
Klyher, Johan Anton 200
Knapton, George 198, 200
Kneller, Sir Godfrey, Bt. 33
Königsmarck, Count Philipp
   von 33–5, 75–6

Lacam, Isaac 214
Lee, Matthew 204
Leibniz, Gottfried von 24–6, 38–41
Leicester, 2nd Earl of 77
Leicester, 4th Earl of 77
Leicester, 6th Earl of 186
Leicester, 7th Earl of 186
Lely, Sir Peter 32, 201
Le Nôtre, André 19, 39, 113
Lepel, Hon. Mary (Lady
   Hervey) 78, 118, 169
Lifford, 2nd Earl of 126
Lorrain, Claude, see Claude
Lorraine, Duke of 104
Louis XIV of France 22, 39, 60
Louisa (third daughter of FL) 199,
   210
Louisa (youngest sister of FL)
   84–5, 167, 196
Louise, Abbesse of Maubuisson 20
Lumley, Viscount 115
Lüneberg-Celle, Duchess of 43
Lüneberg-Celle, Duke of 40, 43
Lyttleton, Sir George, Bt. (Lord
   Lyttleton) 116, 164–5, 178, 216

Macdonald, Flora 193
Maingaud, Martin 195
Malmesbury, 1st Earl of 172
Malpas, Lord 165
Mann, Sir Horace, Bt. 183–4,
   186–7, 189–91, 193, 216
Mansel, Bussy 121
Mar, Earl of 60–2
Marchmont, Lord 164
Maria Theresa, Empress 181–2
Marlborough, 1st Duke of 25,
   27–8, 53, 66, 116, 118
Marlborough, 2nd Duchess
   of 100–1
Marlborough, 3rd Duke of 142, 190

Marlborough, Sarah Duchess
   of 23, 57, 76, 118–20, 122,
   128, 141–2, 160, 164, 166, 191
Mary I 76
Mary II 20–1, 76, 108
Mary, consort of George V 194,
   200, 205
Mary (fourth sister of FL), 84–5,
   196
Mary of Modena, second wife of
   James II 20, 27–8
Matthews, John 85
Maximilian of the Palatine 18
Mercier, Philippe 107–8, 195–7
Middlesex, Earl of (2nd Duke of
   Dorset) 175, 209
Miller, Sir Oliver 107
Mohamet 51
Monmouth, Duke of 55
Montagu, Duchess of 58
Montagu, George 192–3, 216
Montrose, 1st Duke of 130
Morell, Thomas 192–3
Morier, David 200
Murray, Lady 100
Mustapha 51

Nash, Beau 176, 198
Nelson, 1st Viscount 180, 213
Newcastle, 1st Duke of 73, 101,
   114, 145, 181, 207, 209
Newton, Sir Isaac 38
Norfolk, Duchess of 163, 185
Norfolk, 3rd Duke of 201
Norfolk, 7th Duke of 163
North, Lady 174–5
North, 7th Lord 162, 173, 204,
   211, 217, 219
Nottingham, Countess of 54
Nottingham, 2nd Earl of 52
Old Pretender, *see* James Francis
   Edward
Orkney, Countess of 51, 64
Orkney, 1st Earl of 164
Ormonde, Duchess of 81
Ormonde, 1st Duke of 60, 78, 84,
   136
Ossory, Countess of 112

Oxford and Mortimer, 1st Earl
   of 30, 52, 81, 179

Pelham, Henry 207
Pembroke, 9th Earl of 161
Pesne, Antoine 195
Philippe II, Regent of France 191
Philips, Charles 196–7, 200
Pickering, Countess von 31
Pitt, William (1st Earl of
   Chatham) 116, 144, 208, 215,
   219
Platen, Countess von, mistress of
   Ernst August, 1st Elector of
   Hanover 34–5
Platen, Countess von, mistress of
   George I 63
Pomfret, Countess of 115, 175
Pomfret, 1st Earl of 175
Pope, Alexander 78, 109, 178,
   205
Porteous, John 147–8
Portland, 1st Duke of 72
Portsmouth, Duchess of 51
Potter, Archbishop John 168
Poussin, Nicolas 201–2
Pulteney, William (Earl of
   Bath) 118, 178, 198, 207

Queensberry, 3rd Duke of 199
Quennell, Sir Peter 106, 185

Radcliffe, John 21
Regency, Act of (1706) 26, 29
Rich, John 127
Richard III 37
Richards, James 110
Richmond, 2nd Duke of 100, 196
Rights, Bill of (1688) 19
Robinson, Sir Thomas 113
Rosebery, 5th Earl of 173
Rubens, Peter Paul 201
Rupert, Prince Palatine 20, 32, 55
Russell, Edward (Earl of Orford by
   first creation) 183
Russell, Lord John (4th Duke of
   Bedford) 120, 163
Ryder, Dudley 58

Saint-Simon, Duc de 75–6
Savile, Sir George 186
Saxe, Maréchal 190
Scarborough, 2nd Earl of 130, 184
Schaub, Sir Luke 203
Schulenburg, Melusine von der
  (Duchess of Kendal) 34, 49, 50,
  65, 77, 79, 88–9, 91
Schulenburg, Petronilla von der
  (Countess of Walsingham) 79,
  91, 119
Schutz, Baron Ludwig von 25, 29,
  30
Scott, George 211–13
Settlement, Act of (1701) 17, 20,
  22–3, 27–9, 59, 145
Shakespeare, William 196
Shrewsbury, 12th Earl and 1st
  Duke of 48, 52
Smith, Mary 170
Smollett, Tobias 206, 220
Snowe, Revd J. 120
Somerset, 4th Duke of 76
Sophia, Electress of Hanover
  17–21, 23–6, 29, 30, 32, 38–41,
  43, 45, 47–8, 73, 213
Sophia Dorothea of Lüneburg-
  Celle, divorced wife of George I
  (grandmother of FL) 33–6, 43,
  75–6
Sophia Dorothea, queen consort of
  Prussia 86–7, 91–2
Sophie Charlotte, Electress of
  Brandenburg and queen consort
  of Prussia 38–9, 41
Southwell, Sir Edward 141
Spencer, Lady Diana (Lady John
  Russell and Duchess of
  Bedford) 57, 101, 119, 120,
  122, 128, 166
Spencer, 1st Earl 199
Spencer, John 199
Sprimont, Nicholas 210
Stair, 2nd Earl of 130, 152, 160,
  188–9
St Albans, Duchess of 55
Stanhope, 1st Earl 66, 70, 83
Strafford, Earl of 114

Sunderland, 3rd Earl of 83, 119
Sundon, Viscountess 115–16
Swift, Dean 81, 97

Talbot, Lord 208
Tankerville, 2nd Earl of 125
Teniers, David 201
Thackeray, William Makepeace 35
Thornhill, Sir John 50, 69, 70
Tintoretto, Jacopo 202
Titian (Tiziano Vecellio) 202
Toland, John 18, 24
Torrington, Lady 139
Townshend, 2nd Viscount 62, 71,
  77, 87, 90, 139, 207
Townshend, Hon. William 139,
  158, 161
Turner, J.M.W. 201
Tyers, Jonathan 186

Vanbrugh, Sir John 105–6, 114,
  175
Van Dyck, Sir Anthony 195,
  200–201
Vane, Hon. Anne 120–1, 133–6,
  157, 160, 197
Vane, Hon. Henry (Earl of
  Darlington) 121, 197
Van Loo, Jean-Baptiste 198–9
Velázquez, Diego de Silva y 202
Vendôme, Maréchal 28
Vernon, Admiral Edward 180–1
Vertue, George 194–5, 199,
  205–6, 216, 218
Victoria, Queen 37, 39, 170, 179,
  194
Voltaire 24

Wager, Sir Charles 151
Waldegrave, 1st Earl 141
Walmoden, Amelia-Sophia,
  Baroness von 133, 138, 156,
  169
Walmoden, Baron von 133
Walpole, Horace (4th Earl of
  Orford) 35, 47, 88–90, 94,
  111–12, 173, 183–7, 189–91,
  193, 206, 215–17, 219

Walpole, Lady 79, 88
Walpole, Mary 213
Walpole, Sir Robert (1st Earl of
  Orford) 52–3, 66, 68, 70–1, 77,
  79, 83–6, 88, 90, 93–4, 96–7,
  104, 106, 108, 116–17, 119,
  120, 129, 130–2, 141, 144,
  148–50, 152, 154–6, 167, 169,
  180–5, 190, 192, 207–8, 213
Walsingham, Countess of, *see*
  Schulenburg, Petronilla von der
Wentworth, Hon. Peter 114–15,
  164, 166
Wickes, George 203–4
Wilhelmina of Prussia 85–8, 92, 119
Wilkes, John 117
Wilkins, W.H. 118
William III 18, 20–2, 51–2, 62–3,
  65, 76, 78, 95, 108
William IV 56–7, 188, 194
William Augustus, Duke of
  Cumberland (younger brother
  of FL) 83–5, 88, 114–15, 120,
  125, 142, 156–7, 161, 164, 167,
  170, 175, 177, 186, 189–93,
  195–6, 199, 207, 218

William, Duke of Gloucester (son
  of Queen Anne) 21–3, 26
William, Duke of Gloucester (third
  son of FL) 187, 189, 199, 200,
  216
William of Orange (husband of
  Princess Royal) 46, 122–5,
  130–1
William I of Prussia 86–7
Williams, Professor Basil 206
Wilson, Richard 211
Wilson of Rievaux, Lord 96
Wolfenbüttel, Duke of 91
Wolsey, Cardinal Thomas 18
Wootton, John 108, 173, 199
Wortley Montagu, Edward 67
Wortley Montagu, Lady Mary 67,
  78, 96
Wren, Sir Christopher 49, 62, 110,
  175
Wüttenberg, Duke of 131
Wyndham, George 156

Young Pretender, *see* Charles
  Edward